HEAR THE
BOAT SING

HEAR THE BOAT SING

OXFORD AND CAMBRIDGE ROWERS KILLED IN WORLD WAR I

NIGEL McCRERY

For Rebecca and Joe, with all my love. You have
brought me nothing but pleasure and pride.

First published 2017

The History Press
The Mill, Brimscombe Port
Stroud, Gloucestershire, GL5 2QG
www.thehistorypress.co.uk

© Nigel McCrery, 2017

The right of Nigel McCrery to be identified as the Author
of this work has been asserted in accordance with the
Copyright, Designs and Patents Act 1988.

British Library Cataloguing in Publication Data.
A catalogue record for this book is available from the British Library.

ISBN 978 0 7509 6771 6

Typesetting and origination by The History Press
Printed and bound by TJ International Ltd

Contents

Acknowledgements

My many thanks go to: Alan Clay, historian and researcher; Ashley McCrery for advice and research; Richard Black and Roan Hackney, London Medal Company; Hal Giblin, my inspiration; Dennis Ingle, for his hours of calm advice; William Ivory, friend and advisor; Phil Nodding, friend and advisor; Pearce Noonan, Nimrod Dix Auction House; Richard Steel for hours of calming advice and for being one of the kindest people I have ever met, a very true friend; Great War Forum; M. Brockway; R. Flory; Charles Fair; Heritage Plus (first-class research); R. Braverei; Patrica Anne Pedley; Tom Gooden; Kate Wills; IPT; L. Booth; Izzy Melliget; John Hartley; J.D. Ralph; D. Owen; Coldstreamer, tullybrone; Medals Forum; Cambridge University; Oxford University; Trinity College and Trinity College Boat Club; Jesus College, Cambridge; Balliol College, Oxford; Magdalen College, Oxford; Merton College, Oxford; St John's College, Cambridge; Lady Margaret Boat Club; Corpus Christi, Oxford; New College, Oxford; Trinity College, Oxford; Christ Church College, Oxford; University College, Oxford; Brasenose College, Oxford; King's College, Cambridge; Caius College, Cambridge; Christine McMorris, my editor, for all her hard word and sound advice; The History Press for agreeing to publish the book; Michael Leventhal for agreeing to take the book on; 'Hear the Boat Sing' and Göran R. Buckhorn; Putney Council London; Diarmuid Byron O'Connor; Richard Parkin, friend and the person I've been closest to for over fifty years, who is still looking after me – without you life would be a much greater struggle; Nelly Khmilkovska for her time, beauty and patience; Professor John Lonsdale, Trinity College, Cambridge, for changing my life; eBay, one of the finest sources of photographs, books and information on the subject I have ever found.

If there is anyone I have forgotten I can only apologise and I promise to put you into the next edition.

Foreword

I'm a big believer in the saying that history is 'us then'. When writing any of these books, I find myself becoming emotionally involved with the characters I am writing about. In the case of the Oxbridge rowers, for me it becomes even more poignant. I was lucky enough to go to Trinity College and know many of the Boat Club rowers. Young, full of energy and with a zest for life that I had rarely experienced before. Most have gone on to achieve remarkable things in the worlds they have chosen and are a credit to the country they live in. The rowers of 1914–18 never had that chance, their lives cut short before most had chance to achieve anything. For me the epitaph (from *Henry V* by William Shakespeare) on Raymond Asquith's grave (son of the prime minister) sums up my feeling on the loss of these young men: 'Small time, but in that small most greatly lived this star of England.'

We lost around 1 million people during the First World War and when dealing with numbers like this we are in danger of seeing them as numbers not as people. People who had lives, were loved and loved. To this end, I hope the book will at least help people remember that and remember them so they do not die in memory.

Because of the nature of the book there has been some repetition when talking about the various Boat Races, as several men from particular boats were killed, such as the five rowers from the 1914 race. This way you can dip into the book or, if reading from beginning to end, just skip the race you have already read about. I am sure, although I have tried to avoid this, I will have made some mistakes and apologise for this in advance. If you feel I might have missed someone please make your case and I will consider including them in future editions.

I also make one small request: whenever you take a group photograph please name the people in the picture in some kind of order. It really helps later generations. More than anything, I hope you enjoy *Hear the Boat Sing* and it makes a good reference work for future generations to read, consider and, most of all, remember.

Nigel McCrery,
2017

1

LIEUTENANT HUGH JOHN SLADEN SHIELDS

Boat position: Stroke
Race: 67th Boat Race, 23 March 1910
College: Jesus College, Cambridge
Served: Royal Army Medical Corps, attached to 1st Battalion, Irish Guards
Death: 25/26 October 1914, aged 27

He died, killed in action doing his duty, like the brave man he was.

Hugh John Sladen Shields.

Hugh John Sladen Shields (more popularly known as 'Willoughby', a nickname he picked up at school) was born in Calcutta in India on 16 June 1887, the eldest son of the Reverend Arthur John Shields, later rector of Thornford in Dorset, and Mary Forbes, daughter of the Reverend W.B. Holland, rector of Brasted, Kent. Hugh was educated at Orleton Scarborough, before being sent to the Loretto School, Musselburgh, Scotland, where he was a prefect and boarded between 1899 and 1906.

From Loretto he went up to Jesus College, Cambridge to read Natural Sciences. A practising Christian, he was a committee member of the Cambridge Church Society and took part in philanthropic works in both Cambridge and London, giving up many of his evenings and weekends to assist in good causes in Camberwell. The Reverend E.G. Selwyn (the warden of Radley College) later said of Shields:

> I always felt about him at Cambridge that he was absolutely fearless about his religion – not a common thing in that atmosphere; and that the thing he cared most about was the service of his Lord and Master.

A fine all-round sportsman, he was soon in the college's first XV where he was described as a very talented player – 'the cleverest of the forwards', as someone later wrote. He later became captain of the XV. In 1908 Shields rowed in the 'rugger boat'. He enjoyed the experience so much he began to take his rowing seriously, improving to such an extent that he was selected to stroke for the Cambridge crew during the 1910 Boat Race.

67th Boat Race, 23 March 1910

The Oxford coaches were G.C. Bourne (New College), who had represented them between 1882 and 1883; Harcourt Gilbey Gold (Magdalen), who represented Oxford University on four occasions between 1896 and 1899 and was also president of Oxford for the 1900 race; and W.F.C. Holland (Brasenose), who also rowed for Oxford on four occasions between 1887 and 1890. Cambridge was coached by William Dudley Ward (Third Trinity), who rowed for Cambridge in 1897, 1899 and 1900; Raymond Etherington-Smith (First Trinity), who had represented Cambridge in 1898 and 1900; and David Alexander Wauchope (Trinity Hall), who had rowed in the 1895 race.

The race was controversial from the start. As a result of 'awkward' tides it was decided to hold the race in Holy Week. This caused a great deal of disquiet amongst several of the Christian rowers (including Shields) and controversy in the papers. For a while it looked like the race either wouldn't go ahead or its date would have to be moved. It wasn't until the Bishop of Bristol gave his permission, under the express condition that there weren't any celebrations after the race, that the event went ahead. As a committed Christian it would have been doubtful whether Shields would have taken part even if the race had gone ahead.

Race day was beautiful with a warm sun and a mild breeze. Cambridge won the toss and chose to take the Middlesex station, with Oxford on the Surrey side. For the seventh year in a row Fredrick I. Pitman (Third Trinity) was umpire;

Hugh John Sladen Shields.

he had rowed for Cambridge in 1884 (Cambridge), 1885 (Oxford) and 1886 (Cambridge). Pitman, to the cheers of the assembled crowd, started the race promptly at 12.30 p.m. Cambridge made a quick start and began to leave Oxford behind until one of the Cambridge crew caught a crab and the Oxford crew pulled quickly past them. By Craven Steps, and despite being the slower boat, the Oxford crew were ¼ of a length ahead. However, Cambridge put on a spurt and by the Mile Post were in the lead. But the Cambridge crew began to lose ground to Oxford as they rounded an unfavourable bend in the Thames. Oxford began to push hard, gaining a length in 10 strokes. By The Dove pub, Oxford had a 1-length lead, which they finally extended to a 3½-length lead by the end of the race. Their time was 20 minutes 14 seconds, the slowest winning time since 1907. Oxford's overall lead was now thirty-six to Cambridge's thirty.

★★★

In the same year, rowing with Eric Fairbairn (Jesus), Shields won the Lowe Double Sculls. He also rowed at Henley in the Jesus Grand Challenge Cup crew, and was runner-up for three years in succession. He did, however, win the Ladies' Plate in 1905. He also rowed No. 2 in the Jesus boat, which against all the odds won the International Race at Ghent in 1911 against a Belgian crew which had never been beaten before.

In 1910 Shields graduated with honours in Natural Sciences, going on to become a 'scholar and a prizeman' at Middlesex Hospital, where he also captained the XV. He became a Bachelor of Medicine in 1913.

Having always been interested in military matters, Shields was commissioned into the Royal Army Medical Corps in 1912. In 1913 he boxed as a light heavyweight for the army and was runner-up at his weight, being beaten by fellow RAMC officer and rower M.R. Leahy, a former Irish heavyweight champion, having won the crown in both 1908 and 1909. Leahy was also one of the Eight that won

The Cambridge 1910 Eight, with Shields sitting on the far right.

the Thames Cup at the 1903 Henley Royal Regatta, having been introduced to rowing by Bram Stoker (author of *Dracula*) while at Trinity College, Dublin. During this time Shields also became engaged to his cousin Dorothy Hornby, the third daughter of Colonel John Hornby, 12th Lancers, and they were due to be married in October 1914.

He became attached to the 1st Battalion Irish Guards and was with them in Caterham when war was declared. He travelled with them to France on 12 August 1914 as part of the 4th (Guards) Brigade of the 2nd Division. The battalion played an important part in the Battle of Mons and the subsequent rearguard actions during the British army's retreat. They were involved in the actions at Landrecies, and then at Villers-Cotterets on 1 September during the Battle of Le Cateau. During the latter engagement their commanding officer (CO), Lieutenant Colonel the Honourable George Morris, and the second-in-command, Major Hubert Crichton, were killed. It was also during this action that Hugh Shields was taken as a prisoner of war by the Germans after insisting on staying behind to tend the wounded. Interestingly he was captured along with his former boxing rival, Leahy, who was also attached to the Irish Guards. Leahy was badly wounded in the right leg and had to have it amputated. He was eventually repatriated in July 1915 and died in 1965, keeping his interest in rowing to the very end of his life.

The French eventually overran the German camp in which Shields was being held. Shields, together with another RAMC officer, Lieutenant H.C.D. Rankin, managed to escape by stealing a German officer's horse and riding back to their own lines. Quite an adventure. Shields rejoined his regiment on

12 September 1914. For his actions over this period he was mentioned in Sir John French's dispatches of 8 October 1914. On 25 October 1914 Shields wrote home to his parents: 'I must say it was very frightening work running up and down behind the trenches to see men who were wounded, as the bullets were rather thick at times.'

A few days later on 27 October 1914 he was shot and killed while attending a wounded man in the open. Shields was recommended for the Victoria Cross by his brigadier, Lord Cavan, for his behaviour on this day.

His commanding officer, Lieutenant Colonel Lord Ardee, wrote a moving letter to his parents about his death:

He was killed while attending to a wounded man in the firing line during an attack on Rentel, eight to ten miles east of Ypres ... The way in which he insisted on attending to wounded men under fire was the admiration of all of us. On more than one occasion I have advised him not to expose himself so much, but he always would do it, out of a sense of duty. He was shot in the mouth and through the neck while bending down and was killed instantly.

Another wrote:

The battalion were in action in Polygon Wood four and a half miles due east of Ypres. There were two companies in reserve: two in the main line of trenches, and a few outposts (rather a risky job unless in very good cover). Needless to say, the usual place of medical officers is with the reserves, or further back. On this occasion the cover for the outposts was rotten. They were fairly crawling along like caterpillars under rather a bad fire, till one of them was laid out, and lay there in the open thrashing about. Orr-Ewing (Scots Guards), at present commanding us, said at dinner the other night that he was appalled to see Shields strolling out across our trenches (all our men in the trenches with their heads down), and go and fish out some bandages and tie him up. Needless to say, that he was hit before he had been there one moment; the shot hit him in the neck and killed him outright.

The most interesting of the letters comes from Captain the Honourable H. Alexander who wrote:

I think the nicest thing I ever heard was said by one of our men, who said, 'Mr. Shields is the bravest man I ever saw.' The officers said he was too brave and told him but he always said he felt it was his duty to help wounded men whenever he could. If anyone has done his duty and a great deal more, he has.

He rejoined us again at Soupir. It was here that we went up the Castle together. It was at Soupir where Hugh did such frightfully good work by carrying the wounded, both English and German, out of a burning farm which was being very heavily shelled. We moved from there about 20 Oct to Ypres. Hugh died in front of a place called Roulers; he was attending to a wounded man in the open during an attack not more than 200 yards from the enemy. We are all very sorry, as he was so popular in my regiment, but there is consolation in the thought that he himself would not have wished a better death, and he could not have died more gallantly.

Shields was initially buried in the grounds of Huize Beuckenhrost, Zillebeke. However, over the years his body was lost or destroyed and he is now commemorated on the Ypres (Menin Gate) Memorial, panel 56. His name also appears on the Thornford War Memorial.

An edition of his diaries written between 12 August and 25 October 1914 was later privately printed and can now be seen on the Wellcome Library website.

2

SECOND LIEUTENANT REGINALD WILLIAM FLETCHER

Boat position: Bow
Race: 72nd Boat Race, 28 March 1914
College: Balliol College, Oxford
Served: 118th Battery, 26th Brigade, Royal Field Artillery
Death: 31 October 1914, aged 22

In their death they are not divided: they were swifter than Eagles!
They were Stronger than Lions.

Reginald William Fletcher.

Reginald William Fletcher (more commonly known as Reggie) was born on 18 March 1892 at Norham End, Oxford. He was the third son of Charles, a history tutor at Magdalen, and Katharine Fletcher. He was educated at the Dragon School, Oxfordshire, before ill health forced his parents to send him to Mr Pellatt's at Durnford, Langton Matravers, Dorset, where the climate and fresh air was considered better for his health.

A bright, determined boy, he gained a scholarship to Eton College in 1905, remaining there until 1910. While at Eton he rowed in the Eight and served in the Artillery OTC (Officers' Training Corps). He went up to Balliol College, Oxford (1910–14), where he obtained a Second in Honour Moderations in 1912 and later a Second-Class BA in 1914. A great one for the classics, he knew quantities of Homer and Aeschylus by heart and was a fine writer of Latin and Greek verse. Although his second-class degree was a good one, he was expected to get a First and the result was a disappointment to both him and his tutors. He once again became a member of the artillery section of the OTC, later becoming second in command of the corps. He was also a keen Freemason. He stroked for the Trial Eight at Oxford in three successive years, 1911, 1912, 1913, and for four years was stroke of his college boats, both Eights and Fours. He also rowed for the Leander Four at Henley Regatta in 1913 and was selected for the Oxford University boat to take part in the 1914 Boat Race.

72nd Boat Race, 28 March 1914

Oxford went into the 72nd Boat Race as reigning champions having beaten Cambridge the previous year, 1913, by ¾ of a length. However, due to problems with their crew order they were not the favourites, despite having five returning racers in their boat. Sidney Swann (Trinity Hall – number two), who was making his fourth appearance for Cambridge, L.E. Ridley (Jesus – cox), C.S. Clark (Pembroke – number six), G.E. Tower (Third Trinity) and C.E.V. Buxton (Third Trinity). The Oxford boat had four crew members with previous Boat Race experience: E. Horsfall (Magdalen – number four), H.K. Ward (New College – number three), E.F.R. Wiggins (New College) and H.B. Wells (Magdalen). Horsfall also won gold medals in the Men's Eight at the 1912 Olympic Games, rowing for the Leander Club (Horsfall survived the war, having served with the RFC (Royal Flying Corps) and winning an MC (Military Cross) and DFC (Distinguished Flying Cross), before going on to win a silver medal rowing stroke for the Leander Eight during the 1920 Olympic Games. In 1948 he managed the British rowing team.

For the eleventh year in succession the umpire was Frederick Islay Pitman (Third Trinity), the former Cambridge stroke who had raced between 1884 and 1886. The Oxford coaches were: G.C. Bourne (New College) who had raced for Oxford between 1882 and 1883, both Oxford victories; his son Robert Bourne (New College) who had rowed four times for Oxford in 1909 (Cambridge), 1910 (Oxford), 1911 (Oxford) and 1912 (Oxford) and Harcourt Gilbey Gold (Magdalen) who had stroked Oxford to victory in 1896, 1897, 1898, losing in 1899. Gold was made president of the Oxford University Boat Club in 1898. Cambridge were coached by Stanley Bruce who had rowed number two for them in 1904 (Cambridge).

Cambridge won the toss and decided to take the Surrey side, leaving the Middlesex side to Oxford. It was a beautiful day with a light wind and smooth water.

Cambridge Eight 1914 with Fletcher as bow.

The sun shone warmly on both rowers and bystanders as Pitman started the race precisely at 2.20 p.m. Cambridge started strongly and were ¾ of a length ahead by Craven Steps. The rumours of their speed and strength were not exaggerated and by the Mile Post the Cambridge crew had increased their lead to 1¼ lengths. They had increased their lead still further by Hammersmith Bridge, finally winning the race by 4½ lengths ahead, in a time of 20 minutes 23 seconds. It was the first time Cambridge had won the race since 1908, reducing Oxford's overall lead 39–31.

The 1914 race was the last one for six years and they didn't commence again until 1920, the First World War putting an end to the event for the first time since 1853. Five of the 1914 crew died during the war, four from Cambridge and one from Oxford.

***

Fletcher was gazetted to the 8th Brigade, Royal Field Artillery, on the day war was declared, sailing for France on 20 August. He got to the Front during the Battle of the Aisne serving with the 116th Battery. On 21 October he transferred to the 118th Battery, Royal Field Artillery, and was with them when he met his death on 31 October 1914 at Gheluvelt, about 6 miles east of Ypres. It was later learnt that a shell exploded close to him while he was returning from a forward observation post. He was buried where he fell the same evening.

His obituary later said of him:

Regie was never so happy as when he was in lands where the Eagles had never been carried, Iceland, Norway, the far west of Scotland or Ireland. He loved to sleep in the open air, and would sleep quite comfortably under several degrees of frost. As in face and coloring, so in his fierce independence of character, he seemed like some old Norse Rover; and it was this same independence that made one of his schoolmasters compare him to Achilles. In truth the oldest Greece was almost as much a source of inspiration to him as were the Sagas; extraordinarily well-read as he was, for a man of twenty-two, in the best modern literature, his highest delight was in Greek poetry; he knew enormous stretches of Homer and Aeschylus by heart, and would chant them, to the amazement of his crew, in the Balliol barge.

The master of Balliol College wrote:

However, fiercely he might have been growling at the said crew in the afternoon, there was not a room in the College in which he would not have been the most welcome of all guests an hour or two afterwards.

His major wrote shortly after his death:

I have lost a very charming and cheery comrade and a very gallant and capable officer. From a military point of view his death is a great loss to the Battery and from a personal point of view it has been a great shock and grief to his brother officers.

Reginald's body was never recovered or identified and he is commemorated on the Ypres (Menin Gate) Memorial, panels 5 and 9.

His older brother Walter George Fletcher was killed on 20 March 1915 serving with the Royal Welsh Fusiliers. He was also at Eton and Balliol and rowed for both, but not to his younger brother's standard.

Both brothers are also commemorated in the cloisters at Eton College, Windsor. The inscription on the memorial reads:

REMEMBER WITH THANKSGIVING
TWO BROTHERS BOTH SCHOLARS OF THIS COLLEGE
WALTER GEORGE FLETCHER
CAPTAIN OF THE SCHOOL 1906. ASSISTANT MASTER 1913 – 1914
SECOND LIEUTENANT ROYAL WELCH FUSILIERS.
KILLED AT BOIS GRENIEN MARCH 20TH 1915 AGED 27
REGINALD WILLIAM FLETCHER
SECOND LIEUTENANT ROYAL FIELD ARTILLERY
KILLED AT GHELUVELT OCTOBER 31ST 1914 AGED 22.

He is also commemorated on the Langton Matravers and Durnford School War Memorial.

3

CAPTAIN BERNARD RIDLEY WINTHROP-SMITH

Boat position: Number Six
Race: 62nd Boat Race, 1 April 1905
College: Trinity College, Cambridge
Served: 1st Battalion, Scots Guards
Death: 15 November 1914, aged 31

His body was returned to lie in English soil.

Captain B.R. Winthrop-Smith

Bernard Ridley Winthrop-Smith was born on 19 December 1882 at Little Eton, Derbyshire. He was the only son of Francis Nicholas Smith and Constance Ella Winthrop (daughter of the late Reverend Benjamin Winthrop of No. 82 Cromwell Road, London) of Wingfield Park, Ambergate, Derbyshire. He was educated at Carters in Farnborough, before moving on to Eton College (Evans House) and then on 25 June 1901 went up to Trinity College, Cambridge, as a pensioner (without a scholarship), where he obtained his degree in 1904 (BA).

At 6ft 5in tall, broad and strong, Bernard had rowed successfully in the Eight at Eton and for Trinity College, Cambridge. As a result of his success he was selected to row number six for Cambridge in the 1905 Boat Race.

62nd Boat Race, 1 April 1905

Having won the race in 1904 by 4½ lengths Cambridge went into the 1905 race as reigning champions. However, due to various misfortunes and illness they were not the favourites. The Cambridge coaches were John Edwards-Moss (Third Trinity) who had rowed number seven in 1902 and 1903, Francis Escombe (Trinity Hall) and David Alexander Wauchope (Trinity Hall) who both stroked for Cambridge in 1895. The Oxford coaches were William Fletcher (Christ Church) who had stroked and rowed number six and seven for Oxford between 1890 and 1893; C.K. Philips (New College) who had rowed number three for Oxford during their four victories between 1895 and 1898. Frederick I. Pitman (Third Trinity), who had stroked the Cambridge between 1884 and 1886 was the umpire again for the third year running.

The Cambridge crew had four returning rowers including P.H. Thomas (Third Trinity) who replaced Stanley Bruce (who himself had replaced W.P. Wormald due to illness) at the last minute due to illness. Despite making his fourth appearance in the race, having been in the winning crew during the previous three years, 1902–04, he joined straight from an African expedition. Not the best preparation for such an important race. The other three were H. Sanger (Lady Margaret Boat Club – bow), R.V. Powell (Third Trinity – number seven) and B.C. Johnson (Third Trinity – number three). The Oxford crew contained five rowers with previous experience including A.K. Graham (Balliol – number seven), E.P. Evans (University – number six), A.R. Balfour (University – number four), A.J.S.H. Hales (Corpus Christi – number three) and R.W. Somers-Smith (Merton – bow).

Cambridge University won the toss and chose the Middlesex station, leaving Oxford with the Surrey side. Pitman began the race at 11.30 a.m. Oxford took the lead quickly and by the Mile Post they were in a commanding position. They continued to dominate the race and eventually won by 3 lengths in a time of 20 minutes 35 seconds. It was Oxford's first victory in four years.

★★★

Bernard decided on a career in the army. As the nephew of Sir Gerald Smith KCMG, a former lieutenant colonel of the Scots Guards, strings were pulled and he was gazetted into that regiment as a second lieutenant on 1 August 1905, and promoted to lieutenant on 14 May 1910. On 13 August 1913 he was seconded for service under the Colonial Office and appointed aide-de-camp (ADC) to Sir

Harry Belfield KCMG, the governor and commander-in-chief of the East African Protectorate (Kenya). At the outbreak of the First World War Bernard managed to get leave from the Colonial Office and rejoined the 1st Battalion, Scots Guards, who formed part of the 1st (Guards) Brigade, British 1st Division, in October 1914, just in time to take part in the First Battle of Ypres (14 October–30 November). On 8 November 1914, whilst his regiment was at the Front near to Ypres, he was given orders to attack and retake a trench on the battalion's flank that had been occupied by some German troops after it had been vacated by *Zouaves* (light French light infantry distinctive because of their short open-fronted jackets, baggy [serouel] trousers, sashes and oriental head gear). Attacking over open ground and leading his platoon from the front he was hit and badly wounded by a bullet from a shrapnel shell and sustained a compound fracture to the base of his skull. Carried back to his own lines by his men, he was evacuated a few hours later to the Popering field hospital. Three days later, on 11 November, and in need of better medical attention, he was evacuated to the Christol base hospital in Boulogne. Unfortunately, despite receiving the best medical attention, Bernard's condition worsened and his parents were sent for. He died without regaining consciousness on 15 November 1914 with his parents by his side. He was promoted to captain on the day of his death. A total of 281 officers and 6,237 other ranks were killed during the First Battle of Ypres. Bernard alas was one of them.

Winthrop-Smith Memorial, South Wingfield Park (Burial Ground), Wingfield Park, Ambergate, Derbyshire.

Colonel A. Clutterbuck in his book *Bond of Sacrifice* describes Captain Winthrop-Smith as:

> an exceptionally fine man, 6' 5" tall and broad in proportion. He was much liked
> by the men of the right flank company of the 1st Battalion of the Scots Guards
> and by his brother officers.

Unusually Bernard's body was returned to England, travelling back with his parents. He was buried in South Wingfield Park (Burial Ground), Wingfield Park, Ambergate, Derbyshire.

As a lasting memorial to their son, his mother and father paid for a memorial in the form of a stained-glass window at St Matthew's, the parish church of Pentrich. The window at St Matthew's was by Christopher Whitworth Whall (1849–1924). The inscription below the window reads:

> To the Glory of God and in loving memory of our son Bernard Winthrop-Smith, Captain, 1st Scots Guards, died of wounds received at Ypres, Belgium, Nov.15.1914.

He is also commemorated on the war memorial in the cemetery at Wingfield Park, the Eton College War Memorial and Cambridge's Trinity College Chapel.

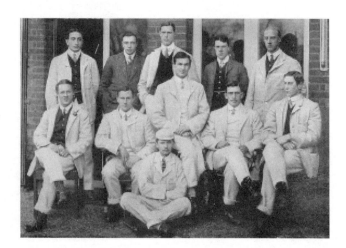

Cambridge 1905 Eight. Standing from left to right: E. Wedd, R. Winthrop-Smith, G. Cochrane, W. Savory, unknown. Middle row: P. Thomas, H. Sanger, C. Taylor, B. Johnstone, P. Powell. Front row sitting: R. Allcard.

4

SECOND LIEUTENANT CYRIL FRANCIS BURNAND

Boat position: Number Four
Race: 68th Boat Race, 1 April 1911
College: Trinity College, Cambridge
Served: 1st Battalion, Grenadier Guards
Death: 11 March 1915, aged 23

He was the only Catholic officer in the 1st Grenadiers, and was always of the greatest help to me in my ministrations.

Second Lieutenant Cyril Francis Burnand, Grenadier Guards.

Cyril Francis Burnand was born on 31 July 1891 at No. 1 Cavendish Square, London, the only son of Mr and Mrs Charles Burnand, of the same address, and the grandson of Sir F.C. Burnand, for many years the editor of *Punch*. He attended Mr Roper's School at Bournemouth in 1900, before going to Downside (Roman Catholic) School, Bath, in April 1904. At Downside he was described as a 'bright young boy' who always took a keen interest in participating in school activities. He was in the second XI in football and hockey (1908–09), being so enthusiastic that he snapped a tendon in 1907. He also won the School Challenge Cup for swimming four years in succession (1905–08). In 1909 he passed the Higher Certificate. He sang in the choir and was keen in all musical activities. He was a gifted actor and played Butterman to much acclaim in the Downside staging of *Our Boys* and later Benjamin Goldfinch in *A Pair of Spectacles*.

After Downside he was admitted as a pensioner (a student without any form of scholarship) to Trinity College, Cambridge, on 25 June 1909. He was elected to the Trinity Boat Club and rowed at Henley. Much to the delight of the Fisher Society (the body that runs events each week during term for all Catholic undergraduates and graduates resident in Cambridge), he was selected to take part in the Boat Race in 1911 rowing number four.

68th Boat Race, 1 April 1911

The 1 April was a beautiful day with a light easterly wind and a strong spring tide. The Oxford crew were coached by the former Oxford rower H.R. Barker (Christ Church), who had turned out for the Dark Blues, rowing number seven in 1908 and number two in 1909; the legendary G.C. Bourne (New College), who had rowed bow for Oxford in 1882 and 1883; and the equally famous and four-time Dark Blue (1896–99 rowing stroke on all four occasions) Harcourt Gilbey Gold (Magdalen). Stanley Bruce (Trinity Hall), who had rowed number two during the 1904 race, coached the Cambridge crew, together with William Dudley Ward (Third Trinity), who had rowed number seven between 1897 and 1900; Raymond Etherington-Smith (First Trinity), who rowed number six for Cambridge in 1898 and five in 1900 (Cambridge); and finally, and more unusually, H.W. Willis, the man who had coached Oxford in 1907. The familiar face of the former Cambridge stroke (1884–86) Frederick I. Pitman (Third Trinity) umpired for the eighth year in succession.

Six members of the Cambridge crew had raced before: R.W.M. Arbuthnot (Third Trinity – stroke), J.B. Rosher (First Trinity – number six), F.E. Hellyer (First Trinity – number three) C.R. le Blanc-Smith (Third Trinity – number five), C.A. Skinner (Jesus – cox) and G.E. Fairbairn (Jesus – number seven). Two members of the Cambridge crew came from South Africa, Pieter Voltelyn Graham van der Byl (Pembroke – number two) and C.A. Skinner (Jesus – cox). Six members of the Oxford crew were students at Magdalen College and had won the Grand Challenge Cup at Henley the year before. Three of the Oxford crew had also taken part in the race twice before, Duncan Mackinnon (Magdalen – number seven, 1909–10), Robert Bourne (New College – stroke, 1909–10) and Stanley Garton (Magdalen – number six, 1909–10). Charles Littlejohn (New College – number five) came from Australia.

The 1911 race was made all the more interesting for several reasons. Firstly because it was followed by the Prince of Wales (the future Edward VIII) and his brother Prince Albert. It was also the first race ever to be monitored by an aeroplane. This never-before-seen sight was later reported on by the *Western Argus*, 9 May 1911:

THE BOAT RACE BY AEROPLANE

SIX AIRMEN OVER THE COURSE

Six aeroplanes flew over the course of the Boat Race between Oxford and Cambridge, and one airman followed the race almost from start to finish, sweeping to and fro across the river to keep level with the crews. The machines were welcomed with great enthusiasm by the crowds. The airmen were Graham Gilmour (who followed the race), who came from Brooklands in a Bristol biplane with a Gnome engine, and five others who came from Hendon aerodrome. Graham White (military Farman machine), Mr Hubert (Ordinary Farman), Gustave Hamel, Mr Greswell and M. Prier all used Bleriot monoplanes. Mr Gilmour later recounted his experience:

I left Brooklands at 1.55pm in a military-type Bristol biplane and followed the river until I reached Putney Bridge. I arrived at the start just before the pistol was fired. Overhead as I circled around was a balloon in which was the Hon Mrs. Atsheton Harbord ... As soon as the boats started off I followed them up the river. More than once I turned of my engine and descended as low as 100 feet above the water, but my normal altitude during the flight was about 200 feet. The spectacle below me was most interesting. I could see the crews quite distinctly. From my aerial point of view they had rather the appearance of flies skimming over a pond in the summer. I could distinguish perfectly well between the two crews by the colors of their oars and it was quite apparent to me from above that Oxford was the better crew of the two. Indeed criticizing the race from an aerial standpoint the first time that such a view had been obtained I could see that Cambridge had a hopeless task, because every time Oxford was pressed the crew responded at once and the boat forged ahead ... After flying over the winning post I landed in a little field (Chiswick Polytechnic cricket field) having run out of petrol. A motorist very kindly gave me four gallons from his supply and I again filled up my tank.

A member of the crowd then helped him start his plane up and he flew the 18 miles back to Brooklands for tea. Alas, Gilmour was killed the following year

Cambridge Eight, 1911 Boat Race.

while flying over the Old Deer Park in Richmond. Gilmour had set off from Brooklands at about 11 a.m. to make a trial cross-country flight in a Martin Handasyde monoplane. Flying at about 400ft, his left wing suddenly folded and he crashed to the ground and was killed on impact.

Oxford won the toss and selected the Middlesex side while Cambridge was handed the Surrey side. The race started at 2.36 p.m.

Oxford made a quick start with Bourne, the Oxford stroke, outrating Cambridge by 2 strokes per minute. By the Craven Steps Oxford were ¾ of a length ahead – a lead they maintained past the Mile Post. Oxford had increased their lead by the Crab Tree pub and were even further ahead by Harrods Furniture Depository. As they passed under Hammersmith Bridge, Oxford were 2½ lengths ahead and still pulling away from Cambridge. By Chiswick Steps Oxford had a 4-length lead, which they had increased by Barnes Bridge. Although the Cambridge crew rallied there was no catching Oxford and they won by 2¾ lengths in an all-time race record time of 18 minutes 29 seconds. It was Oxford's third consecutive victory making the overall tally 37–30 in Oxford's favour.

Guy Nicholls later writing about Burnand in the *Morning Post* reported, 'Burnand rowed in better style than anyone in either crew.'

★★★

After obtaining his BA degree in 1912 Burnand left Trinity and joined the Midland Railway Company. He had always had a keen interest in railway engineering, and secured a position as a porter with the intention of making the railway his career. Moving to Nottingham to pursue his career, he became a member of the Nottingham Rowing Club. However at the outbreak of the First World War in

August 1914, he left the company and joined the Special Reserve of Officers, being gazetted into the 1st Battalion, Grenadier Guards, as second lieutenant. He went to France with his battalion on 17 December 1914. At the end of February he was granted a short leave home before returning to his battalion in March 1915. A week later on 11 March 1915 he was killed in action during the fighting at Neuve Chapelle. Between 10 and 13 March 1915 the Indian Army Corps together with IV Corps (which the 1st Battalion Grenadier Guards were a part of) attacked the village of Neuve Chapelle in an attempt to break through the German lines. The attack commenced at 7.30 a.m. on 10 March with a massive bombardment, which was intended to destroy the enemies wire and front-line trenches. The bombardment lasted for 30 minutes, after which at 8.05 a.m. the infantry moved forward. After hard fighting Neuve-Chapelle and over 1 mile of German front-line trenches were captured. However, due to poor communications, they let the Germans reorganise and reinforce, resulting in the British attack being brought to a halt. The 11 March was a dull and misty day, which caused problems for the artillery trying to spot their targets. At 7 a.m. the infantry moved forward, however, with little damage having been caused to the German positions. Moreover, with those that had been hit repaired, the infantry ran into a storm of machine-gun and artillery fire. The offensive finally petered out on 13 March with the British having suffered over 12,000 casualties. Unfortunately Second Lieutenant Cyril Francis Burnand was one of the casualties. A letter from a brother officer later explained:

… the Guards carried out their orders and Cyril had done remarkably well, but in leading his men on to the parapet of the trenches he was shot in the stomach and died almost immediately. He fell into the arms of another officer, but unfortunately he, poor fellow, was killed the next day …

Father Reginald Watt, Catholic chaplain with the 23rd Field Ambulance of the 7th Division, wrote to Cyril's father:

It is with the sincerest personal regret that I consider your son's death. As doubtless you have already been informed, he died gallantly at the head of his men in battle yesterday. He was the only Catholic officer in the 1st Grenadiers, and was always of the greatest help to me in my ministrations; to the Catholics of his regiment, and still more to me, his loss is a great disaster. I intend to say Mass for him to-morrow. God bless you and help you in this great grief.

Cyril's manager at the Midland Railway later wrote to his parents:

Dear Mr. Burnand, I feel that I must write at once to tell you how much I feel for you and Mrs. Burnand in the terrible sorrow that has come to you.

I think perhaps in some ways, I can feel for you more deeply than many of your more intimate friends, for I had watched and tried your boy very carefully, and had come to the conclusion that he was quite the best young man that had ever come to me in the Midland. I miss him very often and very much. He had most unusual gifts for a young man, great force of character, adaptability, capacity for dealing with men both above and below him … the Midland will be very much the poorer for his loss. I never met a younger man in whom I had greater confidence.

Cyril Burnand's body was never discovered or identified and he is commemorated on the Le Touret Memorial, panel 2. He is also remembered on the Nottingham Rowing Club Memorial and his parents presented a brass memorial plaque to Downside Abbey Church. It can still be seen there today.

5

LIEUTENANT SAMUEL PEPYS COCKERELL

Boat position: Bow
Race: 57th Boat Race, 31 March 1900
College: Trinity College, Cambridge
Served: Royal Flying Corps
Death: 20 March 1915, aged 34

His love of flying was as great as his love of rowing.

Samuel Pepys Cockerell.

Samuel Pepys Cockerell was born on 12 May 1880 at No. 1 Halkin Place, Belgrave Square, London, the son of William Acland and Sidney Ada Cockerell. He was educated at Eton College where he rowed for his college, before going up to Trinity College, Cambridge, as a pensioner (without a scholarship) on 25 June 1898. Rowing for Trinity College, he was selected as bow for the 1900 Boat Race. A fine cricketer, Cockerell was also a member of the MCC (Marylebone Cricket Club).

57th Boat Race, 31 March 1900

Cambridge went into the 1900 race as champions having won the 1899 race by 3¼ lengths in a time of 21 minutes 4 seconds. Oxford's crew were hit by injury and illness as Felix Warre (Balliol – number six) caught scarlet fever, M.C. McThornhill was ordered not to race by his doctor and H.J. Hale (Balliol – number four) was injured. The Cambridge crew were trained by the five-time Light Blue Stanley Muttlebury (Third Trinity) who rowed number six and was the first man to win four intervarsity Boat Races between 1886 and 1890. They were also trained by James Brooks Close (First Trinity), who had rowed bow in the Cambridge boat in 1872–73, and number three in 1874, with Cambridge winning all three races. Oxford were trained by the legendary Harcourt Gilbey Gold (Magdalen), a four-time Oxford Blue, stroking the 1896, '97 and '98 boats to Oxford victories (he was also Oxford University Boat Club president in 1898) and Douglas McLean (New College), a five-time Dark Blue during the period 1883–87. The umpire was Frank Willan (Exeter) who was famous for being in the winning boat for Oxford on four consecutive occasions between 1866 and 1869. He also served in the army during the First World War and was still driving motor lorries aged 70. It was his eleventh appearance as umpire.

The Oxford crew had three rowers with previous experience: C.E. Johnston (New College – number three), C.W. Tomkinson (Balliol – number four) and G.S. Maclagan (Magdalen – cox). Oxford also had the only non-British rower in their crew, H.H. Dutton (Magdalen – bow), who was Australian. Cambridge went with success and experience, and included six members of the winning 1899 side: William Dudley Ward (Third Trinity – number seven), Raymond Broadly

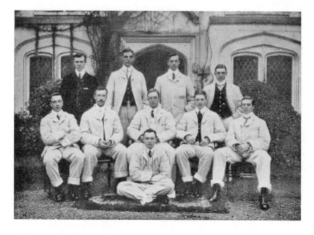

1900 Cambridge Eight with Cockerell standing third from left.

Etherington-Smith (First Trinity – number five), G.A. Lloyd (Third Trinity – cox), J.H. Gibbon (Third Trinity – stroke), R.H. Sanderson (First Trinity – number six) and J.E. Payne (Peterhouse – number four). Interestingly eight of the nine Cambridge crew were Trinity men.

Oxford won the toss and chose the Surrey side, leaving Cambridge the Middlesex station. It was a fine day and promptly at 2 p.m. Willan began the 57th Boat Race. Cambridge got away quickly and took an early lead. By the Craven Steps the Cambridge boat was already 3 lengths ahead. Stroke on stroke they began to pull further away and eventually won the Boat Race by a convincing 20 lengths. The time was 18 minutes 45 seconds, which was the fastest time in the history of the Boat Race (equalling the time made by the Oxford boat in 1893). Overall the Dark Blues now had a lead of 32–24.

$$\star\star\star$$

On leaving Cambridge he became a clerk at the stock exchange before joining the Foreign Office in 1902 serving in the embassy at Madrid as a commercial attaché until 1906 and then the legation at Lisbon until 1910. He then took up aviation and while flying Bristols on Salisbury Plain obtained his RAeC Certificate 132, dated 12 September 1911. He was commissioned into the Royal Engineers Territorial Force (RE [TF]) in February 1912 before becoming a second lieutenant in the Royal Flying Corps Special Reserve (on probation) in January 1914.

Shortly after the outbreak of the war in November 1914, together with Captain W. Massy and Captain S.D. Reilly, Cockerell was sent to Egypt, leaving from Avonmouth aboard the SS *Beethoven* on 4 November 1914 with a RFC detachment equipped with three Maurice Farman aircraft (two 1913-type Longhorns and one 1914-type Shorthorn), plus sufficient equipment to establish a camp. By the end of the year a camp had been established at Moascar, Ismailia. On 21 December 1914 the unit was reinforced by Lieutenant S.C. Parr from the Indian Central Flying School, who brought three additional machines. In March 1915 the detachment became a flight of 30 Squadron – becoming the first RFC squadron outside Western Europe. The squadron flew reconnaissance missions against the Turks who were attempting to cross the Suez Canal. Cockerell served as both a pilot and observer. Samuel didn't die in action but of acute smallpox picked up as a result of service in a foreign land on 20 March 1915. He is his buried in grave A 117, Ismailia War Memorial Cemetery.

He is also commemorated on the Eton War Memorial as well as the war memorial inside the Trinity College Chapel.

6

LIEUTENANT GILCHRIST STANLEY MACLAGAN

Boat position: Cox
Race: 56th Boat Race, 25 March 1899
     57th Boat Race, 31 March 1900
     58th Boat Race, 30 March 1901
     59th Boat Race, 22 March 1902
College: Magdalen College, Oxford
Served: 3rd attached 1st Battalion, Royal Warwickshire Regiment
Death: 25 April 1915, aged 35

The finest Cox the river has ever seen.

Lieutenant Gilchrist Stanley Maclagan.

Gilchrist Stanley Maclagan was born on 5 October 1879 in London, the youngest son of Dr T.J. Maclagan. He was educated at Eton where his ability as a cox was recognised, but not really developed, and he spent his time steering the Eton Second Eight. From Eton he went up to Magdalen College, Oxford. It was while at Oxford that Maclagan's ability as a cox was finally appreciated. He got his Blue as a freshman and coxed the Oxford boat during the Boat Race for the first time in 1899 and then for the following three years.

56th Boat Race, 25 March 1899

Oxford began the 1899 race as champions having won the 1898 race with some ease. Oxford were coached by the former Oxford bow G.C. Bourne (New College), who had rowed for Oxford in both 1882 and 1883, and Douglas McLean (New College), who had rowed number five for Oxford between 1883 and 1887. They were joined by another established Oxford rower, R.P.P. Rowe, who had rowed number two and seven for Oxford on four occasions between 1889 and 1892.

Cambridge University was trained by the former Oxford Blue William Fletcher DSO (Christ Church), who had stroked for Oxford four times between 1890 and 1893, and R.C. Lehmann (First Trinity), a former captain of the First Trinity Boat Club who, although having rowed in the trials on several occasions, never quite made the Cambridge boat. For the tenth year in succession Frank Willan (Exeter) was selected to umpire. Willan had rowed number four, seven and six for Oxford and had been in the winning boat four years in succession between 1866 and 1869.

Cambridge had three rowers with previous Boat Race experience: Claude Goldie (Third Trinity) who had rowed number seven in 1898, William Dudley Ward (Third Trinity) who rowed number seven in 1897 and Raymond Broadly Etherington-Smith (First Trinity) who had rowed number six in 1898. The Oxford crew contained four men with previous Boat Club experience: Harcourt Gilbey Gold (Magdalen) who had stroked the Oxford boat between 1896 and 1899, R.O. Pitman (New College – bow, 1898), F.W. Warre (Balliol – number four, 1898) and A.T. Herbert (Balliol – number seven, 1898).

Cambridge won the toss and decided on the Surrey side, Oxford being handed the Middlesex side of the Thames. It was a fine if cold day with a poor tide. Willan started the race promptly at 12.58 p.m. The crews matched each other stroke for stroke until they reached the Mile Post, by which time the Oxford boat had established a ¼-length lead. However, Cambridge fought back and began to reduce the Oxford lead. With a favourable bend in the river, Harcourt Gold, the Oxford stroke, increased the rate in an attempt to put clear water between the two boats. However, John Gibbon, the Cambridge stroke, was having none of it and matched, then increased, the rate. As a result the Cambridge boat begin to forge ahead and had a good lead by The Dove pub. Cambridge continued to lead, finally winning the race by 3¼ lengths in a time of 21 minutes 4 seconds. It was Cambridge's first win in ten years although Oxford still maintained their overall lead in the race 32–23.

57th Boat Race, 31 March 1900

Maclagan was selected once again to cox in the 1900 Boat Race, with no blame for Oxford's loss in 1899 being attached to him. Cambridge had the unusual distinction of going into the race as champions. Oxford were coached by Harcourt Gilbey Gold (Magdalen), who had stroked in the losing Oxford boat only the year before, and Douglas McLean (New College), who had continued as coach from the previous year. Oxford also suffered more than their fare share of misfortune. M.C. McThornhill (one of the new boys) was instructed by his doctor not to row, the Oxford president Felix Warre (Balliol) caught scarlet fever and H.J. Hale (Balliol) suffered an injury.

Cambridge brought in two new coaches: James Brooks Close (First Trinity), who had been bow and number three in the Cambridge boat on three occasions between 1872 and 1874, and Stanley Muttlebury (Third Trinity), who rowed number six and five for Cambridge between 1886 and 1890. The umpire was once again Frank Willan (Exeter).

Oxford went with three members of the 1899 losing crew: C.E. Johnston (New College – number three), C.W. Tomkinson (Balliol – number four) and

The 1901 Oxford and Cambridge crews. Maclagan bottom right-hand corner.

cox G.S. Maclagan (Magdalen). Oxford's stroke, H.H. Dutton (Magdalen), was an Australian and the only non-British rower. Cambridge, unsurprisingly, went with six members of their victorious crew: William Dudley Ward (Third Trinity – number seven), Raymond Broadly Etherington-Smith (First Trinity – number five), J.E. Payne (Peterhouse – number four), R.H. Sanderson (First Trinity – number six), J.H. Gibbon (Third Trinity – stroke) and finally G.A. Lloyd (Third Trinity – cox). Eight of the nine Cambridge crew were students at Trinity College, the exception being J.E. Payne who was at Peterhouse.

This time Oxford won the toss and chose the Surrey side (as Cambridge had the year before) meaning it was Cambridge's turn to take the Middlesex side of the Thames. For the second year in succession the weather was fine and Willan got the race off on time at 2 p.m. Cambridge pulled hard from the start and took an early lead, being 3 lengths ahead and by the Craven Steps. They continued to pull away from Oxford, finally winning the race by 20 lengths in a time of 18 minutes 45 seconds. It was the fastest winning time in the history of the race (matching the time established by Oxford in 1893). Although overall Oxford still led 32–24, the gap was narrowing.

In the same year as the 1900 Boat Race, Maclagan coxed the Magdalen crew in the Head of River race. He also coxed Leander in the Grand Challenge Cup at Henley from 1899 to 1908. He was part of the winning crew on six occasions, the only man to be able to make such a claim.

58th Boat Race, 30 March 1901

The 1901 race was the first race held under the reign of the new monarch Edward VII, Queen Victoria having died on 22 January 1901. Despite steering the Oxford boat to defeat in both 1899 and 1900, Maclagan was chosen to cox the Oxford boat again in 1901. For the second year in succession Cambridge went into the race as champions. G.C. Bourne (New College) returned as the Oxford coach together with Harcourt Gilbey Gold (Magdalen) from the year before and C.K. Philips (New College) who had rowed number three for Oxford between 1895 and 1898 (all Oxford victories). Cambridge went with two of the coaches that had helped them win the 1900 race: James Brooks Close (First Trinity) and Stanley Muttlebury (Third Trinity). They also brought in John Ernest Payne (Peterhouse) who had rowed number four for the Cambridge winning crew in both 1899 and 1900. The familiar face of Frank Willan umpired the race.

The Cambridge crew only had one rower with previous Boat Race experience: their club president, Bertram Willes Dayrell Brooke (First Trinity), who rowed at number three the year before. Seven of the nine crew were members of Trinity College, the two exceptions being B.C. Cox (Trinity Hall – number two) and

E.F. Duncanson (Emmanuel – number seven). They also suffered problems with injury and illness and were forced to reorganise their boat late into their preparations. One observer commented, 'the crew received a setback from which they never really recovered.' Oxford on the other hand had five returning rowers including their cox Gilchrist Maclagan (Magdalen), F.W. Warre (Balliol – number six), H.J. Hale (Balliol – number four), T.B. Etherington-Smith (Oriel – number seven) and R.H. Culme-Seymour (New College – number two).

This time Cambridge won the toss and decided on the Surrey side, leaving the Middlesex side to Oxford. The day was a poor one and a heavy storm broke over the race; with a strong wind from the south-west it was a difficult race for all concerned. Willan, as efficient as ever, began the race at 10.31 a.m. Oxford started well and, taking advantage of the bend in the river, pulled away to gain a ½-length lead by the Mile Post. Cambridge put on a spurt to try to narrow the increasing gap between the two boats, and the crews levelled as they passed Harrods Furniture Depository. Cambridge then began to pull ahead as the Oxford stroke rate dropped. Hitting rough water the Cambridge crew began to struggle, although it also made it impossible for the Oxford crew to pass them. However, as the boats approached Barnes Bridge Maclagan made his move and the Oxford stroke, Culme-Seymour, began a spurt. They were level by Mortlake Brewery, after which the Oxford crew began to make ground on the Cambridge boat and finally passed it. Cambridge despite their best efforts was unable to respond. Oxford finally won the race by ⅖ of a length in a time of 22 minutes 31 seconds – the slowest winning time since 1877. The overall score was now 33–24 in Oxford's favour. It was the first time Maclagan was in the winning boat and could take much credit for being an important part of their victory. It was a great sadness to all concerned when the Oxford stroke and talented rower Culme-Seymour (New College), who had been largely responsible for the 1901 race win, died the following autumn of pleurisy.

59th Boat Race, 22 March 1902

Oxford went into the 1902 race in a familiar situation as champions, having come back from two defeats. Maclagan, probably because of his fine performance the year before, was selected as cox once again. Oxford retained their winning coaches, G.C. Bourne, Harcourt Gilbey Gold and new boy William Fletcher (Christ Church), who had stroked and rowed number six for Oxford between 1890 and 1893 (all Oxford victories). Cambridge were trained by John Ernest Payne who had been one of the Cambridge coaches the year before. The umpire was once again the reliable Frank Willan. This was his thirteenth and final race as umpire – a fine record.

Cambridge decided on a bit more experience and had four rowers in their boat with previous race training: Wilfrid Hubert Chapman (Third Trinity – bow),

1899 (Cambridge); C.W.H. Taylor (Third Trinity – number four), 1901 (Oxford); H.B. Grylls (First Trinity – number six),1901 (Oxford); and R.H. Nelson (Third Trinity – Stroke), 1901 (Oxford). Six of the nine Cambridge crew members were Trinity men, the three exceptions being T. Drysdale (Jesus – number two), F.J. Escombe (Trinity Hall – number five) and C.H.S. Wasbrough (Trinity Hall – cox).

Oxford selected five former rowers, including their cox Gilchrist Stanley Maclagan (Magdalen), J.Younger (New College – number three), H.J. Hale (Balliol – number four), A. de Long (New College – number six) and F.O.J. Huntley (University – number seven). The Oxford crew also contained the American brothers John George and Devereux Milburn (Lincoln) from Harvard University.

Under a dark sky, with the rain drizzling down, Cambridge won the toss and chose to start from the Surrey side, leaving the Middlesex side of the river to Oxford. At 12.45 p.m., and for the very last time as umpire, Willan got the race under way. Cambridge started quickly and went straight into the lead outrating Oxford from start to finish. Maintaining their lead throughout the race the Cambridge crew won by 5 lengths in a time of 19 minutes 9 seconds. The overall record was now 33–25 in Oxford's favour. This was to be Gilchrist's last race: lost three, won one. However, his rowing career was far from over. In 1908 he was part of the Olympic crew that won the gold medal at the Henley Regatta. He also made honourary secretary of the Amateur Rowing Association shortly before the outbreak of the war and in 1904 Maclagan became a member of the London Stock Exchange.

★★★

In September 1914, shortly after the outbreak of the war, Maclagan was commissioned into the 3rd Battalion, Royal Warwickshire Regiment, later being attached to the 1st Battalion. In December 1914 he went out with a draft of officers to make up the heavy losses and casualties in the 1st Battalion. He served in the trenches for the next four months until he was finally killed in action during the Second Battle of Ypres at Pilckem Ridge, on 25 April 1915 during the first gas attack of the war. It was a disastrous day for the battalion with seventeen officers and 500 other ranks killed, wounded or missing.

On 24 April, the day before the attack, Sir John French ordered counter-attacks towards Kitchener's Wood and St-Julien to restore gaps that had been created in the line. The official history describes the 10th Brigade attack:

> The battalions of the 10th Brigade were able to pass the wire of GHQ Line under cover of the mist but, before they could open out, they came under rifle and machine-gun fire … and it was at once obvious that snipers were out in the

rye grass and other crops that gave cover from view, and that some of the farms
between Wieltje and St Julien were in the hands of the enemy. The brigade,
therefore, shook out into fighting formation somewhat earlier than intended.
Its advance, visible from many points, was carried out in faultless order ... The fire
now came mainly from machine guns hidden in the houses of St Julien and
the upper stories of farm buildings, with cross fire from Kitchener's Wood, and
particularly from two farms south of it (Oblong and Juliet) ... By rushes the
leading lines advanced more than quarter of a mile till they were within one
hundred yards of the outlying houses of St Julien. Then ... the lines paused and
became stationary and for twenty minutes the Germans deluged them with
machine-gun fire, very effective and very heavy. A few men tried to crawl back
into cover, but the majority of those in the leading lines never returned; mown
down, like corn, by machine guns in enfilade, they remained lying dead in rows
where they had fallen. The following lines were pinned to the ground by fire
and, after several efforts to advance ... rose and surged back to cover in the folds
of the ground and hedges behind them ... A new line was quickly organized ...
The losses of the 10th Brigade in its magnificent but hopeless attempt had been
heavy ... mostly irreplaceable, well trained men ... In compensation for the
disaster that had overtaken them, the battalions had the satisfaction of knowing
later that they had stopped any possible enemy advance in the St Julien quarter.

The 10th Brigade front lines had in essence been wiped out.

Maclagan's body was never recovered or identified and he is commemorated
on Ypres (Menin Gate) Memorial, panel 8. He is also commemorated on the Eton
War Memorial and the Stock Exchange Memorial.

The 1902 Oxford Eight with Maclagan
sitting at the front.

7

LIEUTENANT HENRY MILLS GOLDSMITH

Boat postion: Number Three
Race: 63rd Boat Race, 7 April 1906
   64th Boat Race, 16 March 1907
College: Jesus College, Cambridge
Served: Devonshire attached 2nd Battalion, Lincolnshire Regiment
Death: 9 May 1915, aged 29

Tall and apparently slightly built he was an oarsman of unusual power.

Lieutenant Henry Mills Goldsmith.

Henry Mills Goldsmith, known as 'Rosie', was born on 22 July 1885 at Compton Gifford, Plymouth. He was the second son of John Philip, a solicitor with a practice in Devonport, and Elizabeth Goldsmith. He was educated at Sherborne School between 1899 and 1904, House A. In 1905 he went up to Jesus College, Cambridge, and was destined to be one of the great Jesuan oarsman. Considered to be one of the most outstanding oarsmen of his day, he rowed number five in the college first boat from 1906 and in the same year was elected president of the Cambridge University Boat Club – an honour not afforded to a Jesus man for twenty years. He was also selected to row in the Cambridge boat in both 1906 and 1907.

63rd Boat Race, 7 April 1906

Having won the 1905 Boat Race by 3 lengths, Oxford went into the race as reigning champions. For the third year in succession the Cambridge crew were trained by Francis Escombe (Trinity Hall), who rowed number five in 1902, Stanley Muttlebury (Third Trinity) who rowed number six and number five between 1886 and 1890, and David Alexander Wauchope (Trinity Hall) who stroked in the Cambridge boat in 1895. The Oxford coaches were the four-time Oxford rower William Fletcher (Christ Church) who rowed stroke, number six and number seven for his university between 1890 and 1893, and Harcourt Gilbey Gold (Magdalen) who stroked for Oxford between 1896 and 1899, and was Oxford Boat Club president in 1900. The Boat Race umpire for the fourth consecutive year was Frederick I. Pitman (Third Trinity) who had rowed stroke for Cambridge between 1884 and 1886.

The Cambridge crew selected two rowers with previous Boat Race experience: Banner Carruthers Johnstone (Third Trinity – number five) and Ronald Vanneck Powell (Third Trinity – number six). Oxford's crew employed twice that number and had four men in their boat with previous Boat Race experience: E.P. Evans (University College – number six), L.E. Jones, (Balliol – number five), H.C. Bucknall, (Merton – stroke) and L.P. Stedall (Merton – cox).

THE CAMBRIDGE CREW,
1907.

The 1907 Cambridge crew with the number three Henry Goldsmith.

Cambridge went into the race as firm favourites. Oxford won the toss and selected the Surrey side of the Thames, leaving the Cambridge boat with the Middlesex side. There was a strong tide and light wind, which anticipated a fast race. Pitman, as reliable as ever, got the race started at precisely 12 p.m. Cambridge made a quick start and took an early lead. By Barnes Bridge the Cambridge boat was ahead by 4 lengths. They never gave up the lead, winning by 3½ lengths in a time of 19 minutes 25 seconds. It was the fastest winning time since 1902. However, Oxford still held an overall lead of 34–28.

In the same year Goldsmith was not only elected president of the Cambridge University Boat Club but also joined the celebrated and much-publicised Cambridge boat that beat a visiting Harvard crew at the Henley Royal Regatta. The Cambridge crew were challenged by Harvard to a race along the Championship Course. Cambridge beat Harvard by 2 lengths. The student magazine *Granta* (established in 1889) wrote of Goldsmith on 13 October 1906: '… the tact he showed in negotiations with Harvard and the way his genial presence inspired the crew in the sweltering heat of Bourne End and Putney, these things are not written.'

64th Boat Race, 16 March 1907

Goldsmith was selected as part of the Cambridge crew again in 1907. This time it was Cambridge's turn to go into the race as champions. Once again the Cambridge crew were trained by their very successful coaches from 1906: Francis Escombe (fourth consecutive year), Stanley Muttlebury and David Alexander Wauchope. The Oxford coaches were, as with the previous year, Harcourt Gilbey Gold and new boy H.W. Willis (who went on to coach Cambridge in 1911). Once again the umpire was Fredrick I. Pitman (fifth year).

Oxford selected three crew members with previous Boat Race experience: Henry Bucknall (Merton – number two), A.G. Kirby (Magdalen – number six) and A.C. Gladstone (Christ Church – number seven). Six members of the Cambridge winning crew from 1906 were selected once again: Banner Johnstone (Trinity – number six), A.B. Close-Brooks (Trinity – bow), J.H.F. Benham (Jesus – number two), H.M. Goldsmith (Jesus – number three), H.G. Baynes (Trinity – number five) and D.C.R. Stuart (Trinity Hall – stroke).

Winning the toss, the Oxford crew selected the Surrey side of the river, Cambridge being forced to take the Middlesex side. Once again Cambridge made the quicker start and within a couple of minutes were clear of the Oxford boat. The Cambridge boat passed the Mile Post 2 lengths ahead. Their lead increased to 3 lengths by Hammersmith Bridge. However, the Oxford boat wasn't finished yet. Albert Gladstone, the Oxford stroke, put on a spurt and reduced the distance

Cambridge Eight 1906 with Goldsmith standing second left.

between the two boats to 3ft. However, Oxford hit rough water and struggled to keep in touch with the Cambridge Eight and began to fall back once again. By Barnes Bridge Cambridge were 4 lengths ahead, finally winning the race by 4½ lengths in a time of 20 minutes 26 seconds. It was the biggest winning margin since 1904 and moved the overall score to 34–29 still in Oxford's favour.

★★★

Goldsmith missed out on the 1908 race, which Cambridge won by 2½ lengths in a time of 19 minutes 20 seconds. However, this didn't mean he had stopped rowing at the very highest standard. He rowed number five in the Eight during the 1908 Olympic Games, winning a bronze medal after being beaten by the Belgian rowers from the Club Nautique de Gand in the semi-final. Returning to Cambridge he was selected as part of the crew, which revenged themselves on Club Nautique de Gand in May 1911, in the famous race held at Terdonck. Goldsmith wrote home to his family on 17 May 1911 describing the build up to the race. He describes how the team received a warm welcome with receptions, dignitaries (the 'nuts of the town') and visits laid on. He also recounts how the team were spared the ordeal of standing by the bandstand at the zoo while the band played 'God Save the King' as the band had forgotten its music! Arriving at Ghent, they received a rapturous welcome from the locals and had to be escorted through the crowd to find their cars by the local gendarmes. He writes, 'You can't imagine what good fellows these Belgians are. Their great ambition is to be like English "sportsmen" in the best sense of the word.' Seven men from the Terdonck team served and four were killed. The names I have were: E.C. Henty (RASC/ RFA [Royal Army Service Corps/Royal Field Artillery]), H.J.S. Shields (RAMC

[Royal Army Medical Corps], attached Irish Guards) died 25 October 1914, H.C.H. Harland Hudson (11th Hussars), H.E. Swanston (RFA), H.M. Goldsmith (Devon Regiment) died 9 May 1915, G.E. Fairbairn (Durham Light Infantry) died 20 June 1915 and T.M. Crowe (RNVR [Royal Naval Volunteer Reserve]) died 4 June 1915. Another man, F.G. Hudson, saw service in Norway and died there (allegedly killed by German agents in 1916).

On leaving Cambridge, Goldsmith became an articled clerk to a firm of London solicitors. In 1909 he was commissioned into the 5th (Territorial) Battalion Devonshire Regiment. He also found time in 1913 to meet and marry Sybil Elizabeth Perrens, the daughter of the late Mr W. King Perrens of Torquay, and they settled at Rockmoor, Yelverton, Devon. They had one daughter, Elizabeth, born in August 1915; alas several months later Harry met his death.

Harry was promoted to lieutenant in 1910 and on mobilisation he was appointed aide-de-camp (ADC) to the general commanding the Wessex Division. Keen to get to the Front, he was transferred first to the 3nd Battalion, Devonshire Regiment, going to the Front in March 1915. He was then attached to the 2nd Battalion, Lincoln Regiment, and appointed machine gun officer of the battalion, later becoming machine gun officer to the headquarters of the 25th Brigade. Harry was killed in action on 9 May 1915 at Fromelles during the Second Battle of Ypres, one of more than 11,000 casualties sustained on the British side that day.

The dean of Jesus, wrote of him in the *Cambridge Review*:

> Tall and apparently slightly built he was an oarsman of unusual power, not only because of his easy and graceful movements, but on account of the immense strength he put into every stroke. Absolutely unaffected and modest in everything, he is a type of man whose loss makes us feel more poignantly the sacrifices that our struggle with Germany demands.

His remains were never recovered or identified and he is commemorated on the Ploegsteert Memorial, panel 3. He is also commemorated on the war memorial at Marker Church, the Jesus College, Cambridge Memorial, the Crapstone War Memorial and the Sherborne School War Memorial.

8

CAPTAIN OSWALD ARMITAGE GUY CARVER

Boat position: Number Three
Race: 65th Boat Race, 4 April 1908
College: Trinity College, Cambridge
Served: 1/2nd East Lancashire Field Company Royal Engineers
Death: 7 June 1915, aged 28

His widow later married Bernard Montgomery, later field Marshal.

CAPTAIN O. A. CARVER,
ROYAL ENGINEERS.

Captain Oswald Armitage
Guy Carver.

Oswald Armitage Guy Carver, 'Waldo', was born on 2 February 1887 at Marple, Greater Manchester, the second son of William Oswald and Katherine Armitage Carver. His father was a successful cotton goods merchant and founder of Hollins Mill. He made enough money from his business to buy the impressive Cranage Hall, near Holmes Chapel in Cheshire. Carver was educated at Charterhouse before going up to Trinity College, Cambridge, as a pensioner on 26 June 1905. While at Trinity he rowed not only for his college but took part in the 1908 Boat Race, rowing number three.

65th Boat Race, 4 April 1908

After their 1907 victory by 4½ lengths, Cambridge went into the race as champions. They were coached by L.H.K. Bushe-Fox (St John's), a former president of the Lady Margaret Boat Club (1897) and a close friend of the poet Robert Henry Forster. Joining Bushe-Fox were Francis Escombe, who had coached Cambridge to victory in the previous two races (although this was his fifth consecutive year), five-time Light Blue Stanley Muttlebury (Third Trinity, 1886–1990) and David Alexander Wauchope (Trinity Hall), who stroked for Cambridge in the 1895 race. Oxford were trained by the famous and four-time Dark Blue (1896–99) Harcourt Gilbey Gold (Magdalen) and four-time racer (1889–92) R.P.P. Rowe (Magdalen). The former Cambridge Blue (1884–86) Fredrick I. Pitman (Third Trinity) umpired the race for the fifth time in succession.

Four members of the Oxford crew had raced before: Alister Kirby (Magdalen – number five), Albert Gladstone (Christ Church – stroke), E.H.L. Southwell (Magdalen – number three) and A.W.F. Donkin (Magdalen – cox). Cambridge also had four crew members with previous Boat Race experience, Douglas Stuart (Trinity Hall – stroke), Eric Powell (Trinity – number seven), J.S. Burn (Trinity – number five) and R.F.R.P. Boyle (Trinity – cox). Collier Cudmore (Magdalen), the Oxford number two, was Australian and the only non-European in either crew. George Eric Fairbairn (Jesus), the Cambridge number two, was following in his uncle Steven Fairbairn's (Jesus) footsteps: he had rowed four times for Cambridge as number five, six and seven between 1882 and 1887. Both crews were also affected by illness. James Angus Gillian, the Oxford number five (Magdalen), was stopped from taking part in the race by doctors. Influenza affected both crews and A.G. Kirby (Magdalen) went down with jaundice but decided to race anyway against his doctor's advice.

The day was clear and fresh with a strong headwind. Oxford won the toss and decided to take the Surrey side, pushing Cambridge out to the Middlesex side of the river. Pitman started the race at precisely 3.30 p.m. Cambridge made the better start but not by much and began to slowly pull away from the Oxford boat. The rough water favoured Cambridge's style of rowing more so than Oxford and by the Mile Post Cambridge were clear. By Harrods Furniture Depository Cambridge were 2 lengths ahead. Oxford did their best to narrow the gap by continually spurting, but this tactic made very little difference to Cambridge, who were still ahead by Barnes Bridge. Cambridge finally passed the finish post with a 2½-length lead in a time of 19 minutes 20 seconds, the fastest since 1902, although by the narrowest margin since 1901. It was Cambridge's sixth victory in seven years and their third consecutively. The overall record was now 34–30, still in Oxford's favour.

★★★

Being a member of the winning Cambridge crew in 1908 wasn't Carver's only rowing achievement that year. Carver was also selected to row for the Cambridge Eight during the Summer Olympics. The event took place on the River Thames between 29 and 31 July. Six boats took part: Belgium, Royal Club Nautique de Grand; Canada, Toronto Argonaut; Great Britain, Cambridge; Great Britain, Leander; Norway, Norges Roforbund; and Hungarian Boat, Pannonia Evezos Egylet/Magyar Evezos Szovetseg. The Cambridge crew, who had been coached by C.W.H. Taylor and W. Dudley Ward, were eventually beaten in the semi-final by Belgium (who had taken the Grand Challenge Cup in 1906 and 1907) by 1⅓ lengths. The gold medal was eventually taken by the British Leander crew, with Belgium taking the silver, while the British Cambridge crew took the bronze together with Canada.

After getting his BA, Carver became a director of the family company, which owned Hollins Mill at Marple and had offices and warehouses in central Manchester's 'cotton district'. He also became very active in the Scout movement establishing a troop in Marple. In 1911 he married Elizabeth Hobart, daughter of Robert Thompson Hobart of Tunbridge Wells.

On 3 September 1914, shortly after the outbreak of war, he applied for a commission but was rejected by the army medical board because he was having trouble with his hearing. He applied again a month later having had treatment and this time was accepted. He was commissioned into the 1/2nd East Lancashire Field Company, Royal Engineers. Promoted to captain, he was given command of one of the company's four sections. In May 1915 he was sent out to Egypt for training before landing in Gallipoli. During the Third Battle of Krithia, on 4 June 1915, the East Lancashire engineers were ordered to follow the Territorial battalions of the Manchester Regiment in an attack on a strongly defended Turkish position. The engineers were instructed to construct a strong point capable of repelling any Turkish counter-attack, and prepare communication trenches between the front line and the British reserve position. Two sections of engineers, Nos 3 and 4, were behind the 6th Manchesters, while Nos 1 and 2 took up position behind the 8th Battalion. Private Sheldon of 'C' Company, 6th Manchester Regiment, later recounted his experiences during the attack:

> I shall never forget the moment when we had to leave the shelter of the trenches. It is, indeed, terrible, the first step you take – right in the face of the most deadly fire and to realize that any moment you may be shot down; but if you are not hit, then you seem to gather courage and when you see on either side of you, men like yourself, it inspires you with a determination to press forward.

Sheldon was shot in the leg only a few yards from the British trenches. As they advanced, many concealed Turkish snipers (which the Manchesters had missed) started shooting at them from behind. At some point during the advance Captain

The 1908 Cambridge Eight with Carver sitting far right.

Oswald Carver was hit in the back and fell. He was evacuated to 11th Casualty Clearing Station on 'W' Beach but died from his wounds three days later on 7 June 1915. On 2 July 1915 *The Stockport Advertiser* carried a moving tribute:

> The Scout movement has lost a very sincere well wisher and friend. Mr. Carver introduced the movement into Marple and gave it every assistance in his power. He seemed to realize the true spirit underlying it, not the popular one which I am glad to say is dying out, that it kept boys away from street corners, but the higher object, namely, that it gives an opportunity of applying their everyday life and games, the Christian principles they are taught in Church and School. Mr. Carver answered the call of duty immediately the War broke out and had not the opportunity of seeing the Troop since it was re-organized in August last. Now he has answered the higher call and we have lost his personal assistance.

Oswald Carver is buried in Lancashire Landing Cemetery, grave A 7. He is also remembered on the Holmes Chapel War Memorial and in the Trinity College Chapel.

In 1927 Carver's widow married Bernard Montgomery, later a field marshal and national hero in the Second World War.

His brother Basil Armitage Carver, a second lieutenant in the 6th Inniskilling Dragoons, was killed on 21 August 1916, aged 19. His cousin Geoffrey Hamilton Bagshaw, 1st Royal Dragoons, was also killed in action on 13 May 1915.

9

SECOND LIEUTENANT RICHARD WILLINGDON SOMERS-SMITH

Boat position: Number Two & Bow
Race: 61st Boat Race, 26 March 1904
    62nd Boat Race, 1 April 1905
College: Merton College, Oxford
Served: 7th Battalion attached King's Royal Rifle Corps
Death: 30 June 1915, aged 33

The most lion-hearted man that ever sat in a boat.

Richard Willingdon Somers-Smith

Richard Willingdon Somers-Smith was born on 27 October 1882 at Bur Lea, Walton-on-Thames, Surrey. He was the eldest son of Robert Vernon JP CC, clerk to the Grocer's Company, and Gertrude Somers-Smith. From an athletic family, his father, also an Oxford man, ran for his university against Cambridge in 1868 and 1869, and became the AAA ½-mile champion twice. Richard was educated at Eton College and resided with other Etonians on the High Street, as well as Raymond Radcliffe, a clerk in holy orders and schoolmaster, and Radcliffe's wife Mary. He also rowed in the Eton

The 1905 Cambridge crew. Richard Willingdon Somers-Smith is sitting on the far right.

Eight at Henley. On leaving Eton he went up to Merton College, Oxford – his fathers old college. He won the Freshman's mile and could easily have got his Blue for running like his father before him, but rowing became his passion. Richard rowed in the trials and clearly impressed because he was selected to row at number two in the 1904 Boat Race.

61st Boat Race, 26 March 1904

Cambridge went into the 1904 race as champions, having won the previous year's race by an impressive 6 lengths. Oxford were coached once again by G.C. Bourne (New College) who had rowed for Oxford in 1882, 1883 and 1898, four-time Boat Race veteran William Fletcher (Christ Church) 1890–93, and C.K. Philips (New College) who had also rowed for Oxford on four occasions between 1895 and 1898.

Cambridge went with the very experienced Francis Escombe (Trinity Hall) 1902, and three-time race veteran Claude Waterhouse Hearn Taylor (Third Trinity) 1901–03. The umpire was the old Etonian Frederick I. Pitman (Third Trinity) who had rowed for Cambridge between 1884 and 1886. By an unfortunate coincidence both the Boat Club presidents, Monier-Williams (University – Oxford) and Edwards-Moss (Brasenose), were unable to take part in the race due to injury. Monier-Williams had picked up a knee injury; he was never to row again, dying in Africa of fever in 1909. Edwards-Moss damaged his elbow. Two members of the Cambridge Eight had previous Boat Race experience: P.H. Thomas (Third Trinity) rowing number six (1902–04) and B.G.A. Scott (Trinity Hall), the Cambridge cox. They also rowed with two foreign oarsmen, Stanley Bruce (Trinity Hall) number two (Australian, later 1st Viscount Bruce of Melbourne), and the New Zealander Harold Gillies (Caius), number seven. Oxford, on the other hand, only produced one rower with previous race experience, the stroke, A.K. Graham (Balliol).

The morning of the race was cold and foggy with a weak tide and the rowers struggled to keep warm. Cambridge won the toss and decided on the Surrey station, pushing Oxford on to the Middlesex side of the Thames. Umpire Pitman got the race going at precisely 7.45 a.m. A good account of the race was taken from the Cambridge University Boat Club (CUBC) and published by G.C. Drinkwater (Wadham, 1902–03, both Cambridge victories) in his book, *The University Boat Race: Official Centenary History*. This time Drinkwater felt that the 'race was a good one, for the crews were more evenly matched'.

The CUBC Minutes also summarised the race:

We got up and had breakfast at 5.30 and went down to the Leander Boathouse [then on the Embankment at Putney] at about 7 a.m. Notwithstanding the early hour, several old Blues were there. Oxford went out for a preliminary spin, but we stayed at the boathouse as the morning was very cold and there was a slight fog. Oxford left the London R.C. at about 7.45 and we followed at once. We both got to our stake-boats and Mr F. I. Pitman started the race. The tide was not very strong and Oxford rowing the slightly faster stroke, drew away steadily from the start and by the Mile Post were clear of us. But we had settled down to a steady 32 and after this we began to gain steadily upon them. By Harrods, the Oxford cox had come too far across to our shore (the Surrey) and Scott [Cambridge cox] managed to drive him back again and thereby gained a lot of ground for us. We still continued to gain and at Hammersmith Bridge (8 min 24 sec) we were only two thirds of a length to the bad. At The Dove we were level again after 9 min. 40 sec. rowing. Once we got level the race was practically over, for the Oxford crew went to pieces and by Chiswick Ferry we were practically clear; after that it became a procession, we winning by four and a half lengths in 21 min and 37 sec …

This was the slowest winning time since 1898 when Oxford won in 22 minutes 15 seconds (after the Cambridge boat took on too much water and all but sunk). It was Cambridge's third consecutive victory and their fifth in six years. The overall score now stood at 33–27 in Oxford's favour, but Cambridge were beginning to narrow the gap.

62nd Boat Race, 1 April 1905

Despite being in the losing boat the previous year, Richard Somers-Smith (Merton) was selected for the 1905 race. However, this time not as number two, but as bow. Once again Cambridge went into the race as champions. The Cambridge coaches were John Edwards-Moss (Third Trinity) who had rowed number seven for Cambridge in both 1902 and 1903, the experienced Francis Escombe (Trinity Hall – number five, 1902) and David Alexander Wauchope (Trinity Hall – stroke, 1895). The Oxford crew were trained once again by William Fletcher and C.K. Philips. The umpire was the ever-reliable Frederick I. Pitman (Third Trinity). The Cambridge Eight contained four rowers with previous Boat Race experience: H. Sanger (Lady Margaret Boat Club – bow), T.B.C. Johnstone (Third Trinity – number three), T.P.H. Thomas (Third Trinity – number four), who was rowing having still not fully recovered from illness, and R.V. Powell (Third Trinity – number seven). In fact, six members of the Cambridge crew came from Trinity College. Oxford's crew contained five members with Boat Race experience: R.W. Somers-Smith (Merton – bow), A.J.S.H. Hales (Corpus Christi – number three), A.R. Balfour (University – number four), E.P. Evans (University – number six) and A.K. Graham (Balliol – stroke).

Cambridge won the toss and decided on the Middlesex side of the river, leaving Oxford the Surrey side. Umpire Pitman got the race under way at 11.30 a.m. Oxford took an early lead and were ahead by the Mile Post. They never gave up the lead and for the first time in four years won the race by the narrow margin of 3 lengths. Their time was 20 minutes 35 seconds. The overall score was now 33–27 in Oxford's favour.

★★★

As well as rowing in the Boat Race Somers-Smith also won the University pairs with A.K. Graham (Balliol). In 1905 he stroked his college into the final of the coxwainless fours and reached the final of the University pairs, this time with T.G. Brocklebank (Trinity), losing to a heavier crew in the final. He also rowed for his college in four events at Henley.

At Oxford he was said to be a man of remarkable modesty and personal magnetism, with such pluck that, in the words of one of his rowing coaches, he was 'the most lion hearted man that ever sat in a boat'.

After leaving Oxford with his BA he decided to try his luck tea planting in Ceylon. However, at the outbreak of war he returned to England and took a commission into the 7th Battalion, King's Royal Rifle Corps, as a second lieutenant. He travelled to France with his battalion and was involved in heavy fighting around Hooge. Richard Somers-Smith was hit in the head by shrapnel and killed instantly on 7 June 1915 while trying to rescue his sergeant who had been buried alive during a heavy bombardment.

He is buried in Bedford House Cemetery, enclosure No. 2 VI. A 27. He is also commemorated in Trinity Chapel, Eton College, and the Hersham Memorial.

His younger brother, Captain John Robert Somers-Smith, 5th Battalion, London Regiment, won a Military Cross for gallantry in 1915 but was killed in action on 1 July 1916 – the first day of the Battle of the Somme. He was also a fine rower, attending Eton and Oxford, but never took part in a Boat Race. He did, however, win a gold medal in the Coxless Fours during the 1908 London Olympics.

10

SECOND LIEUTENANT GEORGE ERIC FAIRBAIRN

Boat position: Number Two
Race: 65th Boat Race, 4 April 1908
     69th Boat Race, 1 April 1911
College: Jesus College, Cambridge
Served: 10th Battalion, Durham Light Infantry
Death: 20 June 1915, aged 26

*'Ere fiercely upsprang, Eric the mighty; Red was his face, And Blue was his raiment,
Kinsman was he, To Steve the great trainer ...*

Second Lieutenant George Eric
Fairbairn.

George Eric Fairbairn (better known as Eric) was born on 18 August 1888 in Melbourne, Australia. He was the son of Thomas, a pastoralist (concerned with the raising of livestock and animal husbandry), and Lena Fairbairn (née Simpson). They later moved to No. 9 Wilton Street, Westminster, London. He was educated at Geelong Anglican Boarding School, Corio Bay, before going to Eton College as a 'Wet Bob' (rower). In October 1906 he went up to Jesus College, Cambridge. The Fairbairn family was already well known at Jesus College. His uncle was Steven Fairbairn who created the

'Fairbairn style' of rowing and whom many credited as being the man who turned the fortunes of the Jesus College boat around. Steven Fairbairn, although a fine rower, was better known for his coaching. Fairbairn wanted his crews to slide in their seats, which helped them use the power of their legs to much greater effect during the stroke. To this end he wanted longer slides fitted to the boats. He also wanted his oarsmen to concentrate on their oars and blade work, and not how gracefully they moved in the boat. He called the advocates of the 'orthodox style' the 'Pretty-Pretty Brigade', pointing out that crews never won medals and cups for style. Steven Fairbairn also took part in the Boat Race rowing number five in 1882–83 (Oxford victories) and 1886–87 (Cambridge victories).

It's also worth pointing out that Eric was not only a first-class rower, but also a good rugby player, turning out for Rosslyn Park FC. A popular character, a *Cock of the Roost* article gave us a small insight into the man: 'Like all geniuses, he has idiosyncrasies. He hates collars, takes no milk in his tea through fear of dead flies, and is a confirmed Peripatetic after bump-suppers.'

Eric quickly established himself in college rowing. He was Head of the Lent Bumps 1907, won the coxswainless four, took part in the trials, and was finally selected to row number two in the 1908 Boat Race.

65th Boat Race, 4 April 1908

Cambridge put together a formidable coaching team for the 1908 race: L.H.K. Bushe-Fox (St John's) for the fifth year in succession, Francis J. Escombe (Trinity Hall – number five, 1902), the five-time Blue Stanley Muttlebury (Third Trinity) who had rowed number five and six between 1886 and 1890, and David Alexander Wauchope (Trinity Hall) who had stroked for Cambridge in 1895. Oxford was equally well represented by their coaching staff: Harcourt Gilbey Gold (Magdalen) who had stroked for Oxford on four occasions between 1896 and 1899 and was Boat Club president in 1900, and R.P.P. Rowe (Magdalen) who raced for Oxford between 1889 and 1892. Frederick I. Pitman (Third Trinity), the old Etonian and Boat Race veteran (1884–86), was selected to umpire for the fifth year.

Cambridge selected four rowers with previous Boat Club experience: Douglas Stuart (Trinity Hall – stroke), Eric Powell (Third Trinity – number seven), J.S. Burn (First Trinity – number five) and R.F.R.P. Boyle (Trinity Hall – cox). The Oxford crew also contained four members with previous Boat Race experience: Alister Kirby (Magdalen – number five), Albert Gladstone (Christ Church – stroke), A.W.F. Donkin (Magdalen – cox) and E.H.L. Southwell (Magdalen – number three).

Cambridge went into the race as favourites, with the writer and former Oxford rower George Drinkwater describing them as 'better and stronger than the previous year'. This was largely due to the illness and injury that swept through the Oxford crew. James Gillan, their number five, was banned from racing by his doctors. Influenza affected several members of the crew and A.G. Kirby still raced despite not being fully fit, having suffered from a bout of jaundice.

Race day was cold with a strong headwind but good tide. Oxford won the toss and chose the Surrey side of the Thames, leaving the Middlesex side to Cambridge. Umpire Pitman got the race going at precisely 3.30 p.m. Cambridge made the better start, outrating Oxford by 39½ to 38 strokes and began to pull ahead. The rough water also suited Cambridge's smoother, easier style and by the Mile Post they were clear. At Harrods Furniture Depository, Cambridge were a full 2 lengths ahead. Oxford spurted several times but the tactic failed and they were unable to close the gap, with Cambridge well ahead by Barnes Bridge. For the third time in a row Cambridge finally won the race, this time by 2½ lengths in a time of 19 minutes 20 seconds (the fastest time since the 1902 race). It took the overall record to 34–30 in Oxford's favour. Eric had been a member of the winning crew in his very first Boat Race, which is more than his uncle Steven could achieve with Cambridge, having been beaten by 7 lengths in 1882.

Eric Fairbairn's next triumph came in the Summer Olympics in 1908. This time not in the Eight, which went on to win the bronze medal, but in the Coxless Pairs with another Jesus man, Philip Verdon, going on to win the silver medal, beaten by another British pair, John Fenning and Gordon Thomson (Trinity Hall), in a time of 9 minutes 41 seconds. Thomson went on to row number three in the Boat Race of 1909 for Cambridge.

In 1909 Fairbairn captained the Jesus boat and was selected to row for Cambridge again in the Boat Race. However, a week before the race Eric was forced to pull out due to illness. The Jesus boat also entered the Grand Challenge at Henley only to be beaten in the final by the Belgian Eight 'those pesky Men of Ghent'. They would have to wait until 1911 for another chance to take on the Belgians.

68th Boat Race, 1 April 1911

After missing the 1909 Boat Race because of illness and then again in 1910, Eric was eventually recalled to the Cambridge boat in 1911, once again in the number two position. Oxford were the reigning champions having defeated Cambridge the year before by a convincing 3½ lengths. The Oxford boat was coached by H.R. Barker (Christ Church), who had raced for Oxford as number seven in 1908 and number two in 1909, the famous G.C. Bourne (New College), who rowed bow for Oxford in 1882 and 1883, and Harcourt Gilbey Gold (Magdalen), who rowed for Oxford four times between 1896 and 1899. He was also president for the 1900 race. Cambridge chose to be coached by Stanley Bruce (Trinity Hall), who rowed number two for Cambridge in 1904, William Dudley Ward (Third Trinity), who rowed number seven in 1897, 1899 and 1900, Raymond Etherington-Smith (First Trinity), who had rowed number six in 1898 and number five in 1900, and finally H. W. Willis, who had coached the Oxford losing crew in 1907. For the eighth year Frederick I. Pitman (Third Trinity), who had rowed stroke in the Boat Race between 1884 and 1886, was the umpire.

There was a particular buzz to this year's race due to the presence of Edward, the Prince of Wales and his brother Prince Albert who were to follow the race. To add to the excitement, it was also the first race to be followed by an aeroplane – quite a rare sight in those days. Six of the Cambridge crew – F.E. Hellyer (Trinity – number three), C.A. Skinner (Jesus – cox), R.W.M. Arbuthnot (Trinity – stroke), J.B. Rosher (Trinity – number six), C.R. le Blanc-Smith (Trinity – number five) and G.E. Fairbairn (Jesus – number seven) – and three of the Oxford crew – Duncan Mackinnon (Magdalen – number seven), Robert Bourne (New College – stroke) and Stanley Garton (Magdalen – number six) – had previous Boat Race experience. Charles Littlejohn (New College), who rowed number five for Oxford, came from Australia. Pieter Voltelyn Graham van der Byl (Pembroke – number two) and C.A. Skinner (Jesus – cox) came from South Africa.

It was a clear day with a slight breeze and a strong tide. Oxford won the toss and selected the Middlesex side of the river giving Cambridge the Surrey side of the Thames. The race began at 2.36 p.m., started by Umpire Pitman. Oxford set off at the faster rate. By the Craven Steps Oxford were ¾ of a length ahead, a lead they maintained to the Mile Post. By the Crab Tree pub Oxford were clear, and by the time the Oxford boat reached Harrods Furniture Depository they were a further length ahead. At Hammersmith Bridge Oxford were 2½ lengths ahead and by the Chiswick Steps the Oxford crew were 4 lengths clear. Despite a late surge by Cambridge, Oxford maintained their lead, winning by 2¾ lengths in a time of 18 minutes 29 seconds (the winning time was the fastest in Boat Race history). The overall record was now 37–30 in Oxford's favour. Eric had now won one and lost one. The disappointment of losing the Boat Race, however, was quickly put behind him as the greatest challenge of his rowing career loomed.

★★★

In May 1911 the Jesus Eight set out for what their coxswain, Conrad Skinner, called 'the Belgian Expedition', rowing against the Belgian crew that had beaten them in 1909 in the Grand Challenge at Henley. Given the power of the Belgian Eight, the idea of a crew from a single college taking them on, never mind beating them, was greeted with a great deal of cynicism by the rowing world. *The Sportsman* wrote of the challenge:

The 1911 Cambridge Eight.

Once more it is necessary to point out that the Eight which has just left to row the Belgians is not a representative English crew. It is just Jesus College that is going to race a combined Belgian crew, with the knowledge that the Belgians have won three of the last four occasion they have visited Henley – and when they were beaten it took one of the finest amateur Eights, the Leander crew at the Olympic regatta. It is difficult to think that the Jesus men will win, but they carry with them the good wishes of their countrymen.

However, the crew did not lack experience or enthusiasm and contained six rowers that had been beaten by the Belgians in the 1909 Grand Challenge. They were itching for revenge. They were coached by the highly experienced Steven Fairbairn and Stanley Bruce (later prime minister of Australia). Thanks to the two coaches the Jesus Eight started the race in great condition, able to produce between 43 and 47 strokes per minute. On the day of the race, 25 May 1911, over 100,000 spectators lined the length of the Terdonck Canal. Skinner later recounted his experience:

Cheering broke out as the Belgian crew seized the lead on the first half dozen strokes, but then having set the boat moving in four quick but gradually lengthening strokes, we settled into our stride, and speedily drew level … we gave a 'ten' which let daylight in between our rudder and their bows, and with steady confidence this was increased to a lead of a length and a half before the bridge was reached. This huge structure marking the mile, witnessed the decisive struggle. Under cover of its shadow and hidden for perhaps a hundred feet from our opponents under our respective arches, we raised our stroke slightly and gave such a 'ten' that we leaped ahead … we both battled on to the finish, amid an uproar that was little short of deafening.

Much to everyone's surprise the Jesus crew defeated the Belgians. The victory was hailed all over Cambridge and England:

And these young fellows who had come down from Cambridge … to meet a picked Belgian crew just for the honor of English rowing … It was a thoroughly sportsmanlike piece of work on the part of the Jesus men. Their College may well be proud of them.

Such was the excitement that a set of postcards was produced and over 170,000 copies were sold in a week. A march was also composed to the victory and thousands waited outside the banqueting hall just to glimpse their heroes. Skinner later commented:

No crew was ever feted as we were and many of us took shame at the poverty of England's welcome to Belgian crews at Henley in past times. Never will any member of the crew forget the amazing generosity of the Gantois, in fact of the Belgians as a nation.

Later a poem was written to celebrate the Terdonck victory. Fairbairn's part in the race was described:

> 'Ere fiercely upsprang,
> Eric the mighty;
> Red was his face
> And Blue was his raiment
> Kinsman was he
> To Steve the great trainer …

Of the Jesus crew that beat the Belgians that day, four were not to survive the war: Lieutenant Hugh John Sladen Shields, Royal Army Medical Corps (attached 1st Battalion Irish Guards) died 25/26 October 1914; Lieutenant Henry Mills Goldsmith, Devonshire Regiment (attached 2nd Battalion, Lincolnshire Regiment) died 9 May 1915; Sub-Lieutenant Thomas Mervyn Crowe, Royal Naval Volunteer Reserve, Anson Battalion, Royal Naval Division and Eric Fairbairn of the Durham Light Infantry, died 10 June 1915.

On 5 August 1914, a day after war was declared, Eric enlisted into the ranks of the Artists Rifles. On 24 October 1914, he received a commission as a second lieutenant into the 10th Battalion, Durham Light Infantry. After training, on 22 May 1915 Eric travelled with his battalion to France. Unfortunately after only being at the Front for a week, Second Lieutenant Eric Fairbairn was badly wounded by shrapnel from a rifle grenade. The War Diary for 20 June records: 'All companies returned from trenches early this morning … D. Coy reports 2/Lt Fairburn dangerously wounded.' Unfortunately Eric Fairbairn died of his wounds.

He is buried at Bailleul Communal Cemetery Extension, Nord, grave I. C. 135. He's also commemorated on the Jesus College Memorial and the Eton College Memorial.

11

CAPTAIN WILFRID HUBERT CHAPMAN

Boat position: Bow
Race: 56th Boat Race, 25 March 1899
     59th Boat Race, 22 March 1902
     60th Boat Race, 1 April 1903
College: Trinity College, Cambridge
Served: 6th Alexandra Princess of Wales' Own Yorkshire Regiment
Death: 7 August 1915, aged 35

Comparatively light and slightly built, he is an extraordinarily hard worker who never shirks his duties.

Wilfrid Hubert Chapman.

Wilfrid ('Teddy') Hubert Chapman was born on 13 December 1879, in Whitby, Yorkshire. He was the fourth and youngest son of Joseph John and Fanny Chapman of No. 17 St Hilda's Terrace, Whitby. He was educated at Eton College where he was popular in Eton Society (more commonly known as Pop) and was whip of the school's Beagles hunting pack. His talent for rowing was quickly recognised and developed with him seated in bow and he became second captain of boats. He won the Ladies' Plate in 1897 and 1898. He was also a first-class athlete and quick on his feet, winning the School Mile, Steeplechase and Half-Mile. He went up to Trinity

College, Cambridge, as a pensioner on 25 June 1898. There was a rumour at the time that he, together with others, was especially selected (for entrance into the university) and trained by Cambridge in an attempt to put a crew together that would stop Oxford winning the Boat Race again for the tenth year running. As a result Chapman was selected to row bow in the 1899 Boat Race.

56th Boat Race, 25 March 1899

Oxford went into the race having been undefeated in the ten previous years –having won the 1898 race by about ¼ of a mile in 22 minutes 15 seconds. The Oxford crew were coached by the experienced Oxford rower G.C. Bourne (New College) who had been bow in both 1882 and 1883, Douglas McLean (New College) who had raced number five between 1883 and 1887, and finally R.P. Rowe (Magdalen) who had rowed number two and seven for Oxford between 1889 and 1892. Cambridge decided on William Fletcher (Christ Church) who had rowed number six and seven between 1891 and 1893, R.C. Lehmann who, although he had been captain of the Trinity Boat Club and rowed in the Trials Eights, was never selected for the Boat Race. The ever-present Frank Willan (Exeter), who had rowed for Oxford between 1866 and 1869, was selected as umpire for the tenth year in succession. The Oxford crew contained four rowers with previous Boat Race experience: Harcourt Gilbey Gold (Magdalen – stroke), R.O. Pitman (New College – bow), F.W. Warre (Balliol – number four) and A.T. Herbert (Balliol – number seven). Cambridge decided on three experienced rowers: Claude Goldie (Third Trinity – number three), William Dudley Ward (Third Trinity – number seven) and Raymond Etherington-Smith (First Trinity – number five). The Cambridge boat also contained the only non-British rower in N.L. Calvert (Trinity Hall – number two), who was Australian. Cambridge also had a last-minute disaster when their highly experienced number four, John Ernest Payne (Peterhouse), was taken ill with influenza and was unable to race.

The weather was bright and clear, with what breeze there was coming from the south-west. The tide was poor. Cambridge won the toss and selected the Surrey side of the river, leaving the Middlesex side of the Thames to Oxford. Frank Willan started the race at 12.58 p.m. The crews were well matched and by the Mile Post Oxford had a narrow ¼-length lead. As Cambridge began to make up ground Gold, the Oxford stroke, increased the crew's rate. However, Gibbon, the Cambridge stroke, responded and began to slowly pull away from Oxford and by The Dove pub were ahead. It was a lead they were not to lose and they passed the winning post 3¼ lengths ahead in a time of 21 minutes 4 seconds. It was Cambridge's first victory for ten years. It reduced Oxford's overall lead to 32–23.

Chapman was described as:

Comparatively light and slightly built, he is an extraordinarily hard worker who never shirks his duties. He is quaint and original, not particular about dress, and a good friend, who is much liked by all who know him and by many who do not.

Chapman would certainly have been chosen for the Cambridge boat in 1900 had he not taken a commission as a second lieutenant (10 July 1900) into the 4th (Militia) Battalion, North Yorkshire Militia, and sailed to South Africa to

Cambridge Eight in 1899 with Chapman bottom centre.

take part in the Second Boer War 1899–1902. He was promoted to captain on 25 February 1901 but only managed a year in Africa before he was invalided home with fever in 1902.

He returned to Cambridge to continue with his studies. He also coached the Third Trinity May Boat to the Head of the River, and demonstrated his abilities again when Third Trinity won the University Fours. After missing the Boat Race in both 1900 (Cambridge Victory) and 1901 (Oxford Victory) he was selected as bow for the 1902 race.

59th Boat Race, 22 March 1902

Having won the 1901 race by ⅖ of a length, Oxford went into the 1902 race as champions. Once again Oxford were trained by the highly experienced G.C. Bourne (New College), William Fletcher (Christ Church) and another former Oxford rower and four-time Blue 1890–93, Harcourt Gilbey Gold (Magdalen). Cambridge went with the two-time Blue, 1899–90, John Ernest Payne (New College). Once again the umpire was the former Oxford rower (1866–69) Colonel Frank Willan (Exeter). This was his thirteenth and last appearance as umpire in the Boat Race. He died in March 1931. The former Cambridge rower

The 1899 Cambridge Boat Race crew. Chapman sits far right.

Frederick I. Pitman (Third Trinity) who raced three times for Cambridge between 1884 and 1886 was to take his place the following year. Pitman went on to umpire the race thirteen times between 1903 and 1926, dying in January 1942.

Oxford brought back five experienced rowers for their boat, in the hope of emulating their success the year before: Gilchrist Maclagan (Magdalen – cox), F.O.J. Huntley (University – stroke), J. Younger (New College – number three), A. de L. Long (New College – number six) and H.J. Hale (Balliol – number four). The Oxford crew also contained the Milburn brothers; D. Milburn (Lincoln – number two, who was also a noted polo player winning the prestigious Westchester Cup on six occasions) and J.G. Milburn (Lincoln – number five) were both American and Harvard graduates. They were the only foreign rowers that year. Seven of the nine Cambridge rowers came from Trinity College, with four having previous Boat Race experience: Wilfrid Hubert Chapman (Third Trinity – bow), C.W.H. Taylor (Third Trinity – number four), H.B. Grylls (First Trinity – number six) and R.H. Nelson (Third Trinity – stroke).

The day of the race was overcast and raining heavily. Cambridge won the toss and decided on the Surrey side, leaving the Middlesex side of the Thames to Oxford. Umpire Willan got the race going at 12.45 p.m. Cambridge made the better start and went into an early lead. Outrating them, the Cambridge crew were clear of Oxford within a few minutes. Cambridge never gave up the lead and won the race by 5 lengths in a time of 19 minutes 9 seconds. It took Oxford's overall lead to 33–25.

In the same year Chapman was in the Third Trinity Eight, which won the Grand Challenge Cup at Henley, then in the four that won the Stewards' Challenge Cup beating a Leander crew on both occasions. Because of his success in the 1902 Boat Race, and his continuing success after that, Chapman was selected once again to row bow in the 1903 Boat Race.

60th Boat Race, 1 April 1903

Oxford selected the very experienced G.C. Bourne to coach the crew once again, together with the four-time Blue C.K. Philips (New College), 1895–98. Cambridge put their faith in Charles John Bristowe (Trinity Hall) who had rowed bow for Cambridge in 1886–87 and Claude Goldie (Third Trinity) who had rowed number seven twice for Cambridge in 1898 and 1899. Later the former Cambridge rower William Dudley Ward (Third Trinity), who had rowed number seven in 1897, took over the training. The race umpire for the first time was Frederick I. Pitman (Third Trinity).

Oxford's preparation was hampered by a series of accidents and illnesses including influenza, which created problems with crew selection. Despite that Oxford went into the race with four rowers who had previous Boat Race experience: A. de L. Long (New College – number three), G.C. Drinkwater (Wadham – number seven), H.W. Adams (University – number five) and the American (the only foreign rower in the race) D. Milburn (Lincoln – number six). Cambridge selected six rowers from the 1902 winning crew: W.H. Chapman (Third Trinity – bow), H.B. Grylls (First Trinity – number six), C.W.H. Taylor (Third Trinity – number four), R.H. Nelson (Third Trinity – stroke), P.H. Thomas (Third Trinity – number three) and J. Edwards-Moss (Third Trinity – number seven).

On the day of the race there was a strong tide running up the river. However, the 1903 race is probably best known for its poor start, which affected the entire race. Oxford won the toss and chose to row from the Surrey side, leaving the Middlesex side of the river to Cambridge.

Umpire Pitman, starting his first race, tried to get the boats under way at 3.35 p.m. Tom Tim handed him the antique gun, which he had for as long as anyone could remember. However, as Pitman pulled the trigger the pistol struck a half cock and refused to go off for several seconds. As Pitman had shouted his instructions, 'are you ready' the Cambridge crew had squared their blades and against the strong tide the man in the stakeboat was unable to hold them back. The Oxford crew on the other hand were held more firmly and Cambridge took an early ⊠ of a length lead. Pitman, still trying to sort out his faulty firearm, failed to notice. The dismayed Oxford crew did what they could to try to make up the distance but never really got it together. Cambridge crossed the finishing line with a 6-length lead in a time of 19 minutes 33 seconds. Oxford's overall lead was now reduced to 33–26.

★★★

In the same year Chapman became captain of the University Boating Club. At Henley, rowing for Third Trinity, he won the Stewards' Challenge Cup. It was said that this was the best four ever seen at Henley up to that date. He was also in the Third Trinity Eight that were runners up in the Grand Challenge Cup, being beaten by only 6ft. However, he was back in 1904, and won the Grand Challenge Cup once again, this time with the Leander Eight. He also won the Stewards' Challenge Cup again with the Third Trinity four.

In 1905 Chapman travelled to India with the Bombay Company becoming their manager in Karachi. It was in the same year that Chapman's older brother Lieutenant Percy Chapman, 21st Lancers, died of enteric fever while serving in the Sudan. In 1909 he married May Campbell Chapman and they had two daughters, Elizabeth Mary, born 22 April 1911 (Karachi) and Ann Sinclair, born 31 December 1913 (Karachi). At the outbreak of the First World War Chapman took a commission into the Sind Volunteer Field Artillery. However, when his company refused to allow him to go to France, he left his position and returned to England in June 1915, becoming a captain in the 6th Battalion, Yorkshire Regiment (his cousin commanded the battalion). The family resided at Home Farm, Cromer. He travelled with his battalion to Gallipoli and was killed in action during the abortive attack on Lala Baba on 7 August 1915. It was during this attack that the battalion were ordered to use their bayonets only and despite showing great bravery were cut to pieces. At the end of the day the battalion had casualties numbering sixteen officers and 250 other ranks. Ten of the officers were killed instantly or later died of their wounds. Not only was Wilfrid Chapman killed in this attack but so was his cousin, Lieutenant Colonel Chapman, the battalion's commanding officer.

Captain Wilfrid Chapman is commemorated at Azmak Cemetery, Suvla, Special Memorial 35. He is also commemorated on the North Yorks Memorial at St Mary's Church in Whitby, Trinity College Chapel and Eton College Memorial.

12

LIEUTENANT EDWARD GORDON WILLIAMS

Boat position: Number Six
Race: 65th Boat Race, 4 April 1908
    66th Boat Race, 3 April 1909
    67th Boat Race, 23 March 1910
College: Trinity College, Cambridge
Served: 2nd Battalion, Grenadier Guards
Death: 12 August 1915, aged 27

A famous rower from a famous rowing family.

Lieutenant Edward Gordon Williams.

Edward Gordon Williams was born on 20 July 1888 at Ottery St Mary, Devon (some records say Honiton), the son of Edward Gordon and Louise Davies Williams. He was educated at Eton College where he rowed in the First Eight before going up to Trinity College, Cambridge, as a pensioner on 25 June 1907. A talented and established rower he rowed for his college and was selected to row number six in the Cambridge Eight during the 1908 Boat Race.

65th Boat Race, 4 April 1908

Cambridge took part in the 1908 race as champions, having beaten the Oxford boat in 1907 by a convincing 4½ lengths. Oxford were trained by the highly experienced former Oxford stroke Harcourt Gilbey Gold (Magdalen), who rowed between 1896 and 1899, as well as the equally experienced R.P.P. Rowe (Magdalen), who had rowed number two and seven four times for Oxford between 1889 and 1892. For the fifth consecutive year Cambridge selected Francis J. Escombe (Trinity Hall), who rowed number five in the Cambridge victory in 1902 (he later became a Boat Club umpire), L.H.K. Bushe-Fox (St John's), Stanley Muttlebury (Third Trinity), who had rowed number five and six for Cambridge between 1886 and 1890, and David Alexander Wauchope (Trinity Hall), who rowed stroke in the Oxford victory of 1895. The umpire was Frederick I. Pitman (Third Trinity), a Boat Race veteran himself who had rowed for Cambridge as stroke between 1884 and 1886.

Despite a number of the Oxford rowers being laid low by illness and injury, they did just about manage to put a crew together, although maybe not their best. Four of Oxford's rowers were Boat Race veterans: Alister Kirby (Magdalen – number five), who rowed despite not having fully recovered from jaundice, Albert Gladstone (Christ Church – stroke), H.R. Barker (Christ Church – seven) and A.W.F. Donkin (Magdalen – cox). The Australian Collier Cudmore (Magdalen – number two) was the only non-British rower in the race. Cambridge matched Oxford by also having four veterans in their boat: Douglas Stuart (Trinity Hall – stroke), Eric Powell (Third Trinity – number seven), J.S. Burn (First Trinity – number five) and R.F.R.P. Boyle (Trinity Hall – cox). G.E. Fairbairn (Jesus), the Cambridge number two, was following in the steps of his famous uncle, Steven Fairbairn. Steven Fairbairn rowed number six and seven for Cambridge between 1882 and 1883 and number five between 1886 and 1887. He also developed a revolutionary style of rowing called 'Fairbairnism'. Fairbairn wanted his crews to slide in their seats to facilitate leg drive. To this end he wanted longer slides fitted into boats, allowing better use of the legs. This led him to develop a revolutionary rowing style featuring concurrent use of the legs, back and arms at the catch. He was also keen for crews to not focus unduly on positioning their bodies. He adopted the policy that no crew won a race by looking good. Such was his influence on rowing that there is a memorial bust of him on the Mile Post of the race's course.

The day was clear but blustery with a strong headwind. Oxford won the toss and selected the Surrey side of the river with Cambridge therefore forced to take the Middlesex side of the Thames. Pitman started the race at 3.30 p.m. with no mishaps. Cambridge made the better start, getting away quickly and outrating Oxford from the start. The Cambridge crew were also better in the rougher water and by the Mile Post Cambridge were clear. By Harrods Furniture Depository Cambridge

Edward Gordon Williams.

were 2 lengths ahead. Oxford tried a series of spurts to try to get back but failed to make ground. By Barnes Bridge, Cambridge were still ahead and passed the winning post 2½ lengths ahead. The time was 19 minutes 20 seconds (the quickest since the 1902 race). The overall lead was now 34–30 in Oxford's favour.

This wasn't to be Williams' only success that year as he was selected for the Eight to take part in the 1908 Summer Olympics. Williams' boat was well beaten by the Belgians but they still shared the bronze medal with Canada. However, the second British boat, the Leander crew, beat the Belgians into second place and took the gold.

As a result of his two successes, Williams' was chosen again to row in the 1909 Boat Race.

66th Boat Race, 3 April 1909

After the resounding victory in 1908, Cambridge started the 1909 race as champions. For this year's race Oxford decided to bring in G.C. Bourne (New College) who had rowed twice for the university as bow in 1882–83, the highly experienced Francis Escombe (his sixth consecutive year), the celebrated Harcourt Gilbey Gold (Magdalen) who had stroked for Oxford between 1896 and 1899 (Oxford president in 1899), the equally experienced W.F.C. Holland (Brasenose) who had been both bow and stroke for Oxford between 1887 and 1890, and finally the very popular Felix Warre who had rowed number four in the 1898–99 races. The Cambridge crew went into the race as favourites. They were coached by Stanley Muttlebury (Third Trinity – number six), who rowed for Cambridge between 1886 and 1890, and David Alexander Wauchope (Trinity Hall – stroke), who rowed for Cambridge in 1895. Once again for the sixth year the ever-popular Frederick I. Pitman (Third Trinity) was selected as umpire.

On a beautiful, clear day Cambridge won the toss and selected the Surrey side of the river leaving the Middlesex side of the Thames to Oxford. Pitman began the race at 12.38 p.m. This time both crews made a strong start but it was Oxford that managed to take a slight lead, extending to a ⅓ of a length after a minute. They continued to pull hard and extended their lead to ½ a length. The Cambridge crew did not give up and their stroke, D.C.R. Stuart (Trinity Hall), increased their stroke rate. By Harrods Furniture Depository they had drawn level. By Hammersmith Bridge Cambridge had taken a narrow lead. Oxford spurted several times in an attempt to get back in contention. Although Oxford managed to take the lead briefly, a Cambridge spurt put them back in front once again. However, Oxford were not finished and pushing hard passed the Cambridge boat before Barnes Bridge taking a clear lead and winning to everyone's surprise by 3½ lengths in a time of 19 minutes 50 seconds. It took Oxford's overall lead to 35–30.

In the same year, Williams, partnered by Banner Johnstone, won the Coxless Pairs Silver Goblets at Henley. In 1910, and for the third time in a row, Williams was selected once again to row number five for Cambridge in the Boat Race.

67th Boat Race, 23 March 1910

Oxford started the 1910 race, much to everyone's surprise, as champions. Oxford went with the coaches that had proved so successful the year before: G.C. Bourne (New College), Harcourt Gilbey Gold (Magdalen) and W.F.C. Holland (Brasenose). Two of the Cambridge coaches, however, were new: William Dudley Ward (Third Trinity) who had rowed number seven in 1897–99 and 1900, Raymond Etherington-Smith (First Trinity) a three-time Blue, rowing number six between 1898 and 1900 and David Alexander Wauchope (Trinity Hall) who had stroked the 1895 boat. The latter was the only coach kept on from the year before. The familiar face of Fredrick I. Pitman (Third Trinity) umpired yet again.

Cambridge only kept three members of the crew that had lost in 1909: R.W.M. Arbuthnot (Third Trinity – bow), J.B. Rosher (First Trinity – number six) and Edward Gordon Williams (Third Trinity – number five). Oxford included four members of their 1909 winning crew: Duncan Mackinnon (Magdalen – number five), Stanley Garton (Magdalen – number six), Robert Bourne (New College – stroke) and A.W.F. Donkin (Magdalen – cox). Three overseas Blues raced: M.B. Higgins (Balliol – bow) and C.P. Cooke (Trinity Hall – number four) were both Australian and C.A. Skinner (Jesus – cox) was from South Africa.

The race was controversial from the start. As a result of 'awkward' tides it was decided to hold the race in Holy Week. This caused a great deal of disquiet amongst several of the Christian rowers and controversy in the papers. For a while it looked like the race either wouldn't go ahead or its date would have to be moved. It wasn't until the Bishop of Bristol gave his permission, under the express condition that there weren't any celebrations after the race, that the event went ahead. The day was bright with a warm sun and slight breeze. Cambridge won the toss and decided on the Surrey side, leaving Oxford the Middlesex side of the Thames. Pitman started the race at precisely 12.30 p.m. Cambridge made a very quick start and went into the lead. However, one of the Cambridge crew caught a crab, allowing Oxford to push into the lead. They were ¼ of a length ahead by Craven Steps. Cambridge spurted and by the Mile Post went into the lead. As Cambridge rowed around an unfavourable bend in the river, Oxford began to make ground and then spurted, gaining almost a length in 10 strokes. By the time the crews reached The Dove pub Oxford spurted again and went 1 length clear. They continued to extend their lead, finally winning the race by 3½ lengths in a time of 20 minutes 14 seconds (the slowest winning time since 1907). Oxford now had an overall lead of 36–30.

★★★

On leaving Cambridge Williams became a colonial administrator in north-western Rhodesia (Zimbabwe). However, at the outbreak of the First World War Williams returned to England and was commissioned into the 2nd Battalion, Grenadier Guards. He was killed in an accident near Béthune on 12 August 1915.

He is buried in the St-Venant Communal Cemetery, French civilian plot. He is commemorated on both the Eton and Trinity College memorials.

13

SECOND LIEUTENANT DENNIS IVOR DAY

Boat position: Bow
Race: 72nd Boat Race, 28 March 1914
College: St John's College, Cambridge
Served: 106th Battery, Royal Field Artillery
Death: 7 September 1915, aged 23

By the faint sound of your untroubled breath,
Proving your presence near,
in spite of death.

Dennis Ivor Day.

Dennis Ivor Day was born on 10 February 1892 in St Ives, Cornwall. He was the second son of four children born to George Dennis, a solicitor and town clerk, and Margaret Jade (Meta) Day (née Bryn-Derwen), of 'Rheola', St Ives. Dennis was educated at Sandroyd Prep School, Rushmore Park, on the border between Dorset and Wiltshire, and was then sent to Repton School in Derbyshire.

He later went up to his father's old Cambridge college, St John's, to read mathematics. The Day family already had a sporting reputation at St John's. His father, although having tried his hand at rowing, became better known for cycling. He achieved his Blue in 1880, and while racing at the Crystal Palace, broke the world speed record over 13 miles during a race to see if a man could cover 20 miles in an hour. Alas, he was involved in an accident before he could complete the full distance.

Dennis began his rowing together with his brother, George Lewis Day, at the St Ives Rowing Club. Dennis stroked the St Ives Junior 'A' Four in 1909, before taking the bow seat for the seniors in 1910 and 1911, and taking part in various invitation events and against local rivals. In 1912 the Day brothers won the Light Pairs, Double Sculls and Senior Sculls, with Dennis rowing bow and George stroking. They also competed at Henley Regatta. In 1913 Dennis won the Single Sculls against A. Swann (Trinity Hall). This was the first time a St John's man had won the event since it was instituted by another St John's student, Sir Patrick Colquhoun, in 1837. It had only taken thirty years. Such was the excitement at the victory that a poem was penned in celebration entitled, 'Sir Patrick's Sculls'. The poem is a parody of the old Scots ballad 'Sir Patrick Spens'.

Sir Patrick's Sculls

Sir Patrick sate in the College Hall,
Drinking the blue-red wine,
And quoth he
Have we never a man at all
That can win those sculls of mine?

Sir Patrick sate at the table high,
(And a genial ghost was he),
And the rowing men passed under his eye
By one and two and three.

Sir Patrick up and he said his say,
And a straight spoke man was he.
I have chosen a lad by the name of Day
To win those sculls for me!

They have taken their boaties adown the stream,
They have raced them up forbie;
And there's never a man got the better of Day
For as hard as they might try!

To all came Sir Patrick, as was his way
And he's called for the blue-red wine;
And quoth he I give you my good friend Day,
Who has won those sculls of mine!

W.H.

Dennis went on to become captain of the Lady Margaret Boat Club, and secretary of both the Cambridge University Boat Club and the Blues Committee. Rowing with his brother George he won the Fairburn-Foster Pairs, the Magdalene Pairs, the Lowe Double Sculls and stroked the victorious Wyfold Fours at Henley. He also stroked the Leander Eight, which lost to Harvard University in the final of the Grand Challenge Cup. His rowing success did not go unnoticed and he was selected to row bow in the 1914 Boat Race.

72nd Boat Race, Saturday 28 March 1914

Having won the 1913 race by ¾ of a length, Oxford University went into the race as reigning champions. In fact, Cambridge hadn't won the race since 1908. Oxford selected their veteran rower (bow in 1882–83) and coach G.C. Bourne (New College) as a safe pair of hands, his son Robert (New College) who had stroked for Oxford between 1909 and 1912, and the highly experienced and popular Harcourt Gilbey Gold who had stroked for Oxford between 1896 and 1899. Cambridge brought in a fresh coach in Stanley Bruce (Trinity Hall) who had rowed number two for Cambridge in 1904. Frederick I. Pitman (Third Trinity) was selected as umpire once again.

Oxford went into the race with four rowers who had been in the 1913 winning crew, Henry Wells (Magdalen – cox), H.K. Ward (New College – number three), E.D. Horsfall (Magdalen – number four) and A.F.R. Wiggins (New College – number six), and one that had been in the 1912 Oxford victory, F.A.H. Pitman (New College – stroke). The Cambridge crew matched them with five experienced rowers in the boat: S.E. Swann (Trinity Hall – number two), C.S. Clark (Pembroke – number six), C.E.V. Buxton (Third Trinity – number seven), G.E. Tower (Third Trinity – stroke) and L.E. Ridley (Jesus – cox).

The race was held on a beautifully bright day with a high warm sun, a gentle wind and smooth water. Cambridge won the toss and selected the Surrey side of the river leaving the Middlesex side of the Thames to Oxford. Pitman got the race off promptly at 2.20 p.m. By the Craven Steps, Cambridge had taken the lead by ¾ of a length. By the Mile Post Cambridge had increased their lead to 1¼ lengths and continued to pull away under Hammersmith Bridge. Cambridge went on to win the race by 4½ lengths in a time of 20 minutes 23 seconds. The overall record was now 39–31, still in Oxford's favour.

★★★

Due to the outbreak of the war this was the last Boat Race until 1920 and by then the world would have changed. After five years of the most awful war many of the young men rowing and cheering the rowers on would no longer be with us. It was the first time since 1853 that there was a break in this very popular national event. Five members of the two crews that raced that day were to die in the war. From Cambridge: Dennis Ivor Day (Lady Margaret Boat Club – bow), L.E. Ridley (Jesus – cox), John Andrew Ritson (First Trinity – number four) and Gordon Kenneth Garnett (First Trinity – number five), and from Oxford: Reginald William Fletcher (Balliol – bow).

At the outbreak of the First World War in August 1914, the two Day brothers joined the Royal Naval Division. In December 1914, however, Dennis received a commission into the Royal Field Artillery, subsequently being attached to the 24th Division, 106th Brigade. He was posted to France in the spring of 1915 and in July returned home for a short spell of leave. He was back at the Front in August 1915 and was seriously wounded in the eye by a sniper while artillery spotting at Vermelles, France, on 25 September 1915. The sniper's bullet lodged in Day's skull and, fearing the worst, his parents were sent for. Dennis did not regain consciousness and died of his wounds on 7 October 1915. Unusually for the time his parents brought his body back to his hometown of St Ives. On the day of his funeral all the shops in the town closed for an hour and over 3,000 people either lined the route of the funeral, waited outside his home or attended the church. The entire town felt the loss of one of their own. His body was carried from his parents' home to Pig Lane Cemetery, where he was buried (his parents were later buried by his side). A tall granite cross in the cemetery now marks the spot (left pathway, St Ives Public Cemetery).

His brother George, with whom he had rowed so many races, survived the war despite being badly wounded shortly before the end of the war in 1918. His other brother, Miles Jeffery Day, joined the Royal Navy Air Service and through his writings became one of the conflict's war poets. He became a flying ace (shooting down five or more enemy aircraft) and a flight commander, being awarded a Distinguished Service Cross for bravery in the air. He was shot down and killed while attacking a large German formation on 27 February 1918. His body was never recovered and he is commemorated on the Chatham Naval Memorial, Kent, panel 30. Before he died, however, he penned the following poem, 'To My Brother', in memory of Dennis, his lost brother:

To My Brother by Jeffery Day

This will I do when we have peace again,
Peace and return, to ease my heart of pain.
Crouched in the brittle reed-beds, wrapt in grey,
I'll watch the dawning of the winter's day,
The peaceful, clinging darkness of the night
That mingles with mysterious morning light,
And graceful rushes melting in the haze;
While all around in winding waterways,
The wildfowl gabble cheerfully and low,
Or wheel with pulsing whistle to and fro,
Filling the silent dawn with joyous song,
Swelling and dying as they sweep along;
Till shadows of vague trees deceive the eyes,
And stealthily the sun begins to rise,
Striving to smear with pink the frosted sky,
And pierce the silver mists' opacity;
Until the hazy silhouettes grow clear,
And faintest hints of colouring appear,
And the slow, throbbing, red, distorted sun
Reaches the sky, and all the large mists run,
Leaving the little ones to wreathe and shiver,
Pathetic, clinging to the friendly river;
Until the watchful heron, grim and gaunt,
Shows ghostlike, standing at his chosen haunt,
And jerkily the moorhens venture out,
Spreading swift-circled ripples round about,
And softly to the ear, and leisurely,
Querulous, comes the plaintive plover's cry;
And then maybe some whispering near by,
Some still small sound as of a happy sigh,
Shall steal upon my senses soft as air,
And, brother! I shall know that you are there.

And in the lazy summer nights I'll glide
Silently down the sleepy river's tide,
Listening to the music of the stream,
The plop of ponderously playful bream,
The water whispering around the boat,
And from afar the white owl's liquid note,

Lingering through the stillness soft and slow,
Watching the little yacht's red, homely glow,
Her vague reflection, and her clean-cut spars,
Ink-black against the silverness of the stars,
Stealthily slipping into nothingness;
While on the river's moon-splashed surfaces,
Tall shadows sweep. Then when I go to rest
It may be that my slumbers will be blessed
By the faint sound of your untroubled breath,
Proving your presence near, in spite of death.

The brothers are also commemorated on the Repton Memorial in Derbyshire and the St Ives Memorial in Cornwall.

14

LIEUTENANT CHARLES RALPH LE BLANC-SMITH

Boat position: Number Seven
Race: 67th Boat Race, 23 March 1910
       68th Boat Race, 1 April 1911
       69th Boat Race, 1 April 1912
College: Trinity College, Cambridge
Served: 8th Battalion, Rifle Brigade
Death: 27 November 1915, aged 25

His heart and soul was (sic) rowing.

Charles Ralph le Blanc-Smith

Charles Ralph le Blanc-Smith was born on 3 March 1890 in Paddington, London. He was the son of Herbert le Blanc-Smith. He was educated at Eton (1903–09) where he was in the Reverend R.C. Radcliffe's and C.H.K. Martin's House. While there he played football and rowed in the Eight, number six in 1908 and number seven in 1909. He won the House Fours in 1907 and held the school pulling record in 1909. He was also the second captain of boats in 1908–09, served in the college OTC (Officers' Training Corps) for four years and was a member of Pop in the same year. He went up

to Trinity College, Cambridge, as a pensioner. He joined the University OTC and
served with them for three years. In October 1909 he rowed number four in the
winning Trial Eight. As a result of this success he was selected to take part in the
1910 Boat Race, against Oxford, rowing number six.

67th Boat Race, 23 March 1910

The reigning champions Oxford kept with experience and success and appointed
G.C. Bourne (New College – bow), Boat Race veteran of 1882–83; four-
time stroke between 1896 and 1899 Harcourt Gilbey Gold (Magdalen); and
W.F.C. Holland (Brasenose), who had rowed bow and stroke four times for Oxford
between 1887 and 1890. Cambridge only kept one of their previous coaches:
David Alexander Wauchope (Trinity Hall), who had rowed stroke in the 1895 race.
To assist him they brought in William Dudley Ward (Third Trinity), who had rowed
number seven in 1897, 1899 and 1900, and Raymond Etherington-Smith (First
Trinity), who had represented Cambridge three times between 1898 and 1900.
For the seventh year in succession Frederick I. Pitman (Third Trinity) umpired.

The 1910 race brought to the annual event one of its early scandals. As a result
of a poor tide it was decided to hold the race in Holy Week. Religious festivals
were taken far more seriously than they are now and there was national outcry.
Several of the rowers also expressed serious concerns at racing during this time and
at least one refused to take part. It wasn't until the Bishop of London intervened
and allowed the race to go ahead, on the understanding that there would be no
celebrations afterwards that a compromise was reached and the race went ahead.

Cambridge brought in five new rowers, relying on only three with Boat Race
experience: R.W.M. Arbuthnot (Third Trinity – bow), J.B. Rosher (First Trinity –
number six) and Edward Gordon Williams (Third Trinity – number four). Oxford,
as champions, decided to keep as many of the previous year's rowers as they could.
Four members of the 1909 crew returned: Duncan Mackinnon (Magdalen –
number five), Stanley Garton (Magdalen – number six), Robert Bourne (New
College – stroke) and A.W.F. Donkin (Magdalen – cox). Three non-British rowers
took part in the race. One member of the Oxford crew, M.B. Higgins (Balliol –
bow), came from Australia, as did the Cambridge number four, C.P. Cooke (Trinity
Hall). The Cambridge cox, C.A. Skinner (Jesus), came from South Africa.

It was a bright day with a warm sun and light breeze. Cambridge won the toss
and selected the Middlesex station, leaving the Surrey side of the river to Oxford.
Pitman got the race started at 12.30 p.m. Although Cambridge made the quicker
start, one of the boat's rowers caught a crab and Oxford swept by. By Craven Steps
Oxford were ahead by ¼ of a length. However, recovering, Cambridge spurted and
were ahead by the time they reached the Mile Post. Oxford fought back, and as

they reached The Dove pub Oxford spurted again, going into a 1-length lead. They never gave up the lead and in fact extended it, passing the finishing post 3½ lengths ahead in a time of 20 minutes 14 seconds (the slowest winning time since 1907). Oxford now had an overall lead in the race of 36–30.

In the same year le Blanc-Smith also rowed in the Leander boat for the Grand Challenge at Henley, won that year by Magdalen College, Oxford, in 7 minutes 19 seconds. A year later, in 1911, Charles was chosen to row number five for Cambridge again.

68th Boat Race, 1 April 1911

Oxford were certainly the dominant crew over this period and it was a position they were determined to maintain. Once again they chose the highly experienced coach and rower G.C. Bourne (New College), H.R. Barker (Christ Church), who rowed number two in 1908–09, and the equally experienced coach and rower Harcourt Gilbey Gold (Magdalen), who had stroked for Oxford between 1897 and 1899. Cambridge brought in three new boys who had rowed number two in 1904: H.W. Willis, who oddly had coached Oxford in 1907, and Stanley Bruce (Trinity Hall), who had rowed number two in 1904 and later became 1st Viscount Bruce of Melbourne (1883–1967), the eighth prime minister of Australia (1923–29). They also used two more experienced coaches in William Dudley Ward (Third Trinity), who rowed number seven in 1897, 1899 and 1900, and Raymond Etherington-Smith (First Trinity), who rowed number seven in 1898 and 1900. For the eighth year Frederick I. Pitman (Third Trinity) was umpire.

Cambridge 1912 boat sinks just by Harrods Furniture Depository.

To add to the general excitement of the Boat Race, the Prince of Wales and Prince Albert turned up to watch and follow the race. The race was also tracked by an aeroplane for the first time. As few people had seen a plane in 1911, many felt it was a distraction from the importance of the race.

Oxford decided on three rowers who had helped them win the race the year before in 1910: Duncan Mackinnon (Magdalen – number seven), Robert Bourne (New College – stroke) and Stanley Garton (Magdalen – number six). A little surprisingly Cambridge kept faith with five of their crew who had lost the 1910 encounter: R.W.M. Arbuthnot (Third Trinity – stroke), J.B. Rosher (First Trinity – number six), F.E. Hellyer (First Trinity – number three), C.R. le Blanc-Smith (Third Trinity – number seven), C.A. Skinner (Jesus – cox). Cambridge had two South Africans rowing for them: Pieter Voltelyn Graham van der Byl (Pembroke – number two) and C.A. Skinner (Jesus – cox). Oxford had the Australian Charles Littlejohn (New College – number five).

It was a bright day with a gentle breeze and a strong tide, which boded well for a fast time. As it turned out this was quite right. Oxford won the toss and elected to start from the Middlesex side of the river, leaving the Surrey side to Cambridge. Pitman began the race at precisely 2.36 p.m. Oxford made a good start, outrating Cambridge from the beginning. By the time they reached the Craven Steps, Oxford were ¾ of a length ahead, a lead they maintained as they raced by the Mile Post. By the Crab Tree pub Oxford were clear and by Hammersmith Bridge they were 2½ lengths ahead and pulling away. Passing Chiswick Steps, Oxford were 4 lengths clear. Cambridge made a last-minute spurt but it was much too late and Oxford won the race by 2¾ lengths in a record time of 18 minutes 29 seconds. Oxford now had an overall lead of 37–30.

In the same year le Blanc-Smith rowed for the Cambridge University Boat Club (CUBC), winning the Light Four for the Visitors' Challenge Cup at Henley, and was secretary and then president of CUBC in 1912–13. He also won the Colquhoun Sculls in 1912 and the Magdalene Pairs in 1913. In 1912 Charles was selected once again to row number six in the Cambridge boat.

70th Boat Race, 1 April 1912

Once again Oxford went into the race as champions. The reliable G.C. Bourne (New College) was selected to train the Oxford boat, together with Harcourt Gilbey Gold (Magdalen) and W.F.C. Holland (Brasenose), who had rowed four times for Oxford between 1887 and 1890. Cambridge were trained by the veteran rower John Houghton Gibbon (Third Trinity), who had stroked for Cambridge in 1899–90. Frederick I. Pitman (Third Trinity) was once again chosen as umpire.

Oxford went into the race with five Boat Race veterans from the 1911 winning crew: C.E. Tinne (University – number two), L.G. Wormald (Magdalen – number three), L.W.B. Littlejohn (New College – number five), R.C. Bourne (New College – stroke) and H.B. Wells (Magdalen – cox). Cambridge matched them, retaining five crew members from the previous year's boat: F.E. Hellyer (First Trinity – number three), C.R. le Blanc-Smith (Third Trinity – number six), R.W.M. Arbuthnot (Third Trinity – bow), C.A. Skinner (Jesus – cox) and S.E. Swann (Trinity Hall – stroke). Three rowers were registered as non-British: the Oxford number five Charles Littlejohn (New College) was Australian while the Cambridge cox C.A. Skinner (Jesus) came from South Africa and their number two D.C. Collins (First Trinity) came from New Zealand.

On a cold, blustery day, Oxford won the toss and chose the Surrey side of the river, leaving the Middlesex side of the Thames to Cambridge. Pitman began the race at 11.43 a.m. Although Cambridge had the better start, Oxford quickly caught and then passed them. By the end of the Fulham wall, Oxford were clear of Cambridge. However, in the rough conditions both crews had taken on water. The Oxford crew were obliged to stop and empty their boat of water, while the Cambridge boat sank just off Harrods Furniture Depository. Pitman had no choice but to declare a 'No Race'. It was the first time this had happened since 1859. The writer and veteran rower G.C. Drinkwater described the event as 'the greatest fiasco in the history of the race'. It was eventually decided to hold the race again the following Monday.

Unfortunately the weather hadn't improved by Monday; in fact, if anything, the wind was stronger. But it was blowing in a different direction and that made all the difference to the race. Oxford won the toss once again and decided on the Surrey side of the river, leaving Cambridge the Middlesex side. Pitman started the race at 12.40 p.m. and crossed his fingers. Oxford made a fast start, taking advantage of the shelter offered by the Middlesex side of the river. Although the Cambridge boat outrated the Oxford crew by as much as 6 strokes per second, Cambridge could still not catch them. Oxford finally passed the finishing line with a lead of 6 lengths – the biggest winning margin since 1903. Their time was 22 minutes 5 seconds, the slowest since 1901. Oxford were on a roll and now held an overall lead of 38–30. Despite racing on three occasions, le Blanc-Smith had never been in the winning boat. Although selected for the 1913 boat he became ill and was unable to row.

★★★

Leaving Cambridge in 1912 with his BA, le Blanc-Smith joined the Stock Exchange as a clerk. He also moved to Lordship, Standon, Hertfordshire, and became a petty officer in the Royal Naval Reserve. At the outbreak of war, however, he didn't pursue his naval career and took a commission into the 8th Battalion,

Oxford and Cambridge crews for the 1912 race. Le Blanc-Smith (No. 6) is second from right at the bottom of the page.

Rifle Brigade, as a second lieutenant. He was seriously wounded in action at Hooge on 30 July 1915 during a liquid fire attack and was hospitalised in Versailles until 11 August 1915. He was then based at Étaples before being allowed home on leave on 16 August 1915. Returning to the Front on 23 August, he was appointed as machine-gun officer.

As a well-respected officer one of his jobs was to write to the relatives of the soldiers under his command who were killed. One letter still survives. However, it is not about the death of a soldier but about a great act of bravery. It made a pleasant change:

Dear Mrs Hamilton,

I expect you have already heard of all the wonderful things that your son did during the awful attack we had at Hooge and he fired one of the machine guns over the back of the trench, killing a tremendous number of Germans – at one time there were Germans in the trench on each side of him, only being kept off by one of our bombing parties. How any of them got clear, I cannot imagine; but he did and I am very pleased to say that he is the first man in the battalion to receive the Distinguished Conduct Medal, which he most nobly deserves.

I must say I am most awfully proud of the way the machine gun section behaved; they really did most exceptionally well, especially as most of those round were cowed by the awfulness of the liquid fire.

Your son is so modest; he never says anything about himself and it is all the nicer therefore, to feel that he will now go through life with one of the most coveted things in the world – a medal for outstanding bravery. [Although poor Frederick was sadly to lose his life later.]

Lieutenant le Blanc-Smith was himself severely wounded at the commencement of a German liquid fire attack and sadly died of his wounds on 27 November 1915. He is commemorated in Essex Farm Cemetery, Ypres, grave ref. plot I, row R, grave 9. 2265.

15

CAPTAIN ARTHUR JOHN SHIRLEY HOARE HALES MC

Boat position: Number Three
Race: 61st Boat Race, 26 March 1904
      62nd Boat Race, 1 April 1905
College: Corpus Christi, Oxford
Served: 1st Battalion, Wiltshire Regiment
Death: 5/6 July 1916, aged 34

It was an awful blow to the Regiment and we shall never get over
Captain Hales' loss …

Arthur John Shirley Hoare Hales was born on 27 November 1881 at Sydenham, London. He was the eldest son of Major General Arthur Hales, Royal Inniskilling Fusiliers and commandant of the Straits Settlements (a group of British territories located in Southeast Asia), and Maria Frances. He entered Rugby School in 1895 and was in School House. A good all-round sportsman, he was in the first XV in 1899. Leaving Rugby in 1900, he went

Captain Arthur John Shirley Hoare Hales MC.

up to Corpus Christi College, Oxford, where he read Classics Moderations and later Modern History, receiving his BA in 1904. He was secretary of the Boat Club between 1901 and 1902, and captain between 1902 and 1904. He played football for his college, the Harlequins, and for the Monkstown team of 1902. In 1904 he was selected to row number three in the Oxford boat against Cambridge.

61st Boat Race, 26 March 1904

Cambridge University went in to the 1904 Boat Race as champions, having beaten the Oxford Eight the year before by an impressive 6 lengths. To try to reverse their fortunes, Oxford put together the best coaches they could get. Top of their list was the highly experienced former Oxford rower G.C. Bourne (New College), who was bow for Oxford in both 1882 and 1883, the equally experienced William Fletcher (Christ Church), who had stroked and rowed number six and seven for Oxford between 1890 and 1893, and C.K. Philips (New College), who had rowed number two and three for Oxford between 1895 and 1898. Cambridge went with a fresh coaching team: Francis Escombe (Trinity Hall), who rowed number five in 1902, and the former Cambridge rower Claude Waterhouse Hearn Taylor (Third Trinity), who rowed number four between 1901 and 1903. Once again the umpire was the former Cambridge rower Frederick I. Pitman (Third Trinity). Coincidentally neither of the Boat Club presidents, Monier-Williams (University – number seven) or Edwards-Moss (Third Trinity – number seven), were able to take part in the race due to various injuries (they had both been in the 1903 race).

Only one member of the 1903 Oxford crew returned to row in 1904: A.K. Graham (Balliol – cox). Cambridge brought back two members of the previous year's crew: P.H. Thomas (Trinity – number six) and B.G.A. Scott (Trinity Hall – cox). The Cambridge crew also had one Australian in their Eight, Stanley Bruce (Trinity Hall – number two), and one New Zealander, Harold Gillies (Caius – number seven).

On a cold and misty day with a weak tide, Cambridge won the toss and decided on the Surrey side of the river, leaving the Oxford crew with the Middlesex side of the Thames. Pitman got the race under way at 7.45 a.m. Oxford made a speedy start and outrated the Cambridge crew from the beginning. Although Oxford were clear by the Mile Post, Cambridge began to fight back, largely due to poor steering by the Oxford cox, E.C.T. Warner. As they rowed under Hammersmith Bridge, Cambridge had reduced the Oxford lead to ⊠ of a length and by The Dove pub they were level. Pushing on, Cambridge took the lead and by Chiswick Ferry they were clear. Cambridge finally won the race by 4½ lengths in a time of 21 minutes 37 seconds (the slowest since 1898).

In the following year Hales was selected to row number three again.

62nd Boat Race, 1 April 1905

Although Oxford dispensed with G.C. Bourne's services for the 1905 race, they did hang on to William Fletcher (Christ Church) and C.K. Philips (New College). Cambridge turned to John Edwards-Moss (Third Trinity), the former Cambridge president who had rowed number seven in both 1902 and 1903 but missed the 1904 race through illness, the experienced Francis Escombe (Trinity Hall), who had been part of the 1904 coaching team, and David Alexander Wauchope (Trinity Hall), who had stroked for Cambridge in 1895. The ever-present Frederick I. Pitman was selected to umpire once again.

Cambridge brought back four rowers from the 1904 winning crew: H. Sanger (Lady Margaret Boat Club – bow), B.C. Johnstone (Third Trinity – number three), R.V. Powell (Third Trinity – number seven) and P.H. Thomas (Third Trinity – number four), who was a last-minute replacement for Stanley Bruce who was taken ill (Thomas rowed despite being a novice and having not fully recovered from illness himself). Despite losing the 1904 race, Oxford kept faith with five of their 1904 crew: R.W. Somers-Smith (Merton – number two), A.J.S.H. Hales (Corpus Christi – number three), A.R. Balfour (University – number four), E.P. Evans (University – number six) and A.K. Graham (Balliol – number seven).

Cambridge won the toss and decided on the Middlesex side of the river, leaving the Surrey side to Oxford. Pitman got the race started at 11.30 a.m. Oxford took an immediate lead and held on to it throughout the race, winning by 3 lengths in a time of 20 minutes 35 seconds. It was the first time Oxford had won in four years and by the narrowest margin since the 1901 race.

★★★

On leaving Oxford in 1906, Arthur Hales took a job as a master at Radley College in Berkshire. Considered a conscientious master, he was also popular with the boys. However, when war was declared in August 1914 he felt it was his duty to enlist at once, joining the ranks of the 1st Battalion, Wiltshire Regiment. After training he was posted to France in November 1914, later being promoted to sergeant. He wrote a number of letters from the Front, one of which was later mentioned in his old college magazine, *The Radleian*, as part of an article written about him:

> I have heard several times from Mr. Hales, who is sergeant in the Wiltshires. It will be news to hear that, during his first three days in the trenches, even he was absolutely dead beat, as they had to carry up sandbags to mend the gaps in the trenches. His legs absolutely gave out. On the first night he fell into a Jack Johnson hole and was not dry for a week afterwards. Nor could he use his rifle for a day and a half as it was jammed with mud. He is full of praise for the food

and bully beef. He has been under heavy fire several times, but he claims to be
very good at keeping his head down. When we returned this term we heard that
he had been wounded, but his own account is as follows:

A graze on head and arm from a bullet that splintered through a sand bag. Both
wounds quite dry by the time I left the trenches next day.

Hales was, in fact, wounded in January 1915 only a couple of months after arriving
at the Front. He received a battlefield commission in February 1915. On 31 May
1915 he was mentioned in dispatches for gallantry. The following April he was
decorated with the Military Cross for conspicuous gallantry at Spanbroekmolen
on 1 March 1915. His citation read, 'while leading an attack and being wounded
twice he dragged several of his men to cover. He was only stopped from his work
when he was wounded for a third time in the leg.'

In July 1915 he was promoted to captain. On 5 July 1916, while second in
command of his battalion and during the fighting at Leipzig Redoubt, he noticed
one of the companies was in difficulty and went to their assistance. As he made his
way towards them he was shot and killed by a sniper. His last words were reported
to have been, 'Well done.'

When writing about the heavy losses sustained by the Wiltshires on 5 July,
the general commanding the division mentioned Hales: 'I have lost also a most
excellent Officer in Captain Hales.'

Another wrote:

It was an awful blow to the Regiment and we shall never get over Captain Hales
loss. He was so absolutely splendid in everything he did, and such an example
to us all. I am convinced that it was due to his magnificent leading that the men
went over in such a fine spirit and were able to gain their objective.

His old headmaster at Rugby wrote:

You know how high was the regard in which I held him, and how grateful I
was-and am still-for all the help he gave me; the example he set, and the influence
he exerted, in the School House. It is grievous to think that a man of such high
ideals should have been lost to the Country.

His obituary in the Christ Church magazine was both telling and emotional:

To many years of Corpus men the name of 'Sam' Hales brings recollections
of pain, terror, and admiration. His fame ran ahead of him; and on the first
night of Term the mockers were busily exploiting it to chill the enthusiasm
of those who had devoted themselves to the river-gods. Experience showed

SUPPLEMENT TO THE BYSTANDER, APRIL 5, 1905

Hales sits on the left of the front row.

him no less terrible than his repute, yet more than kind. His voice was a thing of wonder, not often heard in entreaty, sometimes paralysing by reproach or objurgation, sometimes imparting something of his own tremendous driving energy. Many will remember (*forsitan et meminisse iuvabit*) a Bump Supper speech of his, developing at length the single theme that 'the younger members of the College must learn to shove'. Everyone knew he practiced what he preached, and that just because he had 'guts' he had been chosen out of a very bad.

'Varsity crew to row the following year in a good one. And so no one resented the stentorian rebuke, or mistook for slave-driving the masterful determination which was bent on making summer days laborious (Oxford summer days too) in pursuit of ends for which no pots were given, and in scorn of the Lotus Eaters who lay on the banks in a spacious security. Many hearts must have sunk with a 'needle' and knees been loosed when he changed, as he often did, a Free Stone to a full course. But he had his reward in the rise of the boats he coached; at his command men did violent stomach exercises in the vacation, and his crews acknowledged that it was owing to his untiring labours that they were in winning Eights, and reaped the joys that the fraternity of the river gives. When he went down, it was only to Radley, whence he made a regular point of coming over to coach: mellowed in manner, perhaps, yet just as keen. The barge's welcome was symbolically given by the smile on George Best's face, as he ferried him over from the towpath, and prophesised 'You're in for it, Sirs'.

The last time I saw him was in summer days again; but in Flanders at La Brique near Ypres in August, 1915. From the midst of a peaceful slumber suddenly I leapt up as though wakened by the last trump. But it was just Hales walking away down the trench, which he had come to visit before taking over; unchanged save for the uniform, the monocle, and the Military Cross. That night the relief did not work smoothly: there were blocks; and I heard him say, 'Oh come on, let's go over the top'. Communication trenches were against his principles, and made soldiers afraid – moles instead of men. And afterwards when he discovered our sins of omission, committed in ignorance by a new battalion, he wrote a long letter of advice, stern, just, and kindly – like lessons to those given on the towpath (or in Hall), but for a more dreadful service. He belonged to a regiment famous for work and fighting; and he, if anyone, could show an example of courage, endurance, and determination; qualities required in a leader of men, in which character who can doubt he was found approved when he fell?

Hales' body was never recovered or identified. He is commemorated on the Thiepval Memorial, pier and face 13 A. He is also commemorated together with his brother, Lieutenant Charles Edward Hoare Hales, who died as a result of war service on 22 November 1917, at the Church of St Andrew, The Street, Carmouth, Dorset.

16

LIEUTENANT GEOFFREY OTHO CHARLES EDWARDS

Boat position: Number Two
Race: 54th Boat Race, 3 April 1897
      55th Boat Race, 26 March 1898
College: New College, Oxford
Served: 3rd attached 9th Battalion, Duke of Wellington's (West Riding) Regiment
Death: 7 July 1916, aged 39

Part of the greatest Oxford crew to ever row the river.

Geoffrey Otho Charles Edwards was born on 2 October 1876 at Southowram, Elland, Halifax, West Yorkshire. He was one of five children (Barbara Florence, Winifred Delia, Eleanor Churchill and Henry Arthur Rolleston) born to Major Arthur Hancock Edwards JP (2nd West Yorkshire Yeomanry Cavalry, whose painting is in the National Army Museum) and Eleanor Louisa Pease (daughter of Lieutenant Colonel Joseph Walker). He was educated at Eton College where he rowed in the College Eight, before going up to New College, Oxford.

While at Oxford he continued with his rowing and was selected to row in the college boat. As a result of his continual improvement he was chosen to row number two in the University Boat Race of 1897.

The 1897 Boat Race Oxford crew: 'the finest crew that ever rowed'. Standing back row: J.J.J. De Knoop (New College), R. Carr (Magdalen), H.G. Gold (Magdalen), G.O.C. Edwards (New College), D.H. McLean (coach). Sitting left to right: C.D. Burnell (Magdalen), C.K. Philips (New College), W.E. Crum (New College), E.R. Balfour (University College). Sitting at the front: H.R.K. Pechell (Brasenose).

54th Boat Race, 3 April 1897

It was said of the 1897 Oxford crew that it was the finest Eight that had ever rowed. Oxford went into the race as champions, having defeated the Cambridge crew by ²/₅ of a length in 1896. Determined to remain champions, Oxford brought in to coach the team: G.C. Bourne (New College), who was bow for Oxford in both 1882 and 1883, William Fletcher (Christ Church), who had stroked and rowed six and seven for Oxford between 1890 and 1893, and Douglas McLean (New College), who had rowed five and seven for Oxford between 1883 and 1887. Although there is no official record of who coached Cambridge it is likely that it was Stanley Muttlebury (Third Trinity), who had coached Cambridge the previous year and had rowed for Cambridge five times between 1886 and 1890. Initially the Oxford crew were a little rough; however, by the time McLean had finished coaching them at Henley they were beginning to attain great pace. After Henley Bourne took over training them at Putney, where they began to break all records on the ebb.

Cambridge selected four former Blues as part of the 1897 Eight: William Augustus Bieber (Trinity Hall – number five), A.S. Bell (Trinity Hall – number seven), D. Pennington (Caius – number three) and W.J. Fernie (Trinity Hall – stroke). Benjamin Hunting Howell (Trinity Hall) was the only non-British rower, being an American from New York. The Oxford boat only went with one fresh rower, Geoffrey Otho Charles Edwards, who was brought in to row number two, C.K. Philips moving to number three. The umpire for the ninth year was Frank Willan (Exeter), who had rowed for Oxford four times between 1866 and 1869.

Oxford went into the race as clear favourites. Cambridge won the toss and selected the Middlesex station, handing the Surrey side of the river to Oxford. In a light breeze from the east and on a favourable tide, Willan began the race at 2.24 p.m. The Light Blues made the quicker start, with the Cambridge stroke, William James Fernie, taking his crew off at 41 strokes per minute. Cambridge went into a ½-length lead. However, Oxford began to pull back and by the time the boats reached Craven Cottage, Oxford were in the lead. Cambridge spurted back at the Mile Post but despite this were unable to keep up with Oxford's pace. By Hammersmith Bridge Oxford had clear water advantage, crossing the winning line 2½ lengths ahead of Cambridge. Their winning time was 19 minutes 12 seconds, the third fastest time in Boat Race history. It was Oxford's eighth consecutive victory, bringing the overall record to 31–22 in Oxford's favour (excluding the 'dead heat' of 1877).

Despite being in the losing boat, Geoffrey Edwards was selected once again to row in the 1898 race.

55th Boat Race, 26 March 1898

Oxford went into the 1989 race as reigning champions, as they had done since 1890 (Cambridge last won the race in 1889). They continued with their winning coaching team of G.C. Bourne (New College) and Douglas McLean (New College). Cambridge, determined to put an end to Oxford's straight victories, decided to take all necessary measures to stop their old rivals taking the honours for a ninth time. The Cambridge president William Dudley Ward (Third Trinity) decided to take a very professional, some might say ruthless, approach to taking the honours. Despite opposition he pushed through with his plans and appointed the former Oxford coach and Blue William Fletcher (Christ Church). There was method in his madness, however, as he was fully aware that if Cambridge were to have any chance of winning they would have to learn and master a style that would better the Oxford crew. As a result of this rash decision several members of the Cambridge crew refused to row (even Ward was forced to stand down due to illness). Despite all these setbacks Fletcher continued to train Cambridge and turned out a first-class crew, considered by many to be the best Cambridge crew for many years. Oxford's training, on the other hand, did not go as well as it had in previous years.

Cambridge's crew only contained two rowers with previous Boat Race experience: Adam Searle Bell (Trinity Hall – stroke) and Edward Caesar Hawkins (Caius – cox). Oxford, on the other hand, kept largely with their winning 1897 crew, retaining seven members of the eight: C. Burnell (Magdalen), R. Carr (Magdalen), G.O.C. Edwards (New College), C.K. Philips (New College), C.D. Burnell (Magdalen), H.G. Gold (Magdalen) and H.R.K. Pechell (Brasenose). For the tenth year in a row the umpire for the race was Frank Willan (Exeter).

Race day wasn't good: high winds and a spring tide made the water rough and difficult to row. Oxford went into the race as favourites once more. They won the toss and selected the Middlesex side of the river, leaving Cambridge the Surrey side of the Thames. Umpire Willan got the race under way at 3.47 p.m. However, within a few strokes the Cambridge boat was almost full of water. Oxford steered towards the shore and, although they also took on water, were still able to continue with the race. With no real competition they went on to win their ninth race in succession in a time of 22 minutes 15 seconds, the slowest winning time since 1878.

★★★

Geoffrey Otho Charles Edwards graduated from New College, Oxford, as a Bachelor of Arts. He returned to Halifax and became a director of the public company Pyenest. During the First World War, Edwards took a commission into the 3rd Battalion, Duke of Wellington's (West Riding) Regiment, later transferring to the 9th Battalion and being promoted to lieutenant. The battalion was formed in Halifax in September 1914 as part of Kitchener's Second New Army. The battalion

The 1897 Oxford Boat Race crew. Edwards is standing second from the left.

moved to Wareham and became part of 52nd Brigade, 17th (Northern) Division, moving to Bovington and later Wimborne. In June 1915 the battalion moved to Hursley in Hampshire. Edwards landed in France on 24 May 1916. He was involved in heavy fighting in Ypres and then in 1916 at the Battle of Albert and Delville Wood.

He was killed in action only a few weeks later, on 7 July 1916, near Contalmaison. His body was never recovered or identified and he is commemorated on the Thiepval Memorial, face 6A and 6B. He is also commemorated on the Eton College Memorial, the New College Oxford Memorial and on a plaque at St James Church as Geoffrey O.C. Edwards. Probate was given to Roger Greville Hazlerigg, on 22 November with effects of £11,160 9s 6d.

Interestingly, for a time Edwards had lived at Ash Grove, Cromwell Bottom. For many years now both the landlord and several tenants have witnessed the ghost of a gentleman at the bottom of stairwells. Only thought to be seen by other men, he would nod in acknowledgement as he passed by and then vanish. In this part of the building people often smell cigarette smoke, thought to be of the old Woodbine type smoked in the First World War. The ghost is considered to be that of Geoffrey Otho Charles Edwards.

17

CAPTAIN JOHN ANDREW RITSON

Boat position: Number Four
Race: 72nd Boat Race, 28 March 1914
College: Trinity College, Cambridge
Served: 5th Service Battalion, Prince of Wales's Volunteers, South Lancashire
     Regiment
Death: 23 July 1916

The men cannot say enough about his gallantry and the way he led them.

John Andrew Ritson was born on 7 November 1892 in Reading, Berkshire. He was the only son of Robert Ritson, surgeon of Blandford House, Hamilton, Reading, and Molly Ritson. He was educated at Rugby School between 1906 and 1911 before going up to Trinity College, Cambridge, as a pensioner, on 25 June 1911. While at Cambridge he rowed for First Trinity, taking part in all their races during the three years he was there, and helping to win the Ladies' Plate at Henley in 1913. In 1914 he was selected to row number four at the annual Boat Race between the two universities, the last one before the outbreak of the First World War.

John Andrew
Ritson.

72nd Boat Race, 28 March 1914

This was to be the final Boat Race before the First World War and in many ways the most tragic; the race recommenced in 1920. Although the services of H.R. Barker (who had coached the winning Oxford crew in 1913) were dispensed with, the ever-dependable and experienced G.C. Bourne (New College – bow), who took part in the Boat Race in 1882–83, remained. He brought with him his son, Robert Bourne (New College – stroke), who had rowed for Oxford between 1909 and 1912. The four-time veteran Harcourt Gilbey Gold (Magdalen – stroke), who had rowed for Oxford between 1896 and 1899, was also retained. Cambridge also dispensed with the talents of their previous year's coach, John Gibbon, and went with Stanley Bruce (Trinity Hall), who had rowed number two in 1904. The now very experienced Frederick I. Pitman (Third Trinity) was selected as umpire for the seventh year running.

The Oxford crew saw five participants return, with four from the 1913 race and one from the 1912 race. From the 1913 race: H.R. Ward (New College – number three), E.D. Horsfall (Magdalen – stroke), who was also a member of the Eight that won the gold medal at the 1912 Olympic Games rowing for the Leander Club, H.B. Wells (Magdalen – cox) and A.F.R. Wiggins (New College – number six). From the 1912 race: F.A.H. Pitman (New College – number seven). Cambridge's crew included five participants with previous Boat Race experience: S.E. Swann (Trinity Hall – bow), who was also a gold medal winner from the 1912 Olympic Games rowing for the Leander Club, C.S. Clark (Pembroke – number six), C.E.V. Buxton (Trinity – number seven), G.E. Tower (Trinity – stroke) and L.E. Ridley (Jesus – cox).

The weather for the race was perfect: smooth water, bright sunshine and a light wind. Cambridge won the toss and chose the Surrey station, leaving Oxford the Middlesex side of the Thames. Pitman started the race at 2.20 p.m. Cambridge took an early lead and were ¾ of a length ahead by Craven Steps, they extended to a 1¼-length lead by the Mile Post. They continued to pull away from Oxford, finally passing the winning post with a 4½-length lead in a time of 20 minutes 23 seconds. It was the first time the Cambridge Eight had won since 1908. Although Cambridge narrowed the overall lead, Oxford were still well ahead at 39–31.

Five of the two 1914 crews were to die in the First World War. From the Oxford boat: Reginald William Fletcher (Balliol – bow); and from the Cambridge Eight: Gordon Kenneth Garnett (Trinity – number five), L.E. Ridley (Jesus – cox), Dennis Ivor Day (Lady Margaret Boat Club – bow) and John Andrew Ritson (Third Trinity – number four).

★★★

Taking his degree in 1914, Ritson became a member of Inner Temple. At the outbreak of the First World War he took a commission into the 5th Service Battalion, Prince of Wales' Volunteers, South Lancashire Regiment, as a second lieutenant. He was promoted to lieutenant three months later and then captain in February 1915. Together with his battalion, he was posted to France in July 1915. However, in August he was taken ill with appendicitis and returned to the United Kingdom. On recovering he was appointed adjutant to a Cadet Officers' Training Battalion, but was soon bored and requested to be returned to his battalion in France. His request was accepted and he returned to France in April 1916.

He was killed instantaneously by machine-gun bullets while leading his men into action in the Battle of the Somme, near Bazentin-le-Petit, in the early hours of 23 July 1916. His colonel later said of him in a letter to his family:

> Everyone liked him enormously. The men cannot say enough about his gallantry and the way he led them. He has always behaved in an exemplary manner under fire, and been cheerful and willing – the most popular and best beloved Officer in the Battalion.

He wrote again later:

> From all I have heard since I last wrote to you there is no doubt that your son did magnificently, far more than any words of mine can express. Had he not been killed he would undoubtedly have received a suitable recognition.

Other officers also put pen to paper:

> I had only seen him a few minutes before the attack started, and then he was absolutely at his best. His Company, B, was in rather a awkward corner being shelled, but 'Peter' was standing up perfectly cool, with his men in complete order. B Company did not start this attack, but were put in to stiffen it up, when the two leading Companies were checked. 'Peter' was shot through the head and killed instantaneously right in front of his men only a few yards from the German wire, and I know you may be sure that it was just at the best moment of his life, knowing as he must then have known that his men would follow him anywhere. He was one of the very best men I can ever hope to meet.

The captain was buried in Caterpillar Valley Cemetery, Longueval, Somme, plot VI. F. 21. He is also commemorated at Rugby School and at Trinity College Chapel in Cambridge.

18

CAPTAIN THOMAS GEOFFREY BROCKLEBANK

Boat position: Bow
Race: 61st Boat Race, 26 March 1904
College: Trinity College, Oxford
Served: 277th Brigade, Royal Field Artillery
Death: 5 August 1916, aged 33

He was one of the most efficient Officers and one of the nicest men I ever met.

Thomas Geoffrey Brocklebank.

Thomas Geoffrey Brocklebank was born in Toxteth Park, Liverpool, on 3 November 1882. He was the eldest son of Harold and Mary Ellen Brocklebank, of Grizedale Hall, Hawkshead, Lancashire. Harold Brocklebank bought the Grizedale estate in 1903 and rebuilt the hall. During the Second World War the hall was taken over by the military and used as a POW camp for German officers. It later featured in the 1957 film *The One That Got Away* starring the German actor Hardy Krüger, and in the same year the hall was finally demolished.

Thomas' father was formerly been associated with the firm of Messrs Thomas and John

Brocklebank, ship owners, of Liverpool, and he was first cousin of Sir Aubrey Brocklebank, chairman of the Anchor-Brocklebank Line of steamships. He was educated at Farnborough Prep School before attending Eton College between 1895 and 1901. After leaving Eton he went up to Trinity College, Oxford, wehre he earned his MA in 1905. A keen rower while at Eton, he continued to row for his college while at Oxford and was selected as bow for the 1904 annual Oxford against Cambridge Boat Race.

Brocklebank memorial window, St Anne's Church of England Church, Aigburth, Liverpool.

61st Boat Race, 26 March 1904

Cambridge went into the 1904 race as champions, having won the 1903 by 6 lengths in 19 minutes 33 seconds. Oxford were determined to come back at them. Oxford were coached by Dr Gordon C. Bourne (New College), who had rowed for Oxford University in 1882 (both his father and son also rowed for Oxford), William Fletcher (Christ Church), who rowed for Oxford between 1890 and 1893, and C.K. Philips (New College), who had represented the Dark Blues four times between 1895 and 1898. Cambridge were coached by Francis Escombe (Trinity Hall) and Claude Waterhouse Hearn Taylor (Third Trinity), who rowed for Cambridge on three occasions between 1901 and 1903.

Both Boat Club presidents, Monier-Williams and Edwards-Moss, were unable to row, having picked up injuries in training. Two of the Cambridge crew had previous Boat Race experience: P.H. Thomas (Third Trinity – number six, rowing for the third consecutive year) and B.G.A. Scott (Trinity Hall – cox). Oxford had a single returning rower: A.K. Graham (Balliol – stroke). The Cambridge crew had two non-British rowers: Stanley Bruce (Trinity Hall – number two), who came from Australia, and Harold Gillies (Caius – number seven), who was a New Zealander.

Cambridge won the toss and elected to start from the Surrey station, giving Oxford the Middlesex side of the river. The race was umpired and started by the former rower Frederick I. Pitman (Third Trinity), whose disastrous start during the 1903 race was remembered by many. A Trinity College man, he rowed in the Boat Race on three occasions for Cambridge in 1884, 1885 and 1886, when the Cambridge crew took the race despite being behind at Barnes Bridge – a rare feat indeed. He was also president of the Cambridge University Boat Club in the same year. The crews had breakfast at 5.30 a.m. and were at their boathouses by 7 a.m. Race day was cold and misty, and the two crews could be seen warming themselves running and jumping, as well as a series of other warm-up exercises.

In a weak tide, the race commenced at 7.45 a.m. much to the public's disquiet, unhappy about the early hour. This time it was a clean start with no mishaps. Oxford took an early lead, outrating Cambridge from the beginning, and were well clear of them by the Mile Post. At this point it looked liked Oxford would revenge their defeat of the year before. However, the Cambridge crew steadied their rhythm and began to make ground on Oxford. This was largely due to the errant steering from the Oxford cox E.C.T. Warner at Harrods Furniture Depository, which allowed Cambridge to come back at Oxford and begin to reduce the gap. By Hammersmith Bridge Oxford's lead was down to ⅔ of a length and by The Dove pub the crews were level – a remarkable turn of events and a tribute to Cambridge's tenacity and training.

The Light Blues slowly pulled ahead and by Chiswick Ferry were clear of the Oxford boat. Meanwhile Oxford struggled to maintain their technique. Cambridge

Captain Thomas Geoffrey Brocklebank.

finally passed the finishing post with a lead of 4½ lengths in a winning time of 21 minutes 37 seconds (the slowest since 1898). Alas, Brocklebank rowed on the losing crew in his one and only race. Cambridge's dominance in the race continued, this being their third consecutive victory and their fifth in six years. However, Oxford still maintained their lead overall by 33 wins to 27.

★★★

Brocklebank was called to the bar in 1906 and joined the Northern Circuit. In 1913, however, he joined the shipping firm of Messrs Thomas and John Brocklebank Ltd, with whom his father was associated. At the time he was listed as living at No. 4 Fulwood Park, Aigburth, Liverpool.

Always interested in military matters, he served with the Volunteers at both Eton and Oxford. He initially enlisted into the 7th London Brigade, Royal Field Artillery (Territorial Force) (RFA [TF]); however, in 1913 he transferred into the 4th West Lancashire (Howitzer) Territorial Brigade, RFA, and was still serving with them when war was declared in 1914. Mobilised in August 1914, he was sent for training before crossing to France in October 1915. He was wounded in the arm on 2 August 1916, but refused to go to the hospital, insisting on staying with his battery 'to see things through'. Three days later, however, while at Maricourt on 5 August 1916, this brave officer was hit in the head by a shell splinter and died instantly. A popular officer, his family soon began to receive letters of condolence and appreciation.

Lieutenant Colonel James Reynolds of the 277th Brigade, RFA, later wrote:

It is with the greatest regret that I write to tell you of Geoffrey's death. He was killed outright by a shell to-day at 2 p.m. It is merciful that he did not suffer at all. He had been under my command since May, and a better officer of more charming companion I could not wish to find. The care he took for his men's interests was a lesson to all. He threw his whole energy into his duties, and I only heard to-day that he actually enjoyed soldiering. He was buried at Dives Copse field dressing station near Daours, about eleven kilometers from Amiens.

The commanding officer of the 7th London Brigade, RFA, with whom Brocklebank had also served wrote:

He was one of the most efficient officers and one of the nicest men I ever met. He was a born soldier. He never spared himself in any way, and his men would have done anything for him. It was a great loss to us when we returned to Liverpool, and felt it his duty to transfer. We should have been only too glad to keep him. It was a great shock to hear of his death. He was such a pleasing personality. I want you to know how great was the mark he left upon all of us, and upon the standard of his battery and the brigade in the comparatively short time he was with us. You have the most sincere sympathy of all those officers and men who served with him in the 7th London.

Colonel T.E. Topping also added this tribute:

His battery was under my command in the great game. He was wounded one day in the hand when looking for places to observe from. The doctors wanted him to go down but he refused. I would hardly get him to dig his guns and men in at the place allotted to him, he was so anxious and so certain we should advance. Next day but one on his way right up to the front he met his death. He died where he fell. It may be a consolation to his parents that he never knew. I have known him for quite a long time though he had not been attached to me for long. He was a *white man*.

What his fellow officers thought of him is outlined in one of the letters sent to his parents after his death:

I would like to tell you what a very happy recollection I have of Geoffrey ever since I first knew him. Since the war began naturally I had got to know him pretty well, and there are very few friends of whom I could say, as I can say of him, that he never had a single shadow of any sort of disagreement between us. I think he was as nearly perfect as any man I ever knew, and I feel his loss tremendously. At the same time it is a very fine ending to a very fine line, and I feel tremendously proud of him. We all do, as you do too. We all feel that one of our very best men has gone.

He is commemorated in Dive Copse British Cemetery, Sailly-le-Sec, France, grave II. E. 28. In his will he left £47,358 5s 1d. He is further commemorated at Southport Civic Memorial, St Anne's Church of England Church, Aigburth, the Liverpool Exchange Newsroom and the Eton War Memorial. There is also a memorial window at All Saints Church, Satterthwaite, Cumbria, dedicated by his parents. The following words are attached to the window:

To the Dear Memory of Thomas Geoffrey
Elder son of Harold Brocklebank of Grizedale
Captain 4th West Lancashire Howitzer Brigade RFA
Fell in action in France near Maricourt
On August 5th 1916 aged 33 years
He being made perfect in a short time fulfilled a long time for his soul pleased the Lord

Wisdom of Solomon IV 13 & 14.

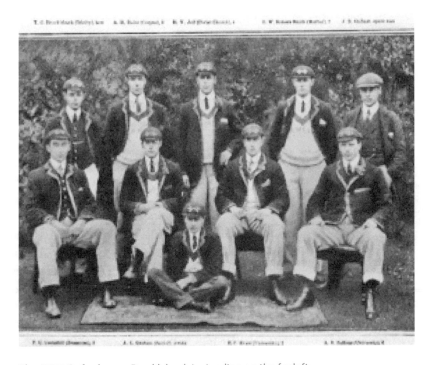

The 1904 Oxford crew. Brocklebank is standing on the far left.

19

MAJOR JOHN JULIUS JERSEY DE KNOOP

Boat position: Bow
Race: 53rd Boat Race, 28 March 1896
     54th Boat Race, 3 April 1897
College: New College, Oxford
Served: 1st Cheshire Yeomanry, attached 6th Company, Imperial Camel Corps
Death: 7 August 1916, aged 40

Fearless commander.

Mr. Jersey de Knoop.

Major John Julius Jersey De Knoop.

John Julius Jersey De Knoop (more commonly known as Jersey) was born on 6 March 1876 in Rusholme, Greater Manchester. He was the son of Baron W. De Knoop and Baroness De Knoop of No. 31 Rutland Gate, London. Interestingly, he was of German decent. His family were industrialists who owned a cotton mill in Manchester. He was educated at Eton College where he was in the Officers' Training Corps and rowed in the Eton Eight. Going up to New College, Oxford, in 1894, he also rowed in his College Eight. He made his girlfriend Evelyn pregnant at the tender age of 13 and she gave birth to a girl named Barbara. He took part in two Boat Races in 1896 and 1897, rowing bow.

53rd Boat Race, 28 March 1896

Oxford went into the race as champions, having defeated Cambridge convincingly in 1895. Despite this Cambridge kept faith with their coach Stanley Muttlebury (Third Trinity), who had rowed number six for Cambridge between 1886 and 1890. Not suprisingly, Oxford also stuck with the same coaching team in G.C. Bourne (New College), who rowed for Oxford in both 1882 and 1883, R.C. Lehmann, a former Cambridge rower and captain of the First Trinity Boat Club who had competed in the trials but never quite made the final Eight, and Douglas McLean (New College), who had rowed number five for Oxford between 1883 and 1887. The well-known and popular former Oxford number four Frank Willan (1866–69) umpired the race for the eighth year.

Five members of Cambridge's 1895 crew were selected once again: Theodore Byram Hope (Trinity Hall – bow), Herbert Aylward Game (First Trinity – number two), Richard Yerburgh Bonsey (Lady Margaret Boat Club – number four), Thomas Jones Gibb Duncanson (Emmanuel – number six) and Adam Searle Bell (Trinity Hall – number seven). Oxford went with three members of their successful 1895 crew: Walter Erskine Crum (New College – number seven), C.K. Philips (New College – number two) and C.D. Burnell (Magdalen – number four).

Despite having been defeated the year before, Cambridge were still the favourites to win the 1896 race. In pouring rain and with a strong westerly wind, Cambridge won the toss and selected the Surrey side of the river, giving Oxford the Middlesex side of the Thames. Willan started the race at 1.03 p.m. Cambridge got away quickly and by Craven Steps were a ⅓ of a length ahead. But by the Mile Post Oxford had drawn level. Cambridge spurted and by Harrods Furniture Depository were in the lead again. By Hammersmith Bridge they were ¾ of a length ahead. By The Dove pub Cambridge were clear and by the Chiswick Steps were 1½ lengths ahead. However, with a supreme effort Oxford fought back and caught up with the Cambridge boat, finally winning the race by ⅖ of a length in a time of 20 minutes 1 second (the narrowest victory since 1877). It was their seventh consecutive victory. Oxford also increased their overall lead to 30–22 in their favour.

54th Boat Race, 3 April 1897

Jersey continued to row for his college and was selected to row for the Oxford Eight the following year. Sticking with a winning team, Oxford were coached once again by G.C. Bourne, William Fletcher and Douglas McLean. For some reason there is no record of the Cambridge coach(es). Frank Willan was once again selected as umpire (ninth year).

The Cambridge Eight included four former rowers: William Augustus Bieber (Trinity Hall – number five), D. Pennington (Caius – number six), A.S. Bell (Trinity Hall – number two) and W.J. Fernie (Trinity Hall – stroke). The only non-British rower was New Yorker Benjamin Hunting Howell (Trinity Hall – number four). Oxford went with seven members of the winning crew from the year before, with the only new face being G.O.C. Edwards (New College – number two).

Oxford went into the race as favourites. With a light easterly breeze and a decent tide, Cambridge won the toss and decided on the Middlesex side, leaving the Surrey side to Oxford. The race started at 2.24 p.m. Cambridge once again made the quicker start, establishing an early ½-length lead. However, once again Oxford fought back and took the lead just before Craven Cottage. Cambridge battled on with a spurt, but despite this by Hammersmith Bridge Oxford were still ahead, a lead they kept, winning the race by 2½ lengths in a time of 19 minutes 20 seconds (the third fastest winning time). Oxford were now up 31–22. Jersey had been in his second winning boat.

★★★

It wasn't until after he left university that Jersey eventually married his long-term girlfriend Evelyn, on 18 July 1898 at St George Hanover Square, London. They moved to Northwich in Cheshire, bought Calveley Hall, Tarpoley, and eventually had four more children. He was an active Mason (Sincerity No. 428, Cheshire). In 1902 he enlisted into the ranks of the Cheshire Yeomanry before being commissioned as a second lieutenant later that year on 25 October. Six years later, in 1908, he was promoted to lieutenant. He was also the Unionist candidate for the Northwich Division in 1910. In August 1914 Jersey was promoted to captain and began training for France, where he was sent in early 1915 as an interpreter (due to his fluent German) serving in Allied Headquarters. However, given the nature of the war, he wasn't even safe there. He was wounded in early 1915, having the top of a finger on his right hand blown off during the Battle of Ypres.

Returning to England to recover from his wounds, he made what *The Times* of London called an impressive speech regarding the 'lack of ammunition for the Cheshire Yeomanry and the entire British Army', further claiming that the British army:

> hung on simply by their eyelids and kept the German's from Breaking through to Calais. Thousands were killed largely because of a lack of ammunition on our side … They have seen in the papers how the brilliant infantry attack north of La Bassee was stopped and thousands of casualties were incurred owing to a lack of ammunition … Ten, 12 and 15 German shells at a time were bursting all up and down the line. Our gunners could do practically nothing.

The speech was reported widely and even brought up in parliament by Sir Arthur Markham MP; it led to Jersey being severely reprimanded by the War Office.

After recovering from his wounds, Jersey returned to his regiment, 1st Battalion, Cheshire Yeomanry, sailing for Alexandria in Egypt. From here the regiment was sent to Wardar in north-east Egypt. On arrival, together with over thirty other men of the regiment, Jersey was transferred and joined the 6th Imperial Camel Corps, where he was put in charge of not only his own company, but also the 4th, 9th and 10th Imperial Corps. For his splendid work with the corps he was mentioned in dispatches. The *London Gazette* said that he 'handled the camel detachment throughout with great skill and judgment'.

Jersey's bravery was to cost him dear: he was shot and killed by a sniper during the Battle of Romani on 7 August 1916. Lieutenant Colonel Verdin, in his history of the Cheshire Yeomanry, later wrote: 'At the Battle of Romani, Jersey risked his own life by walking across a ridge in plain view of the enemy in order to draw fire, to determine their location.' Additionally, he was shot in the arm yet 'was quite unperturbed by the wound and continued leading his troops. He was later killed. At his funeral, his body was lowered into the sand as Lieutenant Houghton recited the Lord's Prayer.' Lieutenant Verdin describes this as a 'simple but moving end to a man who was born to lead'.

Jersey is buried together with thirteen of his men at the Kantara War Memorial Cemetery in north-east Egypt, grave ref. E59. There is also a memorial plaque to him in Calveley Church, Cheshire, together with a photograph. He is further commemorated on the Eton College Memorial, Bunbury War Memorial and the New College Oxford Memorial.

The 1897 Dark Blues. Knoop is standing far left, holding a dog.

20

LIEUTENANT LANCELOT EDWIN RIDLEY

Boat position: Cox
Race: 71st Boat Race, 13 March 1913
      72nd Boat Race, 28 March 1914
College: Jesus College, Cambridge
Served: 1/4th Prince Charlotte of Wales' Royal Berkshire Regiment
Death: 19 August 1916, aged 23

The bravest of the brave.

Lancelot Edwin Ridley.

Lancelot Edwin Ridley was born in 1892 in Ipswich. He was the son of Edwin Perkins Ridley (Mayor of Ipswich) and Charlotte Elizabeth Ridley, of 'Burwood', Westerfield Road, Ipswich. He was educated at the Ipswich school and Eastbourne College, where he was in Wargrave House from 1906 to 1910. He was also a school prefect and a sergeant in the Officers' Training Corps. Good at sports, he played in the second XV. In 1910 he entered Jesus College, Cambridge, taking his BA in 1913. It seems to be while at Cambridge that his interest in rowing developed. A man of small stature, he began coxing for his college. His talent was quickly noticed and he was selected to cox for the university in the 1913 Boat Race.

71st Boat Race, 13 March 1913

To avoid Holy Week, the 1913 race was scheduled earlier than normal, taking place on 13 March 1913. Oxford went into the race as champions, having won the 1912 race by 6 lengths in a time of 22 minutes 5 seconds. For the 1913 race Oxford kept faith with two of their successful coaches from the year before: G.C. Bourne (New College), who had been bow for Oxford in both 1882 and 1883, and Harcourt Gilbey Gold (Magdalen), who had stroked for Oxford between 1896 and 1899 (Oxford president 1900). These two old Oxford hands were supported by two new boys: Alister Kirby (Magdalen), who had rowed number five, six and seven between 1906 and 1909, and H.R. Barker (Christ Church), who rowed for Oxford in 1908 and 1909. Cambridge also went with the previous year's coach, despite losing the race: John Houghton Gibbon (Third Trinity), who stroked for Cambridge in both 1899 and 1900. For the tenth year, Frederick I. Pitman (Third Trinity) umpired the race.

For the 1913 race the Cambridge Eight included two rowers with Boat Race experience: Sidney Swann (Trinity Hall – number two), his third appearance in the race, and Ralph Shove (First Trinity – number six). The Oxford Eight had five returning rowers in its boat: Leslie Wormald (Magdalen – number seven) and Henry Wells (Magdalen – cox), both of whom were taking part in their third race, Ewart Horsfall (Magdalen – stroke), W.H.M. Wedderburn (Balliol – number five) and A.F.R. Wiggins (New College – number six).

It is also worth noting that Edgar Burgess, Sidney Swann, Leslie Wormald and Ewart Horsfall had all won gold medals during the 1912 Olympic Games held in Stockholm, Sweden, in the Men's Eight, rowing for the Leander Club. Arthur Wiggins, rowing for New College, took the silver in the same race.

Cambridge won the toss and elected the Surrey side of the river, leaving the Middlesex side to Oxford. Pitman started the race promptly at 4.38 p.m. The conditions were described as 'almost perfect … with a modest tide'. Oxford outrated Cambridge from the start; however, Cambridge eventually took the lead and were a length ahead within the first few minutes and they were clear by the Mile Post. Oxford spurted and by Harrods Furniture Depository had closed the gap to ½ a length. However, by Hammersmith Bridge Cambridge were clear once again. They extended their lead by The Dove pub and were further ahead by Craven Steps. Cambridge began to tire and Oxford closed in on them. Cambridge spurted just before Barnes Bridge, taking a 1¼-length lead. However, by the time they reached Mortlake Brewery the boats were level. It was now Oxford's chance and they passed the Cambridge boat, going on to win by ¾ of a length in a time of 20 minutes 53 seconds. It was the narrowest margin since 1896. Oxford now had an overall lead of 39–30.

72nd Boat Race, 28 March 1914

Once again Oxford went into the race as champions and they kept with their winning coaches: G.C. Bourne (New College), his son Robert Bourne

Scenes from the 1913 Boat Race.

(New College), who had stroked for Oxford between 1909 and 1912, and the ever-present Harcourt Gilbey Gold (Magdalen). Cambridge were coached by new boy Stanley Bruce (Trinity Hall), who had rowed number two in 1904. Fredrick I. Pitman umpired again for the eleventh year. The Oxford Eight had five returning rowers: Henry Wells (Magdalen – cox [his fourth appearance]), H.K. Ward (New College – number three), E.D. Horsfall (Magdalen – number four), A.F.R. Wiggins (New College – number six) and L.G. Wormald (Magdalen – number seven). The Cambridge boat went with the same number of old hands: Sidney Swann (Trinity Hall – number two), C.S. Clark (Pembroke – number six), C.E.V. Buxton (Third Trinity), G.E. Tower (Third Trinity – stroke) and L.E. Ridley (Jesus – cox).

Cambridge won the toss and decided on the Surrey side of the Thames, with Oxford taking the Middlesex side. The weather was bright with a warm sun, light wind and smooth water. Pitman got the race started at 2.20 p.m. Cambridge took an early lead and were ¾ of a length ahead by Craven Steps. By the Mile Post Cambridge were 1¼ lengths ahead and continued to pull away as they passed below Hammersmith Bridge. Cambridge passed the finishing post 4½ lengths ahead of Oxford in a time of 20 minutes 23 seconds. It was Cambridge's first victory since 1908. However, Oxford still led overall by 39 races to 31. It was the last race before the First World War and the boats of Oxford and Cambridge wouldn't race again until 1920. This would be the first break in the annual Boat Race since 1853. Sadly, five rowers from the 1914 race would lose their lives in the First World War. From the Oxford boat: William Fletcher (Balliol – bow). From the Cambridge boat: John Andrew Ritson (First Trinity – number four), L.E. Ridley (Jesus – cox), Gordon Kenneth Garnett (First Trinity – number five) and Dennis Ivor Day (Lady Margaret Boat Club – bow).

★★★

On leaving Cambridge Ridley served his articles with a firm of solicitors in Ipswich and joined the Officers' Training Corps. On 9 March 1915 he was commissioned into 1/4th Battalion, Princess Charlotte of Wales', Royal Berkshire Regiment. He was killed in action on 19 August 1916 while leading a bombing party in a skirmish near Pozières. His body was never recovered or identified and he is commemorated on the Thiepval Memorial, pier and face 11D.

He is also commemorated on the Jesus College Cambridge Memorial, Ipswich School and Eastbourne College memorials, Ipswich War Memorial and the Chute and Chute Forest Memorial.

21

Boat position: Number Seven
Race: 64th Boat Race, 16 March 1907
　　　　65th Boat Race, 4 April 1908
College: Magdalen College, Oxford
Served: 13th Battalion, Rifle Brigade
Death: 15 September 1916, aged 31

For those who knew them both it is impossible to consider them apart;
the memory of them is single.

Captain Evelyn Herbert
Lightfoot Southwell.

Evelyn Herbert Lightfoot Southwell was born on 19 March 1886 at No. 5 College Yard, Worcestershire. He was the son of the Reverend Canon Herbert Burrows Southwell and Annie. He was a King's Scholar at Eton College, and rowed in the College Eight, before going up to Magdalen College, Oxford, as a demy (a foundation scholar at Magdalen College, Oxford – so called because such a scholar originally received half the allowance of a fellow) in 1904. He stroked the College Eight, was Head of River in 1905 and 1906, and took part in the trials in the same years. In 1907 he also won the Stewards' Challenge Cup. Southwell was selected to crew in two Boat Races: 1907 and 1908.

64th Boat Race, 16 March 1907

Cambridge went into the 1907 race as champions. Once again they selected their successful coaches from the previous four years: Francis Escombe (Trinity Hall) and Stanley Muttlebury (Third Trinity), who had rowed number five and six for Cambridge between 1886 and 1890. They also went with David Alexander Wauchope (Trinity Hall), who stroked for Cambridge in 1895. Oxford selected Harcourt Gilbey Gold (Magdalen), who stroked for Oxford between 1896 and 1899 (Boat Club president 1900) and H.W. Willis. The ever-reliable Frederick I. Pitman (Third Trinity) was chosen as the race umpire for the fifth year. Cambridge selected five rowers who had represented the university before: E.W. Powell (Third Trinity – number seven), Banner Johnstone (Third Trinity – number six), J.H.F. Benham (Jesus – number two), D.C.R. Stuart (Trinity Hall – stroke) and H.M. Goldsmith (Jesus – number three). Oxford decided on three former rowers for their boat: A.C. Gladstone (Christ Church – number seven), A.G. Kirby (Magdalen – number six) and H.C. Bucknall (Merton – number two).

Oxford won the toss and selected the Surrey station, handing the Middlesex side of the Thames to Cambridge. Cambridge pulled away quickly and were clear within the first 2 minutes. By the Mile Post they were 2 lengths ahead and by Hammersmith Bridge they had extended this to 3 lengths. Although Oxford spurted and drew closer, by Barnes Bridge Cambridge were 4 lengths ahead, passing the winning post 4½ lengths ahead in a time of 20 minutes 26 seconds.

The 1908 Oxford Boat Race crew. Southwell sits second from right.

It was the biggest winning margin since 1904. The overall record was now 24–29 in Oxford's favour.

65th Boat Race, 4 April 1908

For this year's race Cambridge kept faith with coaches Francis Escombe (Trinity Hall) (for the fifth year), Stanley Muttlebury (Third Trinity), David Alexander Wauchope (Trinity Hall) and L.H.K. Bushe-Fox (St John's). Oxford also kept faith with their coaches: Harcourt Gilbey Gold (Magdalen) who brought in R.P.P. Rowe (Magdalen), a four-time Oxford rower between 1889 and 1892. For the fifth year the ever-popular Frederick I. Pitman was selected as umpire. Oxford went with four rowers who had represented them previously: Albert Gladstone (Christ Church – stroke), Alister Kirby (Magdalen – number five), E.H.L. Southwell (Magdalen – number three) and A.W.F. Donkin (Magdalen – cox). Cambridge also selected four former rowers for the 1908 boat: J.S. Burn (First Trinity – number four), Eric Powell (Third Trinity – number seven), Douglas Stuart (Trinity Hall – stroke) and R.F.R.P. Boyle (Trinity Hall – cox). Australian Collier Cudmore, the Oxford number two, was the only non-British participant.

Oxford won the toss and chose the Surrey station, with Cambridge taking the Middlesex side of the Thames. Umpire Pitman got things going at 3.30 p.m. The Cambridge crew made the quicker start and began to pull away from the Oxford crew. Cambridge were clear by the Mile Post. By the time they reached Harrods Furniture Depository, Cambridge were 2 lengths ahead. Oxford spurted several times but failed to make any headway. After passing Barnes Bridge Cambridge began to pull further away, passing the finishing post with a 2½-length

The 1907 Oxford Boat Race crew.

Captain Evelyn Herbert Lightfoot Southwell.

lead in a time of 19 minutes 20 seconds, the fastest since 1902. It was Cambridge's third consecutive victory, and their sixth in seven years. However, Oxford still led overall 34–30.

Later in 1908 Southwell was the spare man for the Great Britain (Magdalen) gold-medal-winning Coxless Fours during the 1908 London Olympics.

★★★

Southwell left Oxford with a first-class in Moderations in 1906 and a second-class in Literae Humaniores in 1908, and he became an assistant master at Shrewsbury School in 1910. While at Shrewsbury he met and befriended another master, Malcolm White, who had been educated at King's College, Cambridge, where he had been a member of the college choir and later an assistant master at the King's College Choir School. Always together, many said it was difficult to think of them apart. In 1915, during the First World War, they both took commissions into the Rifle Brigade – White the 6th attached to the first Battalion; Southwell the 13th Battalion. The book *Two Men: A Memoir* by H.E.E. Howson (1919) is probably the best source of information on Southwell and White. The following is an observation of some of their time at the school:

> It is interesting to recall the impressions which they made on their arrival. White had visited Shrewsbury before; he came with experience of teaching at King's College Choir School and afterwards at Marlborough College, and with a reputation as a singer and violin-player: a reputation which was entirely justified by his performances. At first he made no very distinct impression, probably because of his shyness, and he did not seem at once to take very kindly

to Shrewsbury: he was constantly recalling with regret the time he spent at
Marlborough, but this phase did not last long: Shrewsbury soon became to him
the object of reverence which it remained until the end. But several terms passed
before he was valued at his true worth, partly owing to his shyness and partly
owing to his modesty; the latter quality remained to the end as one of his most
striking characteristics; it was so perfectly genuine. He was an excellent violinist,
and he must have known it, and the same may be said of his powers as a singer,
yet his skill in these directions was never obtruded, nor concealed by any false
modesty. If asked to play, he would play, and his 'That's rather jolly, isn't it?'
At the end of the piece suggested that, quite unaffectedly, he considered that the
gratitude of the listeners was due entirely to the composer; in fact he seemed to
join in the gratitude and to regard himself as one of the listeners.

His keen sense of humour did not appear at once. It was of the 'modern' type
which is best illustrated in literature by the work of 'A.A.M.' in *Punch*; though in
some respects perhaps R.L. Stevenson was the forerunner of the type. At any rate,
White's love for the wrong box was infectious, and quotations from that classic
constantly accompanied our meals.

Southwell's arrival in Shrewsbury was somewhat different; before his coming in
May 1910. He was known to no one in Shrewsbury – apart from the headmaster
– except as a first class oars-man. He arrived almost straight from a long visit
to Paris, and seemed at first very French; his love of French literature and the
French nation ('those adorable people' he called them in at least one letter from
the Front) remained constantly with him. He came at about eight o'clock in
the evening of the day before school work began, and when some sort of the
arrangements were being explained to him that night caused some surprise by
inquiring about trains to Liverpool; he wanted to go to see an Oxford friend
who was leaving for America.

Both men were later killed in the war. White was killed first on 1 July 1916 (the
first day of the Battle of the Somme). Shortly before he died he wrote of Southwell:
'Evelyn's soldiering is one of the finest sacrifices of this war, undertaken in spite of
his characteristic distaste for all, or a great deal, that it involves.'

In his last letter to his friend Southwell and knowing he was about to go over
the top, he described himself as feeling like a coach before the Bumping Races,
adding: 'Our new house and Shrewsbury are immortal, which is a great comfort.'
Knowing he might not make it, he wrote to his family: 'It is ... a great comfort to
think of you all going on, living the same happy lives that we have led together,
and of the new generation coming into it all.' He said his death would make up for
small acts of selfishness in his life. White's last words in his diary on 29 June were:
'We go up this afternoon, and this book must not go too.' On 1 July White and his
battalion attacked near the village of Mailly-Maillet. White went ahead of his men

and was hit first. He told his men: 'I'm all right; go on.' At that moment a shell burst near them and White was never seen again. Three days later, Southwell addressed a letter to his old school house, remarking: 'I am in great anxiety about our Man; though I can't say where he is or what he is doing.' Southwell only learned that White was missing in the second week of July. He wrote in anguish to his mother of his friend's death:

> I have faced the casualty list daily without a tremor for two years now, and now, when I am hard hit myself, I cry out! Mum he was such a dear; he was so keen on everything, and the most true 'artist' in the full sense, that I have ever known.

Southwell was only to last a few more weeks, being killed in action on 15 September 1916. A brother officer states that he was killed by sniper fire near Delville Wood, describing his death as 'truly unpleasant' but that Southwell had been 'magnificent throughout' and that 'if he knew what fear was, he never showed it'. Another account states that Sergeant Robert Philip Thomson was binding Southwell's wounds when they were both hit by a shell and killed. It is unclear whether these are two different accounts or one account of the same incident. Such is the confusion of war.

Southwell's remains were never found or identified and he is commemorated on the Thiepval Memorial, pier and face 16B and 16C. He is also commemorated on the Eton College Memorial, Magdalen College Oxford Memorial, Shrewsbury School Memorial and the Worcestershire War Memorial.

22

CAPTAIN THE RIGHT HONOURABLE RICHARD PHILIP STANHOPE

Boat position: Bow
Race: 65th Boat Race, 4 April 1908
College: Magdalen College, Oxford
Served: 3rd Battalion, Grenadier Guards
Death: 16 September 1916, aged 31

Died in the arms of his servant.

The Right Honourable Richard Philip Stanhope.

Richard Philip Stanhope was born on 16 January 1885 at St George, Hanover Square, London. He was the youngest son of Arthur Philip Stanhope, 6th Earl Stanhope (1838–1905), and Evelyn Henrietta Pennefather (1845–1923). He was educated at Eton College where he rowed in the Eight and was a lance corporal in the Eton Volunteers (August 1903) before going up to Magdalen College, Oxford. He rowed bow for his college and was selected to row bow for the 1908 Boat Race between Oxford and Cambridge.

65th Boat Race, 4 April 1908

Cambridge went into the 1908 Boat Race as champions, having won the 1907 race by 4½ lengths in a time of 20 minutes 26 seconds. Cambridge brought in new coach L.H.K. Bushe-Fox (St John's) together with old hands Francis Escombe (Trinity Hall), for the fifth year who had rowed number five in 1902, Stanley Muttlebury (Third Trinity), who rowed number five and six between 1886 and 1890, and David Alexander Wauchope (Trinity Hall), who had stroked for Cambridge in 1895. Oxford kept faith with Harcourt Gilbey Gold (Magdalen), who had stroked the Oxford boat between 1896 and 1899 (president 1900). They also selected new boy R.P.P. Rowe (Magdalen), who had rowed number two and seven between 1889 and 1892. The very popular Frederick I. Pitman (Third Trinity) was umpire for the fifth successive year.

The Oxford Eight contained four members who had rowed in the 1907 race: E.H.L. Southwell (Magdalen – number seven), A.G. Kirby (Magdalen – number six), A.C. Gladstone (Christ Church – stroke) and A.W.F. Donkin (Magdalen – cox). The Cambridge crew also had four returning rowers: E.W. Powell (Third Trinity – number seven), J.S. Burn (First Trinity), D.C.R. Stuart (Trinity Hall – stroke) and R.F.R.P. Boyle (Trinity Hall – cox). The Australian Collier Cudmore (Magdalen – number two) was the only non-British member of either crew.

Cambridge went into the race as favourites, with the writer and former Oxford bow G.C. Drinkwater (Wadham) considering their crew to be 'better and stronger than in the previous year'. The Oxford crew, on the other hand, had been dogged by injuries and illness.

Oxford won the toss and selected the Surrey side of the river, leaving the Middlesex side to Cambridge. Umpire Pitman started the race at 3.30 p.m. and in a strong headwind Cambridge made the quicker start out, stroking and pulling away from the Oxford Eight. By the time they reached the Mile Post Cambridge were clear of the Oxford boat. By the time they reached Harrods Furniture Depository Cambridge were 2 lengths ahead. Oxford spurted several times to try to pull some distance back but failed to make ground on the Cambridge boat and, once the Cambridge crew had passed under Barnes Bridge, they were clear, passing the finishing post 2½ lengths ahead of Oxford in a time of 19 minutes 20 seconds (the fastest since 1902). It was Cambridge's third consecutive victory. The overall record, however, was still 34–30 in Oxford's favour.

★★★

On 13 May 1914 Stanhope married Beryl Franziska Kathleen Le Poer Trench (1893–1957) in St Paul's, Knightsbridge. Moving to Revesby Abbey, Boston, Lincolnshire, Stanhope took a commission as a second lieutenant in the Lincolnshire Yeomanry in 1909. However, on 23 August 1915, he transferred to the 3rd Battalion, Grenadier Guards (commanding 2nd Company), almost certainly to be with his older brother (Major James Richard Stanhope KG DSO MC, 7th Earl Stanhope, Grenadier Guards, 1880–1967) who was already serving with them. He was sent to the Front on 5 October 1915, was wounded during an attack towards Lesboeufs on 15 September 1916 and died the next day of his wounds. The battalion diary explains:

Zero hour was timed for 6.20 a.m. and the Battalion was ready in position by about 3 a.m. The men slept therefore from 3 – 5.45 a.m. when they were given sandwiches and an issue of rum. During this time the 'tanks', which were attached to the Division could be heard making their way up in rear of us. We were in immediate touch with 6th Division on our right. At 6 a.m. our heavy artillery fired about 40 rounds in quick succession. This of course woke up the enemy, who put down his usual barrage on GINCHY village (particularly the NE corner) and started shelling LEUZE WOOD and troops of the 6th Division who were still moving about in that neighborhood. At 6.19 a.m. the whole Brigade rose to it's feet and advanced. Our left front company was met by machine gun fire as soon as it got up and lost Capt MACKENZIE and Mr ASQUITH at once (Asquith was the son of the Prime-Minister and one of the most noted casualties of the war. The words on his head stone, still to be seen, summed up the feeling of the day, 'Small time but in that small most greatly lived this star of England'), 2/Lt H. Williams was wounded a few yards further on. The last remaining officer of that company also fell within 200 yards of our own trenches. Our front company however appeared to get off much more fortunately and did not seem to lose until a considerable way out.

Now owing to the causes which have been set down and owing to the fact that the 6th Division failed to advance and that the tanks were not forthcoming.

(1)   Our left flank was or rather appeared to be in the air as the 1st Brigade had started behind us.

(2)   Our right flank was completely exposed.

(3)   Owing to the closeness of the formation and the irregularity of the assaulting trenches all the waves tended to become mixed.

(4)   Owing to (1) and (2) the tendency was for the Brigade to split up right and left to cover it's exposed flanks.

In addition to the above a German trench or rather a line of shell holes hastily organized and provided with M.G.s was encountered about 250 yards after leaving our own trenches. Every German in this trench was either shot or

Stanhope is standing at the back on the far left.

bayoneted but it helped to break up the regularity of the formation and impaired the cohesion of the assault.

The men however were not to be denied and though the right flank was raked by heavy machine gun fire in enfilade and though the wire and trench on that part of the front owing to impossibility of observation wire untouched by the Brigade continued to advance, but as a Brigade rather than as 4 battalions. The parties who were drawn to the left by the appallingly exposed flank found themselves among the 1st Brigade but did not suffer severely as the wire and trench there had been completely destroyed.

It was on the right flank that our chief casualties were incurred. They included the Commanding Officer Lt Col B.N.S. Brooke D.S.O. and most of the officers except Capts GORDON & HOPLEY.

After reaching the first objective – the German line running through T.8.a.b.2.d it was found that there was a gap between the left parties and the right which was occupied by the enemy who began to enfilade the trench with M.G.s and shell fire.

Composite bombing parties however dislodged them and the whole first objective was in our hands. Our right flank was however completely exposed as the troops on our right were only a short distance, if any, in front of GINCHY TELEGRAPH.

On the right therefore it was impossible to push on but more in the center in composite party of men of the 2nd Gds Brigade under MAJOR ROCKE went forward and established themselves just short of the second line in T.9.b but as that party was only 100 strong and had two open flanks it was impossible to assault the second line. It appeared that LES BOEUFS would have fallen into our hands without opposition or at any rate with only ill-organized resistance if more troops could have been packed on. This was not done doubtless owing to the threat to the right flank of the Division – a threat which would have become more acute with every additional yard forward.

The position was therefore consolidated but the advanced party under Major ROCKE after withholding one counter-attack had both flanks enveloped and being attacked frontally had to fall back on to the first objective. On the evening of the 15th therefore this Battalion held a small frontage on the right of the first objective. This flank was subjected to repeated bombing attacks and the Germans also attempted to work riflemen round it. Fire steps had to be dug in both sides of the trench and bombing parties organized to resist the enemy bombing down. Fighting on a small scale therefore continued throughout the night 15/16th and resulted in all counter-attacks being repulsed. The enemy drove us back at one time about 70 yards but his success was momentary only and the ground was immediately re-taken and 1 machine gun captured.

Stanhope was shot and seriously wounded, dying in his servant's arms the following day, becoming one of the 415 Guards casualties taken during that attack. Stanhope's body was never discovered or identified and he is commemorated on the Thiepval Memorial, pier and face 8D. He is also commemorated on the Eton War Memorial, Magdalen College Oxford Memorial and the memorial at St Mary's Church, Horncastle, Lincolnshire. His probate on 29 December 1916 was £63,044.

23

MAJOR CHARLES PELHAM ROWLEY

Boat position: Stroke
Race: 57th Boat Race, 31 March 1900
College: Magdalen College, Oxford
Served: Royal Garrison Artillery
Death: 29 October 1916, aged 39

The bravest of men who died in a tragic accident.

Major Charles Pelham Rowley.

Charles Pelham Rowley was born on 26 April 1877 in Botley, Hampshire. He was the eldest son of Admiral Charles John Rowley of Botley and Alice, daughter of George Carey Elwes of All Souls College, Oxford. He was educated at the Reverend R.S. Tabor's School at Cheam before going to Winchester College, becoming a commoner prefect and a member of sixth book. He was in C House (Du Boulay's [Cook's]) and was there between 1890 and 1896. In 1896 he went up to Magdalen College, Oxford, graduating in 1900 with honours in Mathematics. A keen rower, he rowed stroke in the Magdalen boat for four years between 1889 and 1900. As a result he was chosen to row in the Oxford boat as stroke in 1900.

57th Boat Race, 31 March 1900

Cambridge went into the race not only as champions but also as favourites, having defeated the Oxford crew during the 1899 race by 3¼ lengths in a time of 21 minutes 4 seconds. It was their first victory in ten years. Writer and former Oxford bow and number seven George Drinkwater (Wadham) said of the Cambridge crew that they 'stand in a class by themselves among University crews'. As for Oxford, he said it was 'one of the poorest that ever came from the Isis'.

Cambridge were coached by James Brooks Close (First Trinity), who had rowed number six, bow and number three between 1872 and 1874, and Stanley Muttlebury (Third Trinity), who had rowed number six for Cambridge between 1886 and 1890. Oxford went with the legendary Harcourt Gilbey Gold (Magdalen), who stroked for Oxford between 1896 and 1899, and Douglas McLean (New College), who rowed number five and seven for Oxford between 1883 and 1887. For the eleventh year in succession the ever-faithful Frank Willan (Exeter), who had rowed number four, seven, six and bow for Oxford between 1866 and 1869, was selected as umpire.

The Oxford crew contained three rowers who had competed before: G.S. Maclagan (Magdalen – cox), C.W. Tomkinson (Balliol – number four) and C.E. Johnston (New College – number three). Not surprisingly Cambridge had six returning rowers: J.E. Payne (Peterhouse – number four), R.B. Etherington-Smith (First Trinity – number five), R.H. Sanderson (First Trinity – number six), W. Dudley Ward (Third Trinity – number seven), J.H. Gibbon (Third Trinity – stroke) and G.A. Lloyd (Third Trinity – cox). H.H. Dutton, Oxford's number three, came from Australia and was the only non-British rower.

On a fine, bright day Oxford won the toss and decided on the Surrey side of the Thames, leaving Cambridge to take the Middlesex side. Willan got the race under way at 2 p.m. Cambridge took the lead immediately and maintained it. By Craven Steps they were 3 lengths ahead and continued to pull away from Oxford with every stroke. Oxford tried spurting several times but were unable to make up the distance. Cambridge finally passed the finishing post, ahead by an impressive 20 lengths, in a time of 18 minutes 45 seconds. It was the fastest winning time in the history of the event, equalling that set by Oxford in 1893. Despite this Cambridge victory, Oxford maintained the overall lead 32–24.

★★★

Major Charles Pelham Rowley.

After leaving Oxford, Rowley went straight into the army, taking a commission into the Royal Garrison Artillery. After training he served for twelve years in India, where he gained a reputation as a first-class shot and photographer. Returning from India, he was stationed in Tynemouth training the New Army. However, at the beginning of 1915 he was sent to France and saw action throughout the Second Battle of Ypres, acting as adjutant to the 13th Brigade, Royal Garrison Artillery, for just under a year. He was then returned to Britain to assist in the training of heavy artillery near Winchester. He was promoted to major and received orders to return to the Front in October 1916. However, on 29 October 1916, the day before he was due to depart, he was accidentally killed at his home in Botley. An elm tree in his garden had been damaged in a fierce gale some days before, and some of its branches were broken and hanging loose. Rowley, watched by his sister, went out into the garden determined to make the tree safe before he went back to the Front. He was cutting the damaged branches away when one fell on him and fractured his skull, killing him instantly. He was 39 years old.

He was given a full military funeral and now lies in the south-west part of All Saints Churchyard, Botley, Hampshire. Inside the church, the last window on the south side (designed by S. Meteyard and executed by Messrs Martyn) is in memory of Rowley and his father. It shows St Michael with children, and was installed in 1920. He is also commemorated on the Winchester College Memorial, the Magdalen College Oxford Memorial and the Botley War Memorial.

24

Boat position: Number Seven
Race: 55th Boat Race, 26 March 1898
   56th Boat Race, 25 March 1899
College: Balliol College, Oxford
Served: 22 Squadron, Royal Flying Corps
Death: 4 November 1916, aged 40

Despite losing a leg in one war, fought with valour in another.

Auberon Thomas Herbert.

Auberon Thomas Herbert, 9th Baron Lucas, 5th Lord Dingwall, was born on 25 May 1876. Herbert was the second but eldest surviving son of the Honorable Auberon Herbert (younger son of Henry Herbert, 3rd Earl of Carnarvon). His mother was Lady Florence, daughter of George Cowper, 6th Earl Cowper. He was educated at Bedford School and, after some time in the house of Mr A.L. Smith, entered Balliol College, Oxford, in October 1895. Although never having rowed at school, he was a fine athlete and became an enthusiast whilst at Balliol. He improved quickly and was selected to row number seven in the Oxford boat for the 1898 Boat Race.

55th Boat Race, 26 March 1898

Oxford started the 1898 race as champions, having defeated Cambridge by 2½ lengths in a winning time of 19 minutes 12 seconds the year before (the third fastest winning time). They were also the favourites, but only just. It was Oxford's eighth consecutive victory, bringing the Boat Race's overall record to 31–22 in Oxford's favour. The Oxford Eight were coached by G.C. Bourne (New College) who had been bow for Oxford in both 1882 and 1883, and Douglas McLean (New College) who rowed number five and seven between 1883 and 1887. In an attempt to stop the rot and bring Cambridge a long-awaited victory, they controversially brought in the former Oxford rower and coach William Fletcher (Christ Church – stroke, number seven and number six). As a result several members of the Cambridge crew refused to row. However, Fletcher did a first-class job and, in the words of the former Oxford rower and writer George Drinkwater (Wadham), 'turned out a crew well above the average …' For the tenth year in succession the ever-reliable former Oxford rower (number four, six and seven 1866 to 1869) Frank Willan (Exeter) was selected to umpire the race.

The Cambridge Eight only went with three rowers with previous Boat Race experience: Adam Searle Bell (Trinity Hall) who had stroked and rowed number seven and two for Cambridge between 1895 and 1898, Edward Caesar Hawkins (Caius) who coxed the Cambridge boat in both 1897 and 1898, and Claude Goldie (Third Trinity) who rowed number seven and three in 1898 and 1899. Oxford, on the other hand, and not surprisingly, stuck with experience and had six rowers in their crew with previous Boat Race experience: G.O.C. Edwards (New College – number two), C.K. Philips (New College – number three), C.D. Burnell (Magdalen – number five), R. Carr (Magdalen – number six), H.G. Gold (Magdalen – Stroke) and H.R.K. Pechell (Brasenose – cox).

In a high wind and with a spring tide making the waters choppy, Oxford won the toss and decided on the Middlesex side of the river, leaving the choppier Surrey side for the Cambridge crew to cope with. Willan started the race at precisely 3.47 p.m. The race was a disaster almost from the start. Within only a few strokes the Cambridge boat was full of water. They made for the smoother waters of the Middlesex side of the river but it was much too late. Although Oxford had also shipped water, the situation wasn't quite so bad and they managed to row on and finish the race, winning by ¼ of a mile in 22 minutes 15 seconds (slowest winning time since 1878). It was Oxford's ninth consecutive victory, taking the overall score to 32–22 in Oxford's favour.

56th Boat Race, 25 March 1899

Seen as part of the successful winning Oxford crew from the previous year, Herbert was selected again for the 1899 race, once again rowing number seven. Oxford stuck with success and experience, selecting G.C. Bourne (New College), together with Douglas McLean (New College) and new boy R.P.P. Rowe (Magdalen), who had rowed number two and seven for Oxford between 1889 and 1892. Cambridge went once again with the controversial William Fletcher (Christ Church), the former Oxford coach who they clearly didn't blame for the previous year's disaster, and R.C. Lehmann, who although a former captain of the First Trinity Boat Club, never rowed in the Boat Race even though he had in the trials. The ever-present Frank Willan umpired the race for the eleventh time.

Cambridge selected two rowers with previous Boat Race experience: C.J.D. Goldie (Third Trinity – number three) and R.B. Etherington-Smith (First Trinity – number five). Oxford selected four former rowers: R.O. Pitman (New College – bow), F.W. Warre (Balliol – number six), A.T. Herbert (Balliol – number seven) and H.G. Gold (Magdalen – stroke). Interestingly, the Oxford number five C.E. Johnston (New College) was the father of the much-loved cricket commentator Brian Johnston who would also become the BBC's principal Boat Race commentator.

On a bright day with a poor tide Cambridge won the toss and selected the Surrey side of the Thames, Oxford being forced to take the Middlesex side. Willan started the race at 12.58 p.m. Both boats got away well and were pretty evenly matched until they reached the Mile Post, at which point Oxford had taken a ¼-length lead. As Cambridge began to make up the distance, Oxford spurted to try to stay ahead. However, the Cambridge crew were having none of it and spurted back; by The Dove pub they were ahead. They maintained this lead for the rest of the race, crossing the finishing line 3¼ lengths ahead in a time of 21 minutes

Herbert sits on the far left.

4 seconds. It was Cambridge's first victory in ten years and took the overall record to 32–23 in Oxford's favour.

***

Herbert was also a member of the famous Balliol Eight of 1899, which contained five Blues. His interests were wide and varied. As well as developing a passion for poetry and music, he also had a keen interest in nature and natural history, and he had an astonishing knowledge of birds. Although he only took a third at Oxford in Modern History, he cultivated many close friendships, befriending scholars like Cuthbert Medd and Raymond Asquith.

At the outbreak of the Second Boer War in 1899 he managed to get himself a position as a war correspondent for *The Times* of London. Although not a military man by nature, he loved the life and the open spaces that South Africa had to offer, not to mention the abundance of wild life and exotic birds. He wrote home: 'When I think what dull things I was doing last year, I am staggered by the luck which has brought me here.'

While keeping up with the army and advancing with them, he was shot and wounded, taking a rifle bullet in the foot. The medical care he received was poor and a serious infection set in. He was returned to England where the doctors were unable to save his leg and he had to have it amputated below the knee. Despite this handicap he continued to ride, play tennis and involve himself in a number of other sports. He became a Liberal candidate for parliament and in 1905, on the death of his uncle, he succeeded to the baronies of Lucas and Dingwall, becoming the 9th Baron Lucas and 5th Lord Dingwall.

When the Liberal government came into power, as one of the few Liberal peers, he was marked down for preferment. He became Mr Haldane's private secretary in 1908 and later undersecretary for war, and in 1911, for a short time, undersecretary for the colonies. In 1911 he went as parliamentary secretary to the Board of Agriculture, where he was a real success. In 1914 he entered the Cabinet as president of the Board of Agriculture and held the post until the formation of the coalition in May 1915.

Keen to do his bit, despite his physical disability and being over age, Herbert took a commission into the Hampshire Yeomanry (Carabineers) before transferring to the Royal Flying Corps and joining 22 Squadron. He became a pilot and served in Egypt before returning to England as an instructor. He went out to France as a flight commander in October 1916. On 4 November 1916 he was killed in action by Lieutenant E. König of Jasta 2 while flying an FE2b, No. 7026, of 22 Squadron over Bancourt. Lord Lucas was hit in the head and legs and died instantly. The plane was eventually landed by his observer Lieutenant A. Anderson who was wounded (22 Squadron lost three aircraft in the same dog fight).

He is buried in Honourable Artillery Company Cemetery, Écoust-St-Mein, grave VIII. C. 17. Lord Lucas never married and his titles passed to his sister Nan Herbert.

His great friend Maurice Baring wrote this elegy:

> IN MEMORIAM. A. H.
>
> O liberal heart fast-rooted to the soil,
> O lover of ancient freedom and proud toil,
> Friend of the gipsies and all wandering song,
> The forest's nursling and the favoured child
> Of woodlands wild –
> O brother to the birds and all things free,
> Captain of liberty!
> Deep in your heart the restless seed was sown.
> The vagrant spirit fretted in your feet.
> We wondered could you tarry long,
> And brook for long the cramping street,
> Or would you one day sail for shores unknown.
> And shake from you the dust of towns, and spurn.
> The crowded market place – and not return.
> You found a sterner guide;
> You heard the guns.
> Then, to their distant fire,
> Your dreams were laid aside
> And on that day, you cast your heart's desire
> Upon a burning pyre;
> You gave your service to the exalted need,
> Until at last from bondage freed,
> At liberty to serve as you loved best,
> You chose the noblest way.
> God did the rest.
>
> MAURICE BARING.

As his epitaph, we may well add to Baring's elegy Robert Louis Stevenson's prose:

> In the hot fit of life, a-tiptoe on the highest point of being, he passes at a bound on to the other side. The noise of the mallet and chisel is scarcely quenched, the trumpets have hardly done blowing, when, trailing with him clouds of glory, the happy-starred, full-blooded spirit shoots into the spiritual land.

He is further commemorated at Bedford School, Balliol College, Oxford, and the House of Commons.

25

LIEUTENANT COMMANDER FREDERICK SEPTIMUS 'CLEG' KELLY DSC

Boat position: Number Four
Race: 60th Boat Race, 1 April 1903
College: Balliol College, Oxford
Served: Royal Naval Volunteer Reserve
Death: 13 November 1916, aged 35

The greatest amateur stylist of all time.

Frederick Septimus 'Cleg' Kelly DSC.

Frederick Septimus Kelly was born on 29 May 1881 at No. 47 Phillip Street, Sydney. He was the fourth son (and seventh child) of an Irish-born woolbroker, Thomas Herbert Kelly and Mary Anne Kelly (née Dick). Not only was Kelly to go on to be a fine rower but he was also a talented musician, playing both Mozart and Beethoven on the pianoforte from an early age. He was educated at Sydney Grammar School before being sent to England to be educated at Eton College. While at Eton he stroked in the Eight, winning the Ladies' Challenge Plate at Henley Royal Regatta in 1899. On leaving Eton he went up to Balliol College, Oxford, where he was awarded the Lewis Nettleship music scholarship. He became president of the university musical club and was taken under the wing of the famous Indian-born English composer, pianist, organist, teacher and writer Ernest Walker (1870–1949).

Kelly continued rowing at Oxford, winning the Diamond Challenge Sculls at Henley in 1902 by beating Raymond Etherington-Smith (First Trinity, who rowed in the Boat Race between 1898 and 1900) in the final. In 1903 he was selected to row number four in the Oxford boat in the annual race.

60th Boat Race, 1 April 1903

Cambridge went into the 1903 race as champions having beaten Oxford the previous year by 5 lengths in a time of 19 minutes 9 seconds. They also went in as favourites partly due to a spate of illness that hit the Oxford crew but also because they were considered to be a very fine and swift crew. Oxford decided on experience and kept faith with G.C. Bourne (New College), who had rowed bow for Oxford in both 1882 and 1883, and C.K. Philips (New College), who had rowed number two and three for Oxford between 1895 and 1898. Cambridge brought in Charles John Bristowe (Trinity Hall), who had rowed bow and stroke for Cambridge in 1886 and 1887, and Claude Goldie (Third Trinity) who had rowed number seven and three in 1898 and 1899. They also later brought in William Dudley Ward (Third Trinity), who had rowed number seven for Cambridge in 1897, 1898 and 1899. Making his debut as umpire was the later legendary Frederick I. Pitman (Third Trinity), who had rowed stroke for Cambridge between 1884 and 1886.

The Oxford Eight went with four rowers who had raced before: H.W. Adams (University – number seven), J.G. Milburn (Lincoln – number five), G.C. Drinkwater (Wadham – bow) and A. de L. Long (New College – number three). Cambridge, sticking with success, decided to bring in six rowers with Boat Race experience: W.H. Chapman (Third Trinity – bow), P.H. Thomas (Third Trinity – number two), C.W.H. Taylor (Third Trinity – number four), H.B. Grylls (First Trinity – number six) and R.H. Nelson (Third Trinity – stroke), along with the only non-British participant, American Oxford rower Devereux Milburn (Lincoln – number six).

On a strong tide, Oxford won the toss and decided on the Surrey station, Cambridge taking the Middlesex side of the river. The race was a disaster from the very beginning. The inexperienced Pitman started the race at 3.35 p.m. However, after calling out 'Are you ready' he failed to discharge his pistol correctly, causing confusion amongst the crews. He also seemed to fail to notice that, despite the misfire, the Cambridge crew pulled away and were ⅓ of a length ahead of Oxford before they even got started. Drinkwater later commented that the Oxford crew 'rowed like a beaten crew from the first stroke'. By Hammersmith Bridge Cambridge were 3 lengths ahead, which they extended to 4½ lengths by Barnes Bridge. They finally swept past the finishing line 6 lengths ahead in a time of 19 minutes 33 seconds. The overall score was now 33–26, still in Oxford's favour. It was the only time that Kelly rowed in the Boat Race.

***

This disappointing Boat Race result didn't stop Kelly continuing with his successful rowing career. The following summer he out-rowed Jack Beresford (who won five successive medals at five Olympic Games – an Olympic record not beaten for sixty years until in 1996 Sir Steve Redgrave won his fifth Olympic medal at his fourth Olympic Games) to win the Diamond Sculls. He also defeated Arthur Cloutte to win the Wingfield Sculls, the Amateur Championship of the Thames.

Kelly left Oxford in 1903 and joined the Leander Club. He was in the Eight that won the Grand Challenge Cup at Henley between 1903 and 1905, and the Stewards' Challenge Cup in 1906. He took the honours in the Diamond Sculls once again in 1905, this time out-rowing Harry Blackstaff (who won the event the following year, and who also won the gold medal in the Single Sculls in 1908 at age 40, making him the oldest sculling champion in Olympic history) in a time of 8 minutes 10 seconds – a record that stood for over thirty years. Kelly's final appearance was in a race during the 1908 Olympic Games held in London. Competing for the Leander Eight, he took the gold medal, defeating the Belgian Royal Club Nautique de Grand in the final. Many people considered Kelly to be the 'greatest amateur stylist of all time', describing his rowing thus: 'his natural sense of poise and rhythm made his boat a live thing under him.'

After leaving Oxford with fourth-class honours in History, Kelly studied the piano under the German composer and teacher Iwan Knorr (1853–1916) at the Hoch Conservatory in Frankfurt. On his return to London he became adviser to the Classical Concert Society. In 1911 he returned to Australia and gave several concerts in Sydney. In 1912 he played in several chamber music concerts in London. He also performed with Pau Casals i Defilló (Pablo Casals 1879–1973), the Spanish cellist and conductor generally regarded as the pre-eminent cellist of the first half of the twentieth century, and one of the greatest cellists of all time. He was also important in organising a series of concerts by Maurice Ravel.

At the beginning of the First World War Kelly was first rejected by the Inns of Court Regiment, then by the Grenadier Guards; however, on the advice of his friend Maurice Bonham Carter, the prime minister's personal private secretary, he applied for a commission in the Royal Naval Division and on 16 September 1914 was accepted, becoming a sub-lieutenant in the Drake Battalion. On learning that Drake were not to take part in the Gallipoli campaign, he transferred to Hood Battalion. It was here that he was to meet and become great friends with, amongst others, the poet Rupert Brooke. Together they formed the 'Latin Club'. Among its members were not only Brooke but Arthur Asquith and Lord Ribblesdale's son, Charles Lister, and the critic and composer William Denis Browne. After the Hood Battalion left England en route to Gallipoli the relationship between Brooke and Kelly deepened and they were seldom out of each other's company.

Frederick Septimus 'Cleg' Kelly DSC.

On 28 February 1915 Brooke developed sepsis from an infected mosquito bite. He was transferred to the French hospital ship moored in a bay off the Greek island of Skyros in the Aegean Sea. His condition worsened and, with Kelly composing Brooke's elegy in the next room, Brooke died on 23 April 1915. His friend and fellow member of the Latin Club, William Denis Browne (who also selected where Brooke was to be buried), later described what happened:

> ... I sat with Rupert. At 4 o'clock he became weaker, and at 4.46 he died, with the sun shining all round his cabin, and the cool sea-breeze blowing through the door and the shaded windows. No one could have wished for a quieter or a calmer end than in that lovely bay, shielded by the mountains and fragrant with sage and thyme.

The expeditionary force had orders to depart immediately. As his friends refused to have Brooke buried at sea, his body was taken to an olive grove at the top of a small hill on Skyros, where he was buried at 11 p.m. Brooke's pall bearers comprised Frederick Kelly, Denis Browne (critic and composer), Arthur Asquith (later Brigadier General Arthur Asquith), Charles Lister (the scholar and son of Lord Ribblesdale), Patrick Shaw-Stewart (scholar and, at the age of 25, a director of Barings Bank) and Bernard Freyberg (later General Lord Freyberg VC and Governor General of New Zealand).

Following the ceremony, Kelly wrote movingly in his diary:

> When the last of the five of us his friends had covered his grave with stones and took a last look in silence – then the scene of the tragedy gave place to a sense of passionless beauty engendered both by the poet and the place.

The poet's death was a great personal loss to Kelly and one he never fully recovered from. With the assistance of his friend and fellow Latin Club member, Denis Browne, Kelly made sure that Brooke's personal effects were recovered from the ship for safe keeping. Kelly even went as far as to copy the contents of Brooke's notebook, fearing it might be lost in transit back to his family.

Kelly landed with his battalion at Cape Helles towards the end of April and was quickly under fire. He was present in the attack of 2 May, when the ferocity of the Turks' retaliatory bombardment on the following night left his batman 'quite unhinged … and completely out of his senses'. During a further attack on 2 June 1915, Kelly was wounded in the right heel by a piece of shrapnel. Evacuated to Alexander, he recovered quickly and was back with his battalion within the month. He was wounded again on 29 June, this time in the head, but once again it wasn't too serious. The Latin Club's actions in Gallipoli were later described in a letter written by Kelly's friend Charles Lister the following July:

Our digging operations, carried out at night within about two hundred yards of the enemy's trenches and under a certain amount of rifle fire, have not only made our own position quite secure but rendered untenable for the Turks a small portion of our sector which they still held in between our extreme right and

Frederick Septimus 'Cleg' Kelly's military and Olympic medals.

our right center. They have also given us a point of vantage from which we can
enfilade Turks retiring before the French on our extreme right. Oc [Asquith]
has been extraordinarily dogged, and is practically responsible for all this corner,
which will be known as Asquith triangle. He hadn't a wink of sleep all the four
days, and Patrick and Kelly also distinguished themselves and in one night dug
a long trench connecting Asquith triangle with our main support. Six men of
this company were killed and wounded, and I think the company of another
battalion working with them lost about as many. Patrick and Kelly remained
above the ground the whole time, and it was a wonder they were not hit. Their
Petty Officer who was doing the same got killed.

After months of stalemate it was eventually decided to evacuate the peninsula. Kelly
together with his friends Freyberg and Asquith formed part of the rearguard, tasked
with covering the evacuation. Kelly was mentioned in dispatches and awarded the
Distinguished Service Cross for his actions with the rearguard by Sir Ian Hamilton
(*London Gazette*, 6 September 1916: 'In recognition of services with the Royal Naval
Division in the Gallipoli Peninsula'). He was also promoted to lieutenant commander.

Kelly was posted with his battalion to France, taking up his duties on the Western
Front. He was appointed second in command of the 2nd Hood Battalion, under
Asquith. Sub-Lieutenant Bentham later wrote an account of his time with the
Hood Battalion in France, which included an account of Cleg Kelly:

The war still seemed a long way off, and Lieutenant Kelly, Sub. Lieutenant
Chapman and myself with 12 Petty Officers and Leading Seamen were sent

The 1903 Boat Race crew. Kelly stands in back row, second
from left.

to Rouen for a bombing course. There was a stir when we arrived at the camp, which contained 5,000 to 6,000 men, and nobody knew who or what we were. We still maintained our naval ranks and Kelly had a full moustache and beard. Kelly stipulated that the navy took precedence on parade, much to the army's annoyance, and we lined up behind the band and led the parade off the parade ground. What a time I had in Rouen: the fortnight went very quickly. It was whilst we were there that I first heard Kelly play the piano. He was a master, and had given recitals at Queen's Hall before the war. He had also won the Diamond Sculls two years running [sic]. But he was very eccentric: he washed his teeth at least 12 times a day, and loathed getting his hands dirty, so he was never without gloves.

The battalion was moved to the Vimy sector and quickly became involved in serious fighting. It was during an attack on Beaumont-sur-Ancre on 13 November 1916 that Kelly was killed while leading his men in a frontal and ultimately successful attack on a German machine-gun position. Freyberg later wrote about the attack and the death of his friend:

At 5.30 a.m., with 15 minutes to go, I went across quickly to see that everything was in order. The patrol in front was in trouble, some bombs were thrown, and it retaliated as it withdrew. On the extreme right I stopped to talk to Kelly, who commanded B Company. We had been daily companions for the last two years, and he, Asquith, Egerton and I were the sole survivors of the Battalion who left Avonmouth for Gallipoli in February 1915. I wanted to take both his hands and wish him 'God Speed', but somehow it seemed too theatrical; instead we talked rather awkwardly, and synchronized our watches. I walked back along our sector, speaking to the men I recognized. The old hands, whom I called by name, answered with a 'Yes sir, I'm here again,' which recalled similar meetings on dark nights, and made me wonder which of them would answer the call at the next attack …

Freyberg was to win a Victoria Cross for the same operation.

A memorial concert was held at Wigmore Hall, London, on 2 May 1919, where Leonard Borwick played some of Kelly's piano compositions and Muriel Foster sang his songs. The one piece that made a lasting impression on all present, however, was Kelly's Elegy for String Orchestra, in memory of Rupert Brooke. An obituary later said of Kelly's Elegy:

No record, however slight, of his [Kelly's] musical life may leave unnoticed the Elegy for String Orchestra written in 1915 and dedicated to the memory of his friend Rupert Brooke. Here he is the poet of deep imagining, finding an

Frederick Septimus 'Cleg' Kelly DSC, sculling.

utterance in music which, linked by its modal inflections to the Past, is no mere expression of personal grief or loss, but, a symbol, rather, of the continuity of life, giving thoughts of Eternity – and as such, for all who knew or loved 'Cleg' Kelly, his own most fitting and perfect memorial.

Kelly is buried in Martinsart British Cemetery, grave ref. I.H. 25. He is also commemorated on the Eton and Balliol college memorials.

26

CAPTAIN MERVYN BOURNES 'BUGGINS' HIGGINS

Boat position: Bow
Race: 67th Boat Race, 23 March 1910
College: Balliol College, Oxford
Served: Adjutant Headquarters, 8th Australian Light Horse
Death: 23 December 1916, aged 29

My grief has condemned me to hard labour for the rest of my life.

Mervyn Bournes 'Buggins' Higgins.

Mervyn Bournes Higgins (known by the nickname 'Buggins') was born in November 1887 in Melbourne, Australia. He was the only son of Mr Justice Henry Bournes Higgins (Australian High Court) and Mary Alice Higgins. He was educated at Ormond College, Melbourne, between 1897 and 1904, where amongst his many other athletic activities he established himself as a fine rower. In October 1906 he went up to Balliol College, Oxford, where he got his BA with honours in the school of jurisprudence. While at Balliol he continued to row, improving dramatically. He stroked the Torpid, which went Head of River in 1907, and was in the College Eight between 1907 and 1910. While in the College Eight they were just beaten to the Ladies' Plate at Henley but did go on to win the Wyfold Cup in 1909. Higgins also rowed bow in the trials in 1909 and was selected for the same position in the Oxford boat to race against Cambridge the following year, on 23 March 1910.

67th Boat Race, 23 March 1910

Oxford went into the 1910 race as champions, having won the 1909 race by 3¼ lengths in a time of 19 minutes 50 seconds (their first win in four races). They also went into the race as favourites. Oxford, not surprisingly, held on to the 1909 winning coaches: G.C. Bourne (New College) who had rowed bow for Oxford in 1882 and 1883, Harcourt Gilbey Gold (Magdalen) who had rowed stroke for Oxford between 1896 and 1899 (Oxford president 1900) and W.F.C. Holland (Brasenose) who had rowed bow and stroke for Oxford between 1887 and 1890. Although Cambridge kept faith with David Alexander Wauchope (Trinity Hall) who had rowed stroke in 1895, they also brought in new boys William Dudley Ward (Third Trinity) who had rowed number seven in 1897, 1899 and 1900, and Raymond Etherington-Smith (First Trinity) who had rowed number six and five between 1898 and 1900. For the seventh year in succession the former Cambridge stroke Frederick I. Pitman (Third Trinity), who after a poor start had become a fine umpire, did the honours once again.

As a result of unfavourable tides, the race was scheduled to be held on the Wednesday of Holy Week, which 'caused considerable controversy', with several rowers refusing to take part. The matter was finally resolved when the Bishop of London gave his permission for the race to go ahead as long as there were no celebrations after the race. The compromise worked and the annual race was on.

The Cambridge crew went with three rowers with previous Boat Race experience: R.W.M. Arbuthnot (Third Trinity – bow), J.B. Rosher (First Trinity – number six) and Edward Gordon Williams (Third Trinity – number five). Williams had also won a bronze medal in the 1908 London Olympics rowing in the Men's Eight. Oxford included four previous Boat Race veterans in their Eight: Duncan Mackinnon (Magdalen – number five), Stanley Garton (Magdalen – number six), Robert Bourne (New College – stroke) and A.W.F. Donkin (Magdalen – cox). Three of the rowers came from overseas: Oxford's M.B. Higgins (Balliol – bow) and C.P. Cooke (Trinity Hall – number four) both Australians; and C.A. Skinner (Jesus – cox) was from South Africa.

Race day was bright with a warm sun and a light northerly breeze. Cambridge won the toss and chose the Middlesex side of the river, giving Oxford the Surrey side of the water. Pitman began the race at 12.30 p.m. Cambridge made the quicker start and pulled away from Oxford quickly. However, one of the Cambridge crew managed to catch a crab. Taking advantage of this, Oxford pushed by Cambridge and took the lead; they were ¼ of a length ahead by Craven Steps. However, Cambridge spurted and by the Mile Post were back in front. Oxford fought back and by The Dove pub a spurt put them 1 length clear. They continued to extend their lead, passing the winning post with a 3½-length lead in a time of 20 minutes 14 seconds (the slowest winning time since 1907). The overall score was now 36–30 in Oxford's favour.

★★★

After leaving Oxford in 1910 Higgins was called to the bar at the Inner Temple in 1911, and in Melbourne and Sydney in 1912. Practising law as a barrister in Australia, he devoted his leisure time to coaching college rowing in Melbourne. A fine cricketer, he also turned out for the Melbourne Cricket Club (Australia). At the outbreak of the First World War he enlisted into the ranks of the 8th Light Horse as a private. However, on 3 February 1915 he was commissioned into the same battalion's 'C' Squadron. He fought with distinction throughout the Gallipoli campaign, including the attack on Lonesome Pine. He was in the second line at the Nek when the attack went in at 4.30 p.m. on 7 August 1915 (made famous in the Australian film *Gallipoli*). Their attack was to be a diversionary action aimed at tying down Turkish troops whilst Allied units to the north (Australians, British, New Zealanders, Gurkhas and Indians) tried to storm the heights of Chunuk Bair and Hill 971.

The first line, led by the battalion's commanding officer, Lieutenant Colonel A.H. White, was shot to pieces by the Turkish defenders who were firing approximately 600 rounds a minute. A young private in the 8th Light Horse, Dave McGarvie, described what happened:

> Out we went – no sooner were we out than they opened fire on us. Our orders were not to fire but to rush up to within 2 yards of the trench, then wait till the bomb throwers cleared the trench with bombs, then go to work and finish the job with the bayonet.
>
> I hadn't gone 10 yards when head over heels I went amongst some wire – rifle one way, helmet the other, the sling was hooked in the wire. I extracted it, put on my helmet and raced on through a hail of bullets. We were under a cross fire from machine guns.
>
> About 20 yards from their trench was a gully about 20 feet deep with fairly thick scrub. Down this I went and got up to the Turks' trench on the other side. The trench was bristling with bayonets and another trench behind the first was full of Turks. I did not happen to be a bomb thrower so I got my rifle ready.

The only thing I could see worth shooting at was a Turk bayonet, 2 yards in front, so I fired and snapped it clean in two. Then the second row of Turks stood up showing heads and shoulders. I got some splendid shots – altogether I fired about 10 shots and I am certain of four or five Turks. Heads and shoulders at 10 or 12 yards was just easy shooting. Every time I fired a man went down. Then I felt a terrible crack on the foot.

Despite having seen what had happened to the first wave, two minutes later the second wave, including Lieutenant Higgins, jumped out of their trenches and followed the first, even though they knew that their chances of survival were slim. Stumbling over the dead bodies of their fallen friends, they met the same fate. By some miracle Higgins was one of the few to survive unscathed. Of the 300 men of the 8th Light Horse that attacked on that fateful day 154 were killed, over 50 per cent of the entire battalion. Higgins was mentioned in dispatches by Sir Archibald Murray, on 18 March 1917, for his actions at the Nek. His colonel later wrote of him: 'He and I are two of only four officers left who laded in this Brigade.'

In January 1916, after the Gallipoli campaign, Higgins was promoted to captain and transferred to Egypt where he became adjutant to Colonel Maygar VC, who later spoke of Higgins as 'a fine officer carrying out trying duties with wonderful tact and ability'. It was during an action in the Sinai on 23 December 1916 that Mervyn Higgins was to lose his life – shot through the head by a sniper in an attack on the Turkish redoubt at El Magdhaba – when the Australians, fighting hard despite having just completed a 20-mile march, destroyed the Turkish forces. It was later explained that Higgins fell at the point of victory. He was a great loss to the battalion; a trooper later wrote:

Our Adjutant led our troop into action in great style. The boys thought a lot of him for his pluck, and the way he took us there saved a squadron from getting cut up.

Brigadier General Antill, on hearing of Higgins' death, wrote:

he had endeared himself to every one with whom he had come in contact; he was one of the few in whom I had implicit confidence not only as an example which had no small effect.

Initially buried where he fell, Captain Higgins' body was later removed to Kantara War Memorial Cemetery, grave A. 190.

His father, who was devastated by the lost of his only son, and who later said very movingly, 'My grief has condemned me to hard labour for the rest of my life', established The Mervyn Bournes Higgins Memorial Trophy for competition in Melbourne University's Inter-Collegiate Boat Race. He spent most of the rest of his life campaigning against war, not wanting any other parent to go through his agonies. He died in 1929.

Mervyn Higgins is commemorated on Oxford's Balliol College War Memorial. He is also commemorated in Dromana Cemetery with a Celtic cross above his parents' graves.

27

CAPTAIN ARTHUR BROOKS CLOSE-BROOKS MC

Boat position: Bow
Race: 64th Boat Race, 16 March 1907
College: Trinity College, Cambridge
Served: 2nd attached 3rd Battalion, Manchester Regiment
Death: 10 January 1917, aged 32

The lost member of a famous Cambridge rowing family.

Captain Arthur Brooks
Close-Brooks MC.

Arthur Brooks Close-Brooks was born on 22 October 1884 in Eccles, Lancashire. He was the son of John and Emily Close-Brooks, of Birtles Hall, Cheshire. He was educated at the Reverend C.L. Cameron's school at Mortimer, before going to Winchester College in 1898, being in I House (Turner's [Hopper's]). On leaving Winchester in 1903 he went up to Trinity College, Cambridge, to read law. While at Trinity, rowing became his passion and he rowed bow in the Trinity boat. In 1907 his talent was noticed and he was selected to row bow in the Cambridge boat to take on Oxford in the annual Boat Race. It was also a proud moment for his father and two uncles, all of whom had raced for Cambridge in the 1870s.

64th Boat Race, 16 March 1907

Cambridge went into the 1907 Boat Race as champions, having defeated Oxford the previous year by a convincing 3½ lengths in a time of 19 minutes 25 seconds (the fastest winning time since 1902). Cambridge not surprisingly then kept faith with their successful coaching staff: Francis Escombe (Trinity Hall) who had rowed number five for Cambridge in 1902 (his fifth consecutive year), Stanley Muttlebury (Third Trinity) who rowed number five and six for Cambridge between 1886 and 1890, and David Alexander Wauchope (Trinity Hall) who had stroked the Cambridge boat in 1895. Oxford kept faith with Harcourt Gilbey Gold (Magdalen) who stroked for Oxford between 1896 and 1899 (he was also Oxford president in 1900). They also brought in new boy H.W. Willis. Frederick I. Pitman (Third Trinity) was selected for the fifth year to umpire the race. Oxford selected three rowers with previous Boat Race experience: Henry Bucknall (Merton – number two), A.G. Kirby (Magdalen – number five) and A.S. Gladstone (Christ Church – stroke). Cambridge not surprisingly selected five members of their 1906 winning crew to race again: Banner Johnstone (Third Trinity – number six), J.H.F. Benham (Jesus – number two), H.M. Goldsmith (Jesus – number three), E.W. Powell (Third Trinity – number seven) and D.C.R. Stuart (Trinity Hall – stroke).

On 8 September 1906 the Cambridge Eight had taken on and beaten by 2 lengths a crew from Harvard University at the Henley Royal Regatta. The 1907 Cambridge crew, with the exception of J.S. Burn (First Trinity), E.W. Powell (Third Trinity) and B.G.A. Scott (Trinity Hall – cox), was the same crew that defeated the Americans.

Oxford won the toss and decided on the Surrey side of the river, handing the Middlesex side of the Thames to Cambridge. Once again Cambridge had the better start and were clear of the Oxford boat within 90 seconds of the race starting. By the time they reached the Mile Post Cambridge were 2 lengths up, which they had extended to 3 lengths by the time they passed under Hammersmith Bridge. However, not to be defeated, Oxford spurted and gradually pulled the deficit back to only a couple of feet. After failing to cope with a section of rough water, however, Oxford began to fall back once again and by Barnes Bridge Cambridge were 4 lengths ahead. Cambridge passed the finishing line 4½ lengths ahead in a time of 20 minutes 26 seconds. The overall score was now 34–29 but still in Oxford's favour. It was to be Close-Brooks' only race but at least he was in the winning boat.

★★★

On leaving Cambridge Close-Brooks practised law in Bolton. In 1912 he married Frances Mary Brown and they had two children, Emily Lois and Arthur Geoffrey Close-Brooks. The family later moved to Glemham Grove, Saxmundham, Suffolk.

At the outbreak of the First World War, and in the rush to join up before it was all over Close-Brooks enlisted into the ranks of the Public Schools Battalion of the Royal Fusiliers. Later, however, and almost certainly because of his background, he was commissioned into the 2nd Battalion Manchester Regiment. He was sent to France in 1915 and was quickly involved in the heavy fighting around the Ypres Salient with the 2nd Manchesters, where they were in the line for almost three months. It was during this time that Lieutenant Close-Brooks won the Military Cross for bravery. Patrolling no-man's-land, especially at night, was a duty performed by both sides as they tried to gather information on each other's activities. His citation read:

> On 10th June 1915 this officer was detailed to obtain information concerning a new piece of trench work in the enemy's lines. With a sergeant and a private soldier, Close-Brooks crawled towards the enemy's front line. Just before daybreak the party came under heavy fire, the private soldier being wounded. All three separated and made their way to the battalion's front line trenches. However, it was discovered that the sergeant had not returned. Immediately, Close-Brooks returned to No Man's Land and crawling across the ground in broad daylight found that the sergeant had been killed within 35 yards of the German lines. He managed to crawl back to his own trenches and when darkness fell returned to No Man's Land and brought the sergeant's body back to the British lines.

Harvard University v. Cambridge University 1906, with Close-Brooks standing far left.

The sergeant in question was 5268 Charles Ernest Kirby, who had previous served with the 1st Lancashire Fusiliers, being discharged in 1904 as being worthless and incorrigible, so he must have changed a lot to make sergeant by 1915. He is buried in Chester Farm Cemetery.

Close-Brooks was promoted to captain and transferred to the 3rd Battalion before being posted to the 1st Battalion and sent to Mesopotamia. On 10 January 1917 he was seriously wounded during an attack near the Shatt-el-Hai Canal, dying from those wounds later the same day at the 8th British Field Ambulance. He was later mentioned in dispatches for his actions on the day he was killed.

He is buried in the Amara War Cemetery, grave ref. XXVIII. A. 2. He is also commemorated in the chapel at Trinity College, Cambridge, and his old School Winchester College, cloister outer B2.

His brother, Lieutenant John Charles Close-Brooks, 1st Life Guards was killed earlier in the war, on 30 October 1914 at Zandvoorde. His body was never discovered and he is commemorated on the Menin Gate Memorial to the missing.

28

SECOND LIEUTENANT ROBERT PROTHERO HANKINSON

Boat position: Number Three
Race: 71st Boat Race, 13 March 1913
College: New College, Oxford
Served: 56th Punjabi Rifles (Frontier Forces)
Death: 23 February 1917, aged 26

Always keen to be close to the action.

Robert Prothero Hankinson was born on 8 December 1890. He was the son of Robert Scott and Emma Mildred Hankinson (daughter of the Reverend Canon George Prothero) of Little Bassett Wood, Southampton (later No. 74 Chelsea Park Gardens, London).

He was educated at West Downs School, going on to Winchester College in 1904. He was in College House and was a school prefect in his last year. He also won the Warden and Fellows Prize for Greek Prose and was in the College XV. In 1909 he was awarded a scholarship to New College, Oxford, where he gained a first in Classical Moderations. While at Oxford he became a keen rower, rowing number three in his college boat. He so impressed

Second Lieutenant Robert Prothero Hankinson.

in that position that he was selected to row in the Boat Race in his final year at Oxford in 1913.

71st Boat Race, 13 March 1913

After the 1912 fiasco with the Cambridge boat sinking during the original race and Oxford winning the re-run by 6 lengths, everyone hoped that the 1913 race would go ahead smoothly. Oxford hung on to their two successful coaches, G.C. Bourne (New College), who rowed bow for Oxford in 1882 and 1883, and Harcourt Gilbey Gold (Magdalen), who rowed stroke for Oxford between 1896 and 1898, and was president in 1900. They were joined by H.R. Barker (Christ Church), who rowed number seven and two for Oxford in 1908 and 1909, and Alister Kirby (Magdalen), who rowed number five, six and seven for Oxford between 1906 and 1909. Despite the disaster and eventual defeat by Oxford, Cambridge kept the faith and kept their coach, John Houghton Gibbon (Third Trinity), who had stroked the Cambridge boat in 1899 and 1900. The umpire for the tenth year in succession was the former Third Trinity rower Frederick I. Pitman. To avoid Holy Week and all the controversy that went with competing over that time, the race was scheduled to be held earlier than normal, on 13 March 1913. Cambridge went with two former Boat Race competitors: Sidney Swann (Trinity Hall – number two) and Ralph Shove (First Trinity – number six). Oxford, having won the 1912 race, not surprisingly decided on five rowers with previous Boat Race experience: L.G. Wormald (Magdalen – number seven), E.D. Horsfall (Magdalen – stroke), H.B. Wells (Magdalen – cox), A.H.M. Wedderburn (Balliol – number five) and A.R.R. Wiggins (New College – number six). Burgess (Magdalen), Swann (Trinity Hall), Wormald (Magdalen) and Horsfall (Magdalen) had all also won gold medals during the 1912 Olympic Games in Sweden rowing in the Men's Eight for the Leander Club.

In almost perfect conditions with a modest tide, Cambridge won the toss and chose the Surrey side of the river leaving the Middlesex side to Oxford. Fredrick I. Pitman got the race under way at 4.38 p.m. Cambridge took an early lead and went into a quick ½-length lead and were clear by the Mile Post. Oxford spurted and by Harrods Furniture Depository had closed Cambridge's lead down to ½ a length. However, Cambridge hung on and began to pull away once again and were almost clear of Oxford as they swept under Hammersmith Bridge. By The Dove pub Cambridge were ¼ of a length clear, extending to a full ½ a length by Craven Steps. Cambridge, however, began to tire and, aided by a spurting from Oxford, by the time the boats reached Mortlake Brewery the crews were level. Notwithstanding their best efforts, Cambridge were unable to hold Oxford and the Dark Blues passed the finishing line ¾ of a length ahead of Cambridge in a

The 1913 Oxford boat crew, with Hankinson standing centre.

time of 20 minutes 53 seconds. It was the slowest time since 1896. Oxford now had an overall lead of 39–30.

★★★

On leaving Oxford in 1913 Hankinson decided on a career with the Indian Civil Service and in 1914, after passing the appropriate exams, was accepted and sent to India. He was appointed as an assistant magistrate and collector. During the First World War he was initially commissioned as a second lieutenant into the 4th Queen's but in August 1915 Hankinson transferred to the Corps of Guides, eager to do his bit. He was then posted to Mesopotamia with the 56th Punjabi Rifles. In his determination to remain in the field he declined an appointment under the political officer at Basra, for which his knowledge of Persian had qualified him, and chose instead to serve in the front line. It was while serving during the Mesopotamian campaign that Second Lieutenant Robert Prothero Hankinson was seriously wounded in action near Kut, dying of his wounds on 23 February 1917.

He is buried in grave XXI.C.15 of the Amara War Cemetery. He is also commemorated at Winchester College outer cloister C6, the New College Oxford War Memorial and the war memorial at Stoneham, Hampshire.

29

CAPTAIN ALISTER GRAHAM KIRBY

Boat position: Number Five, Number Six & Number Seven
Race: 63rd Boat Race, 8 September 1906
     64th Boat Race, 16 March 1907
     65th Boat Race, 4 April 1908
     66th Boat Race, 3 April 1909
College: Magdalen College, Oxford
Serving: 5th Battalion, London Regiment (London Rifle Brigade)
Death: 29 March 1917, aged 29

Won the Boat Race after four attempts.

Alister Graham Kirby.

Alister Graham Kirby was born on 14 April 1886 in Brompton, West London. He was the son of Arthur Raymond Kirby, a bencher of Lincoln's Inn, and his wife Gertrude Fleming. He was educated at Eton College before going up to Magdalen College, Oxford. After developing his talents he was selected to row in the Oxford boat against Cambridge on four occasions. The first was in 1906, rowing number five.

63rd Boat Race, 8 September 1906

Oxford went into the 1906 Boat Race as champions, having won the 1905 race by 3 lengths in a time of 20 minutes 35 seconds. It was Oxford's first victory in four years and the narrowest winning margin since 1901. Despite this Oxford were not the favourites for this year's race. Oxford not surprisingly went with success and selected William Fletcher (Christ Church) who rowed stroke, six and seven for Oxford between 1890 and 1893, and Harcourt Gilbey Gold (Magdalen) who stroked for Oxford between 1896 and 1899 (Oxford president in 1900). Keeping faith with their coaches despite the loss for the third year in succession, Cambridge were coached by Francis Escombe (Trinity Hall) who had rowed number five for Cambridge in 1902. He was joined by Stanley Muttlebury (Third Trinity) who rowed number five and six between 1886 and 1890, and David Alexander Wauchope (Trinity Hall) who had rowed stroke in 1895. The umpire for the fourth year in a row was the ever-popular Frederick I. Pitman (Third Trinity).

The Cambridge University Eight only included two rowers with previous Boat Race experience: Banner Johnstone (Third Trinity – number seven), who rowed number three and seven between 1904 and 1907, and number seven against the Harvard Eight in September 1906; Ronald Powell (Third Trinity – number six), who had rowed number five, six and seven for Cambridge between 1904 and 1906, and was also in the Cambridge Eight that rowed against the visiting Harvard rowers; and Eric Powell (Third Trinity), Ronald's brother, who also rowed in the Cambridge Eight in 1906. The Oxford Eight went with four rowers with previous Boat Race experience: E.P. Evans (University – number six), L.E. Jones (Balliol – number four), H.C. Bucknall (Merton – stroke) and L.P. Stedall (Merton – cox).

Given the conditions, with a strong tide and little wind, the expectation was for a fast time. Oxford won the toss and selected the Surrey side of the river, forcing Cambridge to take the Middlesex side. At precisely 12 p.m. Umpire Pitman got the race under way. Cambridge got away quickly and led from the beginning. Within 2 minutes they were clear of Oxford and by the time they reached Barnes Bridge were 4 lengths clear. Cambridge finally crossed the winning line 3½ lengths clear of Oxford in a time of 19 minutes 25 seconds – the fastest winning time since 1902. The overall score, however, was still 34–28 in Oxford's favour. Despite being in the losing boat, Kirby was selected again the following year, this time rowing number six.

64th Boat Race, 16 March 1907

Cambridge went into the 1907 race as champions. Once again they selected their successful coaches from the previous four years, Francis Escombe (Trinity Hall),

Stanley Muttlebury (Third Trinity) and David Alexander Wauchope (Trinity Hall). Oxford selected Harcourt Gilbey Gold (Magdalen), assisted for the first time by H.W. Willis. The ever-reliable Frederick I. Pitman (Third Trinity) was chosen as the race umpire for the fifth year. Cambridge selected five rowers that had represented the university before: E.W. Powell (Third Trinity – number seven), Banner Johnstone (Third Trinity – number six), J.H.F. Benham (Jesus – number two), D.C.R. Stuart (Trinity Hall – stroke) and H.M. Goldsmith (Jesus – number three). Oxford decided on three former rowers for their boat. A.C. Gladstone (Christ Church – number seven), A.G. Kirby (Magdalen, number six) and H.C. Bucknall (Merton – number two).

Oxford won the toss and selected the Surrey station, handing the Middlesex side of the Thames to Cambridge. Cambridge pulled away quickly and were clear within the first 2 minutes. By the Mile Post they were 2 lengths ahead and by Hammersmith Bridge they had extended this to 3 lengths. Although Oxford spurted and drew closer by Barnes Bridge, Cambridge were already 4 lengths ahead, passing the winning post 4½ lengths ahead in a time of 20 minutes 26 seconds. It was the biggest winning margin since 1904. The overall record was now 24–29 in Oxford's favour.

65th Boat Race, 4th April 1908

Going into the race as champions, Cambridge kept faith with coaches Francis Escombe (Trinity Hall) (for the fifth year), Stanley Muttlebury (Third Trinity), David Alexander Wauchope (Trinity Hall) while bringing in new boy L.H.K. Bushe-Fox (St John's). Oxford also kept faith with Harcourt Gilbey Gold (Magdalen), who brought in R.P.P. Rowe (Magdalen) who had rowed for Oxford between 1889 and 1892. For the fifth year the ever-popular Frederick I. Pitman was selected as umpire. Oxford went with four rowers who had represented them previously: Albert Gladstone (Christ Church – stroke), Alister Kirby (Magdalen – number five), E.H.L. Southwell (Magdalen – number three) and A.W.F. Donkin (Magdalen – cox). Cambridge also selected four former rowers for the 1908 boat: J.S. Burn (First Trinity – number four), Eric Powell (Third Trinity – number seven), Douglas Stuart (Trinity Hall – stroke) and R.F.R.P. Boyle (Trinity Hall – cox). Australian Collier Cudmore, the Oxford number two, was the only non-British participant.

Oxford won the toss and chose the Surrey station, with Cambridge taking the Middlesex side of the Thames. Umpire Pitman got things going at 3.30 p.m. The Cambridge crew made the quicker start and began to pull away from the Oxford crew. Cambridge were clear by the Mile Post. By the time they reached Harrods Furniture Depository, Cambridge were 2 lengths ahead. Oxford spurted several times but failed to make any headway. After passing Barnes Bridge

Cambridge began to pull further away, passing the finishing post with a 2½-length lead in a time of 19 minutes 20 seconds, the fastest since 1902. It was Cambridge's third consecutive victory and their sixth in seven years. However, Oxford still led overall 34–30.

66th Boat Race, 3 April 1909

After the resounding victory in 1908 Cambridge started the 1909 race as champions. For this year's race Oxford decided to bring in G.C. Bourne (New College), who had rowed twice for the university as bow in 1882–83, the celebrated Harcourt Gilbey Gold (Magdalen), the equally experienced W.F.C. Holland (Brasenose), who had been both bow and stroke for Oxford between 1887 and 1890, and finally the very popular Felix Warre (Balliol), who had rowed number four in 1898, number six in 1899 and number six once again in 1901. The Cambridge crew went into the race as favourites. They were coached once again by Stanley Muttlebury (Third Trinity), David Alexander Wauchope (Trinity Hall) and Francis Escombe (Trinity Hall). Once again, for the sixth year, the ever-popular Frederick I. Pitman (Third Trinity) was selected as umpire.

The Cambridge Eight went with three rowers with previous Boat Race experience: H.E. Kitching (Trinity Hall – number four), Edward Gordon Williams (Third Trinity – number five) and Douglas Stuart (Trinity Hall – stroke). Oxford went with six experienced crew members: Alister Kirby (Magdalen – number seven), Albert Gladstone (Christ Church – bow), H.R. Barker (Christ Church – number two), C.R. Cudmore (Magdalen – number three), A.W.F. Donkin (Magdalen – cox) and J.A. Gillan (Magdalen – number six). Australian Collier Cudmore (Magdalen – number three) was the only non-British crew member. Interestingly, several of the rowers had taken part in the 1908 London Olympics. Oxford rowers Mackinnon, Gillan and Cudmore (all Magdalen) had won a gold medal in the Coxless Fours and Cambridge's Edward Gordon Williams (Third Trinity) won a bronze in the Men's Eight.

On a beautiful, clear day Cambridge won the toss and selected the Surrey side of the river, leaving the Middlesex side of the Thames to Oxford. Pitman began the race at 12.38 p.m. This time both crews made a strong start but it was Oxford that managed to take a slight lead, extending to ⅓ of a length after a minute. They continued to pull hard and extended their lead to ½ a length. The Cambridge crew did not give up and their stroke, D.C.R. Stuart (Trinity Hall), increased their stroke rate. By Harrods Furniture Depository they had drawn level and achieved a narrow lead by Hammersmith Bridge. Oxford spurted several times in an attempt to get back in contention. Although Oxford managed the lead briefly, a Cambridge spurt put them ahead once again. However, Oxford were not finished and, pushing hard, passed the Cambridge boat before Barnes Bridge, taking a clear lead and winning to everyone's surprise by 3½ lengths in a time of 19 minutes 50 seconds. It took Oxford's overall lead to 35–30. It was Kirby's fourth race and his first victory. Coincidentally he was Oxford president in the same year.

★★★

in 1909 Kirby was also president of the Vincent's Club, a sports club founded by the rower Walter Bradford Woodgate in 1863 for the use of predominantly but not exclusively Oxford Blues at Oxford University. Kirby also became a prominent member of the Leander Rowing Club. Based in Remenham in Berkshire, the Leander Club was founded in 1818 and is one of the oldest rowing clubs in the world. Selected as captain to lead the Eight in the 1912 Stockholm Olympics, his crew comprising Edgar Burgess, Sidney Swann, Leslie Wormald, Ewart Horsfall, James Angus Gillan, Stanley Garton, Alister Kirby, Philip Fleming and Henry Wells, they defeated the New College, Oxford, Eight to take the gold medal. Germany picked up the bronze. Kirby had an outstanding rowing career by anybody's standard.

At the outbreak of the First World War, Kirby was commissioned into the 5th Battalion, London Regiment (London Rifle Brigade). He was promoted to captain before becoming ill and dying on 29 March 1917. He is buried in Mazargues War Cemetery, Marseilles, grave ref. III.A.3. He is also commemorated on the Eton College War Memorial and Oxford's Magdalen College War Memorial.

Oxford 1908 crew with Kirby seated in the centre.

30

LIEUTENANT KENNETH GORDON GARNETT MC

Boat position: Number Five
Race: 72nd Boat Race, 28 March 1914
College: Trinity College, Cambridge
Served: 111th Battery, Royal Field Artillery
Death: 21 August 1917, aged 25

Such a glorious creature.

Kenneth Gordon Garnett.

Kenneth Gordon Kenneth Garnett was born on 30 July 1892 in Tynemouth, Northumberland. He was the son of Dr William and Rebecca Garnett (daughter of the late John Samways of Southseas, Hampshire) of the Chestnuts, Branch Hill, Hampstead. He won a scholarship to St Paul's School, London, before going up to Trinity College, Cambridge, where he obtained a first-class degree in Mathematics. When he wasn't studying he spent most of his time on the river rowing. He rowed in the Trinity Eight in 1913 when his boat went Head of the Lents. He stroked in the Clinker Fours to victory and rowed in the May Races and at Henley, helping to win the Ladies' Plate for First Trinity. After rowing in the trials at Ely he was selected to row number five in the Cambridge boat during the 1914 Boat Race against Oxford.

72nd Boat Race, 28 March 1914

Having won the 1913 race by ¾ of a length, Oxford University went into the race as reigning champions. In fact, Cambridge hadn't won the race since 1908. Oxford selected their veteran rower and coach, G.C. Bourne (New College –bow, 1882–83), as a safe pair of hands, his son Robert (New College), who had stroked for Oxford between 1909 and 1912, and the highly experienced and popular Harcourt Gilbey Gold, who had stroked for Oxford between 1896 and 1899. Cambridge brought in a fresh coach in Stanley Bruce (Trinity Hall), who had rowed number two for Cambridge in 1904. Frederick I. Pitman (Third Trinity) was selected as umpire again.

Oxford went into the race with four rowers who had been in the 1913 winning crew – Henry Wells (Magdalen – cox), H.K. Ward (New College – number three), E.D. Horsfall (Magdalen – number four) and A.F.R. Wiggins (New College – number six) – and one who had been in the 1912 Oxford victory, F.A.H. Pitman (New College – stroke). The Cambridge crew matched them with five experienced rowers in the boat: S.E. Swann (Trinity Hall – number two), C.S. Clark (Pembroke – number six), C.E.V. Buxton (Third Trinity – number seven), G.E. Tower (Third Trinity – stroke) and L.E. Ridley (Jesus – cox).

The race was held on a beautifully bright day with a high, warm sun, a gentle wind and smooth water. Cambridge won the toss and selected the Surrey side of the river leaving the Middlesex side of the Thames to Oxford. Pitman got the race off promptly at 2.20 p.m. By the Craven Steps Cambridge had taken the lead by ¾ of a length, which they had increased to 1¼ lengths by the Mile Post. They continued to pull away under Hammersmith Bridge. Cambridge went on to win the race by 4½ lengths in a time of 20 minutes 23 seconds. The overall record was now 39–31, still in Oxford's favour.

Due to the outbreak of the First World War this was the last Boat Race until 1920, and by then the world would have changed. Five members of the two crews that raced that day were to die in the war: from Cambridge, Dennis Ivor Day (Lady Margaret Boat Club –bow), L.E. Ridley (Jesus – cox), John Andrew Ritson (First Trinity – number four) and Gordon Kenneth Garnett (First Trinity – number five); from Oxford, Reginald William Fletcher (Balliol – bow).

★★★

On the outbreak of the First World War, Garnett and several of his Cambridge friends and rowing partners didn't follow convention by joining the ranks an infantry regiment or even by taking a commission into one. Instead they joined the crew of the yacht *Zarepha*. This boat was probably chosen because Garnett's brother, Lieutenant Stuart Garnett, who had borrowed it from his friend Steane Price, was already serving on her as a lieutenant commander. Gordon Kenneth Garnett served on her for five months, during which she was mainly engaged in minesweeping duties. However, in January 1915, the crew were dispersed, most going to the *Sagitta* – a much larger yacht. However, rather than do this, and keen to 'do his bit' at the Front, he took a commission into the Royal Field Artillery and was sent out to France the following month, on 3 February. Stationed near La Bassée, he was accidentally shot in the leg and was returned to London on 3 March to recover. He spent several weeks at the nursing home on Bruton Street, London, before arranging to move back into his old rooms at Trinity College. At the end of the six weeks he took his degree with honours in the Mechanical Science Tripos. When he received his degree at the senate house he did so in his khaki and was greeted with a standing ovation as a Blue, a wounded soldier and a dearly loved friend. He was offered several appointments within the government but chose instead to return to the Front and his battery. In a letter home he wrote that he did not 'wish to stay at home and let a married man fight for him'. He returned to France on 16 October 1915, travelling there with his great friend John Deverell, whom he called 'the boy'. He served throughout the winter of 1915 and 1916 in Ypres, never once complaining about the hardship of his conditions.

Occasionally food like cake and chocolates would arrive; these he would share with all the ranks of his company. He never smoked or drank as he 'never really got a taste for either'. He served with his battery for ten months, on occasion writing to his parents. One such letter was sent on Sunday 19 December 1915:

My dear Mother,

We had an interesting experience this morning, which might easily have ended tragically; as it was, it has merely prepared us, so that we shall be safe next time, praise God. However it was not pleasant. At 5.30 a.m. the enemy machine guns started making a beastly noise, and soon afterwards Blakemore, our Captain, came into my room in a tremendous hurry – 'gas attack, tumble out quickly – helmets on.' So I shoved on a coat and a pair of gun boots, a helmet and dashed out to the guns. We had already opened fire when I got there, but the sentry had not warned the men that it was a gas attack – as a result they all got a dose before they returned to put on their helmets. I couldn't get the beastly tube mouth piece for exhaling to work – the rubber had stuck – and so I soon got in a bad way. Meanwhile most of my detachment – I could only look after one gun – through not having on their tube helmets to start with, were pretty bad. So Blakemore dashed into our pit – and it was very bad in the pits – loaded and fired one round, and I carried on 'earthing' the rounds, loading and firing. Luckily No. 2 (the range setter) was all right, and for some time he and I and, afterwards, Thomson, Blakemore's servant ran the guns when I had to give up: I felt sure we were done in though I was not in a funk – I told the men (and I had to shout through the helmet) to trust in Jesus and this was an easy way to die … then just later my helmet started to work and things went better. I am now at our 'O Pip.' Gas would be worse here, but quite withstandable with our helmets. Never mind – many rats and mice here in the trenches have been slain – or rendered inactive – bless the Bosch for that! ... Yes it is a great life – I really thought my end had come this morning – a curious feeling – Heaps of love to all ...

He writes again the next day:

Dear Father,

Just out of the trenches where I've really had a good time. The Bosch had been shelling at the average rate of one per minute for the last twenty-four hours. We've been retaliating too, with much effect – altogether it has been a great spree. The whole ground shakes ... but you know it really is a great game being out here and being shelled is the best fun, if taken in the right spirit. The signal men now copy my catchword, to any very near and noisy crump; 'Come straight on, don't knock.' ... The Babe.

Garnett's mother, in the biography of her son, gives her account:

While the war continues it is not possible to give any account of Kenneth's adventures with his brother in the North Sea. Until Kenneth was recognised by a Lowestoft tradesman, notwithstanding his A.B. dress, as a member of the Cambridge Eight, the University Crew were a puzzle to the East Coast, especially when leave was obtained for an evening off and the men dined in Cambridge fashion in a first-class hotel and discussed University questions, Henley, or Yachting. It is impossible, for the same reason, to describe the mechanical and other contrivances which Kenneth devised for raising the efficiency of his guns. The gas attack at 5.30 a.m. on 19 December took place in the dark, and Kenneth determined that his men should not again be handicapped as they were then. The improvements which he made in his gun-pits extended beyond his own division. He was always ready to volunteer for the position of Forward Observation Officer, and he introduced methods of signalling to his guns which could be used when his telephone wires were cut by shell. The last apparatus he used for this purpose, after an honourable and useful career in the Somme Advance was dissipated by a fair hit from 'Little Willie,' about three months after Kenneth had returned to England.

During his last few months in Flanders Kenneth designed an apparatus for reading quickly from the map at the Observation Station, and accurate to two or three minutes, the angle at which the guns should be trained as well as the range for hitting any object, the position of which could be identified on the map. A rough model was constructed and sent out to him to be tested, but it was not possible at the time to induce London instrument makers to construct a straight-edge 30 inches long which could be folded for the pocket, and the rigid straight-edge, which formed part of the instrument sent out, had to be left behind on the occasion of a trek.

The last scheme which Kenneth had on hand was an apparatus for measuring the direction and intensity of the wind at the height of a dozen or twenty feet by observations which could be taken in the gun-pits. This was in an early experimental stage when he returned from France.

The picture of Kenneth as an artillery officer would not be complete without reference to his fondness for his horses, in which he took great pride …

Garnett was wounded in the neck and paralysed while acting as a liaison officer at Delville Wood on 24 August 1916. He was returned home and nursed at the Empire Hospital, Vincent Square, where he remained on his back for a year. While there it was clear that he was often in considerable pain. However, he never complained and earned the nickname 'the sunshine of the hospital'. He was later moved to Lady Cornelia Wimborne's Hospital, Roehampton. While there he was personally awarded with the Military Cross for bravery by George V. He was also decorated by the French with the Croix de Guerre and palms. Lieutenant Garnett finally succumbed to his wounds on 22 August 1917. On learning of his death, his captain R.B. Purey Cust wrote to his parents:

> I shall never forget his friendship and I know there are many in the 111th who remember him with gratitude. I was told the other day that when he was hit near Waterlot Farm (Deville Wood) and instantly paralyzed, he told his signalers with him not to mind about him, and how glad he was to die for his country and about the better life he was going to … I thought you would like to hear it …

Garnett was buried with full military honours at the Putney Vale Cemetery, grave ref. I.627. He is also commemorated in Trinity College Chapel and at St Paul's School.

His brother, Lieutenant William Hubert Stuart Garnett, who he had sailed so gloriously with, was killed in a flying accident in 1916 and is buried at Upavon Cemetery, Wiltshire.

Garnett in the 1914 Cambridge crew.

31

SECOND LIEUTENANT CECIL PYBUS COOKE

Boat position: Number Four
Race: 67th Boat Race, 23 March 1910
College: Trinity Hall, Cambridge
Served: 5th Battalion, Shropshire Light Infantry
Death: 22 August 1917, aged 29

*The stained glass window to his memory is the most beautiful
in Australia.*

Cecil Pybus Cooke was born on 8 August 1888, in Hamilton, Victoria. He was one of five children born to Herbert Pybus and Agnes Jane Cooke (née Orme) of Koomangoonong, Balldale, New South Wales. He was educated at Geelong Church of England Grammar School, which is situated in Corio, on the northern outskirts of Geelong, Victoria, Australia. While at school he rowed in the Eight, as number six in 1905 and stroke in 1906. He was also captain of boats in the same year. After finishing school he was sent to England to further his education at Trinity Hall, Cambridge. While at Cambridge he continued rowing, being in the College Eight who were Head of the River in 1907. In 1910 he was selected to row number four in the annual Oxford and Cambridge Boat Race.

67th Boat Race, 23 March 1910

Having won the 1909 race by 3½ lengths in a time of 19 minutes 50 seconds, Oxford went into the 1910 race as both champions and favourites. As a result of their success Oxford kept faith with their coaches. Once again they selected G.C. Bourne (New College), who had represented Oxford between 1882 and 1883, Harcourt Gilbey Gold (Magdalen), who had represented Oxford on four occasions between 1896 and 1899, and was president of Oxford for the 1900 race, and W.F.C. Holland (Brasenose), who also rowed for Oxford on four occasions between 1887 and 1890. Cambridge were coached by William Dudley Ward (Third Trinity), who had rowed for Cambridge in 1897, 1899 and 1900, Raymond Etherington-Smith (First Trinity), who had represented Cambridge in 1898 and 1900, and David Alexander Wauchope (Trinity Hall), who had rowed in the 1895 race.

As the race was scheduled to be held during Holy Week, there was much disquiet, especially amongst the Christian members of the crews. Eventually the Bishop of London agreed to allow the race to go ahead provided that all the after-race celebrations were cancelled. Had he not, it is doubtful the race would have gone ahead.

Race day was beautiful with a warm sun and a mild breeze. Cambridge won the toss and chose to take the Middlesex station with Oxford on the Surrey side. Frederick I. Pitman was umpire again for the seventh year in a row. Pitman (Third Trinity) had rowed for Cambridge in 1884 (Cambridge), 1885 (Oxford) and 1886 (Cambridge). Pitman, to the cheers of the assembled crowd, started the race promptly at 12.30 p.m. Cambridge made a quick start and began to leave Oxford behind until one of the Cambridge crew caught a crab and the Oxford crew pulled quickly past them. By Craven Steps and despite being the slower boat,

Cambridge 1910 boat crew. Cook is sitting far left.

Illustrations from *The Graphic* – crews training for the race in 1910.

the Oxford crew were ¼ of a length ahead. Cambridge put on a spurt and by the Mile Post were in the lead. However, the Cambridge crew began to lose ground to Oxford as they rounded an unfavourable bend in the Thames. Oxford began to push hard, gaining a length in 10 strokes. By The Dove pub, Oxford had a 1-length lead, which they finally extended to a 3½-length lead by the end of the race. Their time was 20 minutes 14 seconds, the slowest winning time since 1907. Oxford's overall lead was now 36 to Cambridge's 30.

★★★

In 1916 Cooke enlisted into the ranks of 28th London Regiment (Artists Rifles) before being commissioned into the 5th Battalion, Shropshire Light Infantry, on 26 April 1917 (*London Gazette*, 6 June 1917). Returning to the Front, he only lasted a few weeks and was killed during the Third Battle of Ypres on 22 August 1917, during an attack on a German trench. His body was never found or identified and he is commemorated on the Tyne Cot Memorial, panels 112 to 113.

An obituary in his local paper did much to sum up the character of the man:

> Lieutenant Cooke was endowed with all those forces which make for the exemplary man and the pity is that he in common with many others who represent the flower of the land are cut off before attaining the prime of life. Had Lieut. Cooke seen longer service it is safe to assert that his bulldog courage and his happy knack of proving himself a man amongst men would have been valuable assets to his regiment and covered his name with imperishable glory.

His uncle, Samuel Winter Cooke, had a stained glass window put into St Peters Anglican Church in Tahara, Glenelg Shire, Victoria, Australia, in memory of his two nephews, Cecil Pybus Cooke and William Ventry Gayer. Gayer served with 1st Reinforcements for 4th Artillery Brigade; he transferred to 11th Brigade in December 1915 as gunner and later, in France, he was appointed bombardier. On 9 October 1917, and in charge of a party conveying ammunition to his battery near Zonnebeke, the party came under heavy fire. Another driver and some horses were killed, including Gayer's horse. Taking another mount, Gayer succeeded in delivering the ammunition under adverse conditions and at a critical period for the battery. He was awarded the Military Medal for his bravery in the field. Less than a month later he was wounded in action and taken to 3rd Canadian Clearing Station where he died on the same day, 1 November 1917. He was buried at Lijssenthoek Military Cemetery, Belgium, 931.

32

LIEUTENANT COLONEL ROGER ORME KERRISON

Boat position: Number Seven
Race: 50th Boat Race, 22 March 1893
     51st Boat Race, 17 March 1894
College: Trinity College, Cambridge
Served: Reserve Regiment of Cavalry, attached to 4th Brigade, Australian Field
     Artillery
Death: 18 September 1917, aged 44

As strong as a lion but never in the winning boat.

Lieutenant Colonel Roger Orme Kerrison.

Roger Orme Kerrison was born on 19 April 1874 at Old Lakenham, Norfolk. He was the only son of Roger Kerrison, a banker, and Florence Kerrison (daughter of the Reverend Sir Charles Clark) of Tattingstone Place, Ipswich, and of Glevering Hall, Wickham Market, Suffolk. He was educated at Eton College, rowing in the Eight, before going up to Trinity College, Cambridge, as a pensioner on 7 October 1891. While at Trinity he rowed number seven for his college before being selected to row for his university in the same seat in 1893.

50th Boat Race, 22 March 1893

Oxford went into the 1893 race as both champions and favourites, having won the 1892 race by 2¼ lengths in a time of 19 minutes 10 seconds. It was Oxford's third consecutive victory. For this year's race Oxford changed coaches, selecting G.C. Bourne (New College) who rowed bow for Oxford in both 1882 and 1883, Tom Cottingham Edwards-Moss (Balliol) who had rowed stroke and number seven between 1875 and 1878, and Douglas McLean (New College) who rowed number five for Oxford between 1883 and 1887. Cambridge went with experience, sticking with R.C. Lehmann (First Trinity) who, although having rowed in the trials and been the captain of the First Trinity Boat Club, had never rowed in the Boat Race. He was also happy to coach either side, normally in the latter half of their training.

Cambridge selected two rowers with previous Boat Race experience for their Eight: Graham Campbell Kerr (First Trinity – number six) and Thurstan Fogg-Elliot (Trinity Hall – number three). Oxford kept faith with five of their previous rowers: W.A.L. Fletcher (Christ Church – number six), H.B. Cotton (Magdalen

Cambridge crew, 1894. Kerrison is bottom centre.

– bow), J.A. Ford (Brasenose – number two), V. Nickalls (Magdalen – number five) and C.M. Pitman (Magdalen – stroke).

Due to repairs at Barnes Bridge the race almost didn't take place – for one of the few times in its history it wasn't held on a Saturday but on Wednesday. On a day with a strong spring tide and an easterly breeze, Cambridge won the toss and decided on the Surrey side of the river, leaving the Middlesex side to the Oxford Eight. Frank Willan (Exeter), who had been selected as umpire for the fifth year, got the race started promptly at 4.35 p.m. Although Cambridge made the better start and went into an early lead, Oxford quickly caught up and went ahead. By the Mile Post Oxford were 1 length ahead. By Hammersmith Bridge, however, Oxford's lead had been cut to ½ a length and by The Dove pub the crews were level. Cambridge began to tire and Oxford took advantage, pushing ahead. By Barnes Bridge they were 1½ lengths clear. With rough water slowing the Oxford crew, Cambridge attempted to take advantage but, despite a big effort, were unable to stop Oxford taking the race by 1¼ lengths in a time of 18 minutes 45 seconds (it was the fastest time in the history of the race). Oxford now had an overall lead of 27 races to 22.

51st Boat Race, 17 March 1894

Once again Oxford went into the race as champions and were favourites to take the honours. This year they selected William Fletcher (Christ Church) as their coach; he had rowed stroke, number seven and number six for Oxford between 1890 and 1893. They also selected former First Trinity captain R.C. Lehmann, who had switched sides for the 1894 race, and Douglas McLean (New College). Having lost Lehmann to Oxford, Cambridge were coached by Charles William Moore (Christ's) who had rowed number seven and three for Cambridge between 1881 and 1884. The ever-present Frank Willan (Exeter) was selected as umpire for the sixth year.

Cambridge kept faith with four of their rowers from the previous year's race: Lionel Arthur Edward Ollivant (First Trinity – number five), Charles Thurstan Fogg-Elliot (Trinity Hall – number six), Robert Orme Kerrison (Third Trinity) and Trevor Gwyn Elliot Lewis (Third Trinity – stroke). Oxford went with five members of their 1893 winning crew: Charles Murray Pitman (New College – stroke), Hugh Benjamin Cotton (Magdalen – bow), M.C. Pilkington (Magdalen – number two), J.A. Morrison (New College – number four) and L. Portman (University – cox).

There was a buzz of excitement around this year's race as the Duke of York (later George V) accompanied the umpire Frank Willan in one of the following launches. Willan got the race started at 9.12 a.m. Cambridge got away quickly and took an early lead. However, this lead wasn't to last long and by the Mile Post Oxford had a ½-length lead. By Hammersmith Bridge, Oxford were clear of the struggling Cambridge boat. They extended this lead to over ½ a length by The Dove pub and by the time they reached Barnes Bridge this lead had been extended to 5 lengths. Oxford finally passed the winning post with a 3½-length lead, in a winning time of 21 minutes 39 seconds. It was the largest margin since 1883 and Oxford's fifth consecutive victory. The overall score was now 28 to 22 in Oxford's favour.

★★★

Deciding on a career in the army, Kerrison was commissioned into the Loyal Suffolk Hussars (Yeomanry) in 1896. In 1900 he became a lieutenant and later went on to become a lieutenant colonel and command the regiment, serving with them during the Second Boer War. He later became a Justice of Peace in Suffolk and was a member of the Marylebone Cricket Club. He then became attached to the 6th Secondary Regiment, Australian Field Artillery, which was attached to the 4th Brigade, Australian Field Artillery, and died while still serving with them on 18 September 1917 after contracting dysentery.

He is buried in Wimereux Communal Cemetery, grave ref. IV. N. 4. He left £19,578 2s 12d in his will. He is commemorated on the Eton War Memorial, inside Trinity College's Chapel and on the Tattingstone War Memorial.

33

LIEUTENANT DUNCAN MACKINNON

Boat position: Number Five
Race: 66th Boat Race, 3 April 1909
      67th Boat Race, 23 March 1910
      68th Boat Race, 1 April 1911
College: Magdalen College, Oxford
Served: 1st Battalion, Scots Guards
Death: 9 October 1917, aged 30

Duncan Mackinnon was without doubt one of the finest oars that ever rowed for Oxford.

Lieutenant Duncan Mackinnon.

Duncan Mackinnon was born on 29 September 1887 in Paddington, London. He was the third son of Duncan Mackinnon, of Loup and Balinakill, Argyllshire, who was for many years chairman of the British India Steam Navigation Company, and of Margaret Braid Macdonald. He was educated at Rugby School between 1902 and 1905. After leaving Rugby he went up to Magdalen College Oxford. He rowed for Magdalen's Coxless Four and won the Stewards' Challenge Cup and the Visitors' Challenge Cup at Henley Royal Regatta in 1907 and 1908. The Magdalen crew were chosen to represent Great Britain during the 1908 London Olympics. Rowing with Collier Cudmore, John Somers-Smith and Angus Gillan, Mackinnon took the gold medal, defeating the Leander crew. He was selected to row for the Oxford Eight in the 1909 Boat Race.

66th Boat Race, 3rd April 1909

After the resounding victory in 1908, Cambridge started the 1909 race as champions. For this year's race Oxford decided to bring in G.C. Bourne (New College) who had rowed twice for the university as bow in 1882 and 1883, the highly experienced Francis Escombe (Trinity Hall) (his sixth consecutive year), the celebrated Harcourt Gilbey Gold (Magdalen) who had stroked for Oxford between 1896 and 1899 (Oxford president in 1899), the equally experienced W.F.C. Holland (Brasenose) who had been both bow and stroke for Oxford between 1887 and 1890, and finally the very popular Felix Warre (Balliol) who had rowed number four in the 1898–99 races. The Cambridge crew went into the race as favourites. They were coached by Stanley Muttlebury (Third Trinity – number six) who rowed for Cambridge between 1886 and 1890, and David Alexander Wauchope

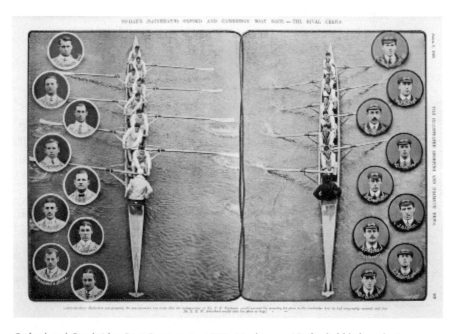

Oxford and Cambridge Boat Race crews 1909. Mackinnon (Oxford) fifth from bottom.

(Trinity Hall – stroke, 1895). Once again, for the sixth year, the ever-popular Frederick I. Pitman (Third Trinity) was selected as umpire.

On a beautiful, clear day Cambridge won the toss and selected the Surrey side of the river, leaving the Middlesex side of the Thames to Oxford. Pitman began the race at 12.38 p.m. This time both crews made a strong start but it was Oxford who managed to take a slight lead, extending to a ⅓ of a length after a minute. They continued to pull hard and extended their lead to ½ a length. The Cambridge crew did not give up and their stroke, D.C.R. Stuart (Trinity Hall), increased their stroke rate and by Harrods Furniture Depository had drawn level; by Hammersmith Bridge Cambridge had taken a narrow lead. Oxford spurted several times in an attempt to get back in contention. Although Oxford managed to lead briefly, a Cambridge spurt put them ahead once again. However, Oxford were not finished, and pushing hard, passed the Cambridge boat before Barnes Bridge, taking a clear lead and winning to everyone's surprise by 3½ lengths in a time of 19 minutes 50 seconds. It took Oxford's overall lead to 35–30.

67th Boat Race, 23 March 1910

Given the unexpected victory over Cambridge the year before, Mackinnon was selected once again to row number five on the Oxford Eight. The reigning champions Oxford stuck with experience and success, and appointed G.C. Bourne (New College – bow), Boat Race veteran of 1882–83, four-time stroke (between 1896 and 1899) Harcourt Gilbey Gold (Magdalen) and W. F. C. Holland (Brasenose), who had rowed bow and stroke four times for Oxford between 1887 and 1890. Cambridge only kept one of their previous coaches, David Alexander Wauchope (Trinity Hall), who had rowed stroke in the 1895 race. To assist him they brought in William Dudley Ward (Third Trinity), who had rowed number seven in 1897, 1899 and 1900, and Raymond Etherington-Smith (First Trinity), who had represented Cambridge three times between 1898 and 1900. For the seventh year in succession Frederick I. Pitman (Third Trinity) umpired. The 1910 race brought to the annual event one of the early scandals. As a result of a poor tide it was decided to hold the race in Holy Week. Religious festivals were taken far more seriously then than they are now and there was national outcry. Several of the rowers also expressed serious concerns at racing during this time and at least one refused to take part. It wasn't until the Bishop of London intervened and allowed the race to go ahead, on the understanding that there would be no celebrations after the race, that a compromise was reached and the race went ahead.

Cambridge brought in five new rowers, relying on only three with Boat Race experience: R. W.M. Arbuthnot (Third Trinity – bow), J.B. Rosher (First Trinity – number six) and Edward Gordon Williams (Third Trinity – number four). Oxford, as champions, decided to keep as many of the previous year's rowers as they could. Four members of the 1909 crew returned: Duncan Mackinnon (Magdalen – number five), Stanley Garton (Magdalen – number six), Robert Bourne (New College – stroke) and A.W.F. Donkin (Magdalen – cox). Three non-British rowers took part in the race. One member of the Oxford crew, M.B. Higgins (Balliol – bow), and the Cambridge number four, C.P. Cooke (Trinity Hall), were from Australia. The Cambridge cox, C.A. Skinner (Jesus), came from South Africa.

It was a bright day with a warm sun and light breeze. Cambridge won the toss and selected the Middlesex station, leaving the Surrey side of the river to Oxford. Pitman got the race started at 12.30 p.m. Despite Cambridge making the quicker start, one of the boats rowers caught a crab and Oxford swept by. By Craven Steps Oxford were ahead by ¼ of a length. Recovering, Cambridge spurted and by the time they reached the Mile Post they were ahead. However, Oxford fought back and, as they reached The Dove pub, Oxford spurted again, going into a 1-length lead. They never gave up the lead and in fact extended it, passing the finishing post 3½ lengths ahead in a time of 20 minutes 14 seconds (the slowest winning time since 1907). Oxford now had an overall lead of 36–30.

68th Boat Race, 1 April 1911

The 1 April was a beautiful day with a light easterly wind and a strong spring tide. The Oxford crew had been coached by the former Oxford rower H.R. Barker (Christ Church) who had turned out for the Dark Blues rowing number seven in 1908 and number two in 1909, the legendary G.C. Bourne (New College) who had rowed bow for Oxford in 1882 and 1883, and the equally famous and four-time Blue (rowing stroke on all four occasions between 1896 and 1899) Harcourt Gilbey Gold (Magdalen). Stanley Bruce (Trinity Hall), who had rowed number two during the 1904 race, coached the Cambridge crew together with William Dudley Ward (Third Trinity) who had rowed number seven in 1897, 1899 and 1900, Raymond Etherington-Smith (First Trinity) who rowed number six for Cambridge in 1898 and five in 1900 (Cambridge), and, finally, and more unusually, H.W. Willis, the man who had coached Oxford in 1907. The familiar face of the former Cambridge stroke Frederick I. Pitman (Third Trinity, 1884–86) umpired for the eighth year in succession.

Six members of the Cambridge crew had raced before: R.W.M. Arbuthnot (Third Trinity – stroke), J.B. Rosher (First Trinity – number six), F.E. Hellyer (First Trinity – number three), C.R. le Blanc-Smith (Third Trinity – number five), C.A. Skinner (Jesus – cox) and G.E. Fairbairn (Jesus – number seven). Two members of the Cambridge crew came from South Africa: Pieter Voltelyn Graham van der Byl (Pembroke – number two) and C.A. Skinner (Jesus – cox). Six members of the Oxford crew were students at Magdalen College and had won the Grand Challenge Cup at Henley the year before. Three of the Oxford crew had also taken part in the race twice before: Duncan Mackinnon (Magdalen – number seven, 1909–10), Robert Bourne (New College – stroke, 1909–10) and Stanley Garton (Magdalen – number six, 1909–10). Charles Littlejohn (New College – number five) came from Australia.

The 1911 race was made all the more interesting for a number of reasons. Firstly, it was followed by the Prince of Wales (the future Edward VIII) and his brother Prince Albert. It was also the first race ever to be monitored by an aeroplane. This never-before-seen sight was later reported on by the *Western Argus*, 9 May 1911:

THE BOAT RACE BY AEROPLANE.
SIX AIRMEN OVER THE COURSE

Six aeroplanes flew over the course of the Boat Race between Oxford and Cambridge with one airman following the race almost from start to finish, sweeping to and fro across the river to keep level with the crews. The crowds welcomed the machines with great enthusiasm. The airmen were Graham Gilmour (who followed the race), who came from Brooklands in a Bristol biplane with the Gnome engine, and five others who came from Hendon aerodrome. Graham White (military Farman machine), Mr Hubert (ordinary Farman), Gustave Hamel, Mr Greswell, and M. Prier all used Bleriot monoplanes. Gilmour later recounted his experience:

I left Brooklands at 1.55pm in a military-type Bristol biplane and followed the river until I reached Putney Bridge. I arrived at the start just before the pistol was fired. Overhead as a circled around was a balloon in which was the Hon Mrs Atsheton Harbord … As soon as the boats started off I followed them up the river. More than once I turned of my engine and descended as low as 100 feet above the water, but my normal altitude during the flight was about 200 feet. The spectacle below me was most interesting. I could see the crews quite distinctly. From my aerial point of view they had rather the appearance of flies skimming over a pond in the summer. I could distinguish perfectly well between the two crews by the colors of their oars and it was quite apparent to me from above that Oxford was the better crew of the two. Indeed criticizing the race from an aerial standpoint the first time that such a view had been obtained I could see that Cambridge had a hopeless task, because every time Oxford was pressed the crew responded at once and the boat forged ahead … After flying over the winning post I landed in a little field (Chiswick Polytechnic cricket field) having run out of petrol. A motorist very kindly gave me four gallons from his supply and I again filled up my tank.

Members of the crowd then helped him start his plane up and he flew the 18 miles back to Brooklands for tea. Alas, Gilmour was killed the following year while flying over the Old Deer Park in Richmond. Gilmour had set off from Brooklands at about 11 a.m. to make a trial cross-country flight in a Martin Handasyde monoplane. Flying at about 400ft, his left wing suddenly folded and he crashed to the ground, being killed on impact.

Oxford won the toss and selected the Middlesex side, while Cambridge was handed the Surrey side. The race started at 2.36 p.m.

Oxford made a quick start with Bourne, the Oxford stroke, outrating Cambridge by 2 strokes per minute. By the Craven Steps Oxford were ¾ of a length ahead, a lead they maintained past the Mile Post. Oxford had increased their lead by the Crab Tree pub and were even further ahead by Harrods Furniture Depository. As they passed under Hammersmith Bridge Oxford were 2½ lengths ahead and still pulling away from Cambridge. By Chiswick Steps Oxford had a 4-length lead, which they had increased by Barnes Bridge. Although the Cambridge crew rallied, there was no catching Oxford, who won by 2¾ lengths in an all-time race record time of 18 minutes 29 seconds. It was Oxford's third consecutive victory, making the overall tally 37–30 in Oxford's favour.

Duncan Mackinnon.

Mackinnon was also president of the Oxford University Boat Club in 1910 and helped his college become Head of the River in the same year. He also won the Grand Challenge Cup twice and the Wyfold Challenge Cup.

★★★

After leaving Oxford Mackinnon joined the family business of Messrs Macneill and Co. and Messrs Mackinnon Mackenzie, Calcutta, and served as a lance corporal in the Calcutta Light Horse. Returning to England at the outbreak of the First World War, he was commissioned into the Royal North Devon Hussars in March 1915, travelling with them to Suvla Bay, Gallipoli, in September 1915. He remained with them in the peninsula until December when he was evacuated to Egypt. Mackinnon remained in Egypt until February 1917 when he was commissioned into the Scots Guards, serving with them as a lieutenant. He was sent to France on 1 August 1917. Surviving for only eight weeks, he was killed in action at Passchendaele near Langemarck on 9 October 1917.

A brother officer later wrote:

> We have lost one who has endeared himself to all ranks and has proved himself a splendid and gallant soldier. We can ill afford to lose such an Officer. His Regiment honor his memory and realize his loss to it.

Another:

> Your son was a most splendid and gallant Officer, absolutely fearless and one whom we can ill spare. I hope it may be some consolation to you to know how devoted all his brother Officers were to him.

And yet another:

> We shall all miss your son dreadfully, as he was most extraordinarily popular and we were all devoted to him. All the men of his Company would have done anything for him. He was commanding his Company in the attack.

Lieutenant Colonel Harcourt Gold OBE, president of the Oxford University Boat Club in 1899, wrote:

> Duncan Mackinnon was without doubt one of the finest oars that ever rowed for Oxford. His strength, stamina and will-power were unsurpassed. It is probably no exaggeration to say that his strength of character and determination had an effect on the crews in which he rowed almost without parallel in the history of modern rowing.

His body was never recovered or identified and he is commemorated on the Tyne Cot Memorial, panel 10. His eldest brother Captain W. Mackinnon, London Scottish Regiment, fell five months before him on 11 May 1917. He is further commemorated at Rugby School and Magdalen College.

34

LIEUTENANT COLONEL GEORGE EVERARD HOPE MC

Boat position: Number Three
Race: 64th Boat Race, 16 March 1907
College: Christ Church College, Oxford
Served: 1st Battalion, Grenadier Guards commanding 1/8th Battalion, Lancashire Fusiliers
Death: 10 October 1917, aged 30

One of the bravest Officers in the Grenadier Guards.

Lieutenant Colonel George Everard Hope MC.

George Everard Hope was born on 4 November 1886 in Buckinghamshire, England. He was the son of Henry Walter Hope of Luffness, Scotland, and Lady Mary Catherine Constance Primrose, sister of the 5th Earl of Roseberry. He was educated at Eton (Mr A.M. Goodhart's and Mr A.C. Benson's houses), before going up to Christ Church College, Oxford, in 1905. Having rowed at Eton and for his college, he was selected to row in the Oxford Eight as number three during the 1907 annual Oxford and Cambridge Boat Race.

64th Boat Race, 16 March 1907

Cambridge went into the race as both champions and favourites. Once again the Cambridge crew were trained by their very successful coaches from 1906: Francis Escombe (fourth consecutive year), Stanley Muttlebury and David Alexander Wauchope. The Oxford coaches were, as with the previous year, Harcourt Gilbey Gold and new boy H. W. Willis (who went on to coach Cambridge in 1911). For the fifth consecutive year, the umpire was Frederick I. Pitman.

Oxford selected three crew members with previous Boat Race experience: Henry Bucknall (Merton – number two), A.G. Kirby (Magdalen – number six) and A.C. Gladstone (Christ Church – number seven). Six members of the Cambridge winning crew from 1906 were selected again: Banner Johnstone (Trinity – number six), A.B. Close-Brooks (Trinity – bow), J.H.F. Benham (Jesus – number two), H.M. Goldsmith (Jesus – number three), H.G. Baynes (Trinity – number five) and D.C.R. Stuart (Trinity Hall – stroke).

Winning the toss, the Oxford crew selected the Surrey side of the river, with Cambridge being forced to take the Middlesex side. Once again Cambridge made the quicker start and within a couple of minutes were clear of the Oxford boat. The Cambridge boat passed the Mile Post 2 lengths ahead. Their lead increased to 3 lengths by Hammersmith Bridge. However, the Oxford boat wasn't finished yet. Albert Gladstone, the Oxford stroke, put on a spurt and reduced the distance between the two boats to 3ft. Oxford hit rough water, however, and struggled to keep up with the Cambridge Eight and began to fall back once again. By Barnes Bridge Cambridge were 4 lengths ahead, finally winning the race by 4½ lengths in a time of 20 minutes 26 seconds. It was the biggest winning margin since 1904 and moved the overall score to 34–29, still in Oxford's favour. After this success Hope went on to win the Grand Challenge Cup in 1908.

★★★

After coming down from Oxford, Hope was commissioned as a second lieutenant on the 15 September 1909 into the 1st Battalion, Grenadier Guards, being promoted to lieutenant on 9 July 1910. On 8 April 1911 he married Margaret Cockton and they had two children: Wilhelmine Mary Margaret and Archibald John George.

Hope went to France with the 1st Battalion, embarking with the battalion at Southampton on 4 October 1914 on board SS *Armenian* and landing at Zeebrugge at 6 a.m. on 7 October 1914. Hope was appointed battalion signalling officer. Involved with his battalion during the First Battle of Ypres, he was awarded the Military Cross for his bravery at the Battle of Kruseik on 24 October 1914. Realising that the King's Company commander, Major Weld-Forester, had failed to receive the order to withdraw, Lieutenant G.E. Hope turned back on his own initiative to warn them. On his way he also managed to persuade some of

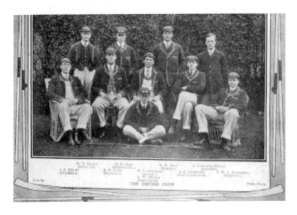

1907 Oxford Boat Race crew. Hope in back row second left.

the 1st Division to come to its assistance. At about 4 p.m. the King's Company fought their way back through the village, taking heavy casualties, especially from machine guns in the windows, including Major Weld-Forester who was killed and Lieutenant Hope who was wounded. Unfortunately the message that the company was about to retire was never received by a platoon of 3rd Company or an isolated King's Company platoon, which were both overwhelmed.

By the end of October the battalion had lost 900 of the 1,000 men they had started with. Hope was wounded again on 4 November 1914 when he was shot in the head by a sniper. As well as being decorated with the Military Cross, Hope was also mentioned in dispatches three times during the war: *London Gazette*, February 1915; serving as a Staff Officer, *London Gazette*, June 1916, and *London Gazette*, 15 May 1917. He also served as an aide-de-camp, staff captain, deputy assistant adjutant and quartermaster general, and general staff officer grade 3. He was given command of the 1/8th Battalion, Lancashire Fusiliers (126th Brigade, 42nd Division), on 16 June 1917, and was promoted to the rank of acting lieutenant colonel. The battalion was positioned north of Ypres, and took part in the Battle of Passchendaele. It was during this battle on 10 October 1917 that Colonel Hope, while on a night patrol, stumbled into an enemy post at Nieuport. At first it was hoped that he had been taken as a prisoner of war and was only initially reported as missing. However, when no news of him was forthcoming it was assumed that he had been killed on that date.

His body was later discovered and he was buried in Ramscappelle Road Military Cemetery, grave ref. VI. A. 1. His mother never accepted the death of her only son and was convinced in her own mind that at some point he would show up. It is a story that was repeated thousands of times during the war.

He is also commemorated on the Eton College War Memorial, Christ Church College Memorial and the Aberlady War Memorial.

35

Boat position: Bow
Race: 35th Boat Race, 13 April 1878
College: University College, Oxford
Served: 1st Volunteer Company, Princess Charlotte of Wales' Royal Berkshire Regiment
Death: 1 November 1917, aged 62

Queen Victoria's surgeon.

W. A. Ellison. 1878.

William Augustine Ellison.

William Augustine Ellison was born in 1855 in Windsor, Berkshire. He was the eldest son of Dr James Ellison. He was educated at Eton College where he played football and was a fine gymnast. He also rowed twice for the Eton Eight. He went up to University College, Oxford, in 1874 where he continued to row. He rowed University College to Head of the River three times during his time there. He also won the Silver Goblets at Henley Royal Regatta in 1878, paired with fellow Etonian Tom Cottingham Edwards-Moss. In 1878 he was also selected to row bow in the Oxford boat during the annual Boat Race against Cambridge.

35th Boat Race, 13 April 1878

Everyone hoped that this year's race would not be as controversial as the 1877 race, which had, after numerous arguments and a meeting in a law court, been declared a dead heat – although Oxford always insisted that they had won by feet. The satirical magazine *Punch* later wrote, 'Oxford won, Cambridge too.' The general feeling was that if Oxford hadn't broken an oar they would have won easily.

Oxford went into the race as favourites to take the honours and were considered one of the best Eights the university had ever produced. Cambridge's coach was once again James Brooks Close (First Trinity) who had rowed bow and number three for Cambridge between 1872 and 1874. Oxford changed their coach from the year before, Reverend William Sherwood, and decided on William Grenfell (Balliol) who had rowed number four for Oxford in 1877 and 1878, A.J. Mulholland (Balliol) who had rowed number six for Oxford in 1877 and Edmund Warre (Balliol) who had rowed number six and seven for Oxford in 1857 and 1858; the latter he was also the only member of Oxford's coaching team from the previous year that was retained. Joseph William Chitty (Balliol), a former Oxford rower, was chosen as the umpire. The starter was Edward Searle and the finishing judge was E.H. Fairrie.

Four members of the Cambridge crew had previous Boat Race experience: L.G. Pike (Caius – number five), C. Gurdon (Jesus – number six), T.E. Hockin (Jesus – number seven) and G.L. Davis (Clare – cox). Oxford went two better and included six rowers with previous Boat Race experience: D.J. Cowles (St John's – number two), W.H. Grenfell (Balliol – number four), H. Pelham (Magdalen – number five), T.C. Edwards-Moss (Brasenose – number seven), H.P. Marriott (Brasenose – stroke) and F.M. Beaumont (New College – cox).

Oxford won the toss and selected the Surrey station, leaving the Middlesex side to Cambridge. Searle got the race started at precisely 10.15 a.m. The Cambridge Eight took an early lead and were ½ a length ahead within the first minute. However, Oxford quickly caught up and by the Crab Tree pub were a ½ a length ahead. Oxford had extended this lead to 4 lengths by the time the boats reached Hammersmith Bridge. Oxford finally crossed the winning line 10 lengths ahead in a time of 22 minutes 40 seconds. It was sweet revenge for the previous year and brought the overall record to 18–16 in Oxford's favour. Ellison had been in the winning boat in his one and only race. His rowing career, however, wasn't over and in 1880 he rowed for the Leander Club, for whom he stroked the winning Eight to the Grand Challenge Cup.

★★★

After taking the diploma of MRCS Eng, in 1882 he graduated MB Oxon in 1884 and proceeded to MD in 1895. Ellison received his medical training at St George's

Hospital, London, later serving as an assistant medical registrar at the same hospital. He must have had a fine reputation because in 1888 he was appointed surgeon apothecary to Queen Victoria's household at Windsor Castle. Popular with the Queen and royal family he also became acting resident physician to Queen Victoria at Balmoral during the 1890s. After the queen's demise he was reappointed as consulting physician to Edward VII and then later again to George V. Ellison also became a member of the Eton College Medical Board, vice-president of the Medical Officers of Schools Association and vice-president and member of council of the National League for Physical Education.

During this time he also joined up and eventually became a lieutenant colonel and commanded the first volunteer battalion of the 4th Royal Berkshire Regiment – a command he kept during the First World War between 1915 and 1916, being mentioned in dispatches for his war service. He died as a result of an illness on 1 November 1917. His funeral took place at Eton Cemetery on 5 November, for which Canon Sheppard, sub-dean of the Chapels Royal, officiated, assisted by the vicar of Eton.

36

SECOND LIEUTENANT GRAHAM FLORANZ MACDOWALL MAITLAND

Boat position: Stroke
Race: 58th Boat Race, 30 March 1901
College: Trinity College, Cambridge
Served: 1st Battalion Irish Guards
Death: 1 November 1914, aged 35

His sense of adventure and devotion to duty put him above most men.

Graham Floranz Macdowall Maitland was born on 20 May 1879 in Kirkcudbright, Dumfries and Galloway. He was the third son of David Maitland of Cumstoun, Kirkcudbright. He was educated at Marlborough College, where he was in the Rifle Corps and shooting VIII between 1896 and 1897 and shot in the Spencer cup in 1897. After leaving Marlborough he went up to Trinity College, Cambridge. He

The Cambridge Boat Race crew 1901. Maitland is sitting second from the right.

was a member of the Pitt Club and in 1900, together with Claude Goldie, won the Silver Goblets at Henley Royal Regatta. In 1901 he was selected to row stroke for the Cambridge boat in the annual Oxford and Cambridge Boat Race.

57th Boat Race, 30 March 1901

The 1901 race was the first held under the reign of a new monarch, Edward VII, Queen Victoria having died on 22 January 1901. For the second year in a row Cambridge went into the race as champions. G.C. Bourne (New College) returned as the Oxford coach together with Harcourt Gilbey Gold (Magdalen) from the year before and C.K. Philips (New College) who had rowed number three for Oxford between 1895 and 1898 (all Oxford victories). Cambridge went with two of the coaches that had helped them win the 1900 race: James Brooks Close (First Trinity) and Stanley Muttlebury (Third Trinity). They also brought in John Ernest Payne (Peterhouse) who had rowed number four for the Cambridge winning crew in both 1899 and 1900. The familiar face of Frank Willan umpired the race.

The Cambridge crew only had one rower with previous Boat Race experience, their club president, Bertram Willes Dayrell Brooke (First Trinity), who rowed at number three the year before. Seven of the nine crew were members of Trinity College, the two exceptions being B.C. Cox (Trinity Hall – number two) and E.F. Duncanson (Emmanuel – number seven). They also suffered problems with injury and illness and were forced to reorganise their boat late into their preparations. One observer commented, 'the crew received a setback from which they never really recovered.' Oxford on the other hand had five returning rowers: their cox Gilchrist Maclagan (Magdalen), F.W. Warre (Balliol – number six), H.J. Hale (Balliol – number four), T.B. Etherington-Smith (Oriel – number seven) and R.H. Culme-Seymour (New College – number two).

This time Cambridge won the toss and decided on the Surrey side, leaving the Middlesex side to Oxford. The day was a poor one and a heavy storm broke over the race; with a strong wind from the south-west it was a difficult race for all concerned. Willan, as efficient as ever, began the race at 10.31 a.m. Oxford started well and, taking advantage of the bend in the river, pulled away, taking a ½-length lead by the Mile Post. Cambridge put on a spurt to try to narrow the increasing gap between the two boats and the crews levelled as they passed Harrods Furniture Depository. Cambridge then began to pull ahead as the Oxford stroke rate dropped. Hitting rough water, the Cambridge crew began to struggle, although it also made it impossible for the Oxford crew to pass them. However, as the boats approached Barnes Bridge Maclagan made his move and the Oxford stroke, Culme-Seymour, began a spurt. The boats were level by Mortlake Brewery after which the Oxford crew began to make ground on the Cambridge boat and finally passed it. Cambridge, despite their best efforts, were unable to respond. Oxford finally won the race by ⅖ of a length in a time of 22 minutes 31 seconds – the slowest winning time since 1877. The overall score was now 33–24 in Oxford's favour. It is also worth noting that, to the shock and great sadness to all concerned, especially the rowers from both universities, the Oxford stroke and talented rower Culme-Seymour (New College), who had been largely responsible for the 1901 race win, died the following autumn of pleurisy.

★★★

After obtaining his degree Maitland was called to the bar at Inner Temple in July 1905. However, always looking for adventure, he headed across the ocean and spent some time in Canada, surveying in British Columbia. Returning home at the outbreak of the First World War, he was gazetted as a second lieutenant into the 1st Battalion, Irish Guards, on 12 August 1914. Travelling to France with his battalion, he was reported missing in action at Klein Zillebeke, Flanders, on 1 November 1914. His death was later presumed to have taken place on that date. Rudyard Kipling in *The Irish Guards in the Great War* (volume 1) describes in some detail what became of Maitland:

> Bombardment was renewed on the 1st November. The front trenches were drenched by field-guns, at close range, with spurts of heavy stuff at intervals; the rear by heavy artillery, while machine-gun fire filled the intervals. One of the trenches of a platoon in No. 3 Company, under Lieutenant Maitland, was completely blown in, and only a few men escaped. The Lieutenant remained with the survivors while Sergeant C. Harradine, under heavy fire, took the news to the C.O. It was hopeless to send reinforcements; the machine-gun fire would have wiped them out moving and our artillery was not strong enough to silence any one sector of the enemy's fire.
>
> In the afternoon the enemy attacked – with rifle-fire and a close-range small piece that broke up our two machine-guns – across some dead ground and occupied the wrecked trench, driving back the few remains of No. 3 Company. The companies on the right and left, Nos. 4 and 1, after heavy fighting, fell back on No. 2 Company, which was occupying roughly prepared trenches in the rear. One platoon, however, of No. 1 Company, under Lieutenant N. Woodroffe (he had only left Eton a year), did not get the order to retire, and so held on in its trench till dark and 'was certainly instrumental in checking the advance of the enemy.'
>
> The line was near breaking-point by then, but company after company delivered what blow it could, and fell back, shelled and machine-gunned at every step, to the fringe of Zillebeke Wood. Here the officers, every cook, orderly, and man who could stand, took rifle and fought; for they were all that stood there between the enemy and the Channel Ports. (Years later, a man remembering that fight said: 'Twas like a football scrum. Every one was somebody, ye'll

understand. If he dropped there was no one to take his place. Great days! An' we not so frightened as when it came to the fightin' by machinery on the Somme afterwards'.) The C.O. sent the Adjutant to Brigade Headquarters to ask for help, but the whole Staff had gone over to the 2nd Brigade Headquarters, whose Brigadier had taken over command of the 4th Brigade, as its own Brigadier had been wounded. About this time, too, the C.O. of the Battalion (Lord Ardee) was wounded. Eventually the 2nd Battalion Grenadiers was sent up with some cavalry of the much-enduring 7th Brigade, and the line of support-trenches was held. The Battalion had had nothing to eat for thirty-six hours, so the cavalry kept the line for a little till our men got food.

The 1901 Oxford and Cambridge Boat Race crews. Maitland is in the centre of the Cambridge crew.

Memorial to Second Lieutenant Graham
Floranz Macdowall Maitland.

A French regiment (Territorials) on the right also took over part of the
trenches of our depleted line. Forty-four men were known to have been killed,
205 wounded and 88 – chiefly from the blown-up No. 3 Platoon – were missing.
Of the officers, Lieutenant K.R. Mathieson had been killed (he had been last
seen shooting a Hun who was bayoneting our wounded); Captain Mulholland
died of his wounds as soon as he arrived in hospital at Ypres; Lieut.-Colonel
Lord Ardee, Captain Vesey, Lieutenant Gore-Langton and Lieutenant Alexander
were wounded, and Lieutenant G.M. Maitland, who had stayed with his handful
in No. 3 Company's trench, was missing. Yet the time was to come when threee
hundred and fifty casualties would be regarded as no extraordinary price to pay
for ground won or held. One small draft of 40 men arrived from home that night.

Maitland was mentioned in dispatches for his bravery on 1 November 1914.

Maitland's body was never found or identified and he is commemorated on the
Ypres (Menin Gate) Memorial, panel 11. Maitland is also commemorated on the
Rerrick Parish War Memorial in Dundrennan, the Trinity Chapel Memorial and
at Marlborough College.

37

CAPTAIN WILLIAM FRANCIS CLAUDE HOLLAND

Boat position: Bow & Stroke
Race: 44th Boat Race, 26 March 1887
    45th Boat Race, 24 March 1888
    46th Boat Race, 30 March 1889
    47th Boat Race, 26 March 1890
College: Brasenose College, Oxford
Serving: 4th Battalion, Durham Light Infantry
Death: 8 November 1917, aged 52

The finest athlete and rower Eton and Oxford has ever produced.

William Francis Claude Holland was born on 14 September 1865 in Paddington, London. He was the son of William James and Lizzie Holland, partners in an upholsterers and cabinet makers partnership of No. 65 Porchester Terrace, Paddington. He was educated at Eton College where he was in Mr E.S. Shuckburgh's House and then in Mr A. Cocksott's House. While at Eton he

The 1889 Oxford Boat Race crew with Holland bottom centre.

won the 100 yards, ½ mile, 1 mile and long jump, clearing an impressive 22ft 10in. Leaving Eton in 1885, he went up to Brasenose College, Oxford, where he not only continued with his athletics but also took up rowing, quickly getting a seat in the College Eight. His talent was quickly noticed and he was selected to row bow in the 1887 race.

44th Boat Race, 26 March 1887

The 1886 race had been one of the most exciting on record. Oxford were ahead at Barnes Bridge, normally a sure indication of victory; however, Cambridge spurted, overtaking Oxford and crossing the finishing line ⅔ of a length ahead of Oxford in a time of 22 minutes 30 seconds. It was the first time the winning crew had come from behind at Barnes Bridge to win the annual race. As a result of their spectacular and surprise victory Cambridge went into the 1887 race as both champions and favourites.

Cambridge stuck pretty much with their winning coaches, bringing back Charles William Moore (Christ's) who had rowed number seven and three for Cambridge between 1881 and 1884, and Herbert Edward Rhodes (Jesus) who rowed stroke and number seven for Cambridge between 1873 and 1876. They also brought in a new boy by the name of Donaldson. In an attempt to reverse their fortunes, Oxford brought in Tom Cottingham Edwards-Moss (Brasenose) who rowed stroke and number seven between 1875 and 1878, R.S. Kindersley (Exeter) who rowed number five for Oxford between 1880 and 1882, and A.R. Paterson (Trinity) who had rowed number three, four and six for Oxford between 1881 and 1884. The umpire was the former Cambridge rower Robert Lewis-Lloyd (Third Trinity).

Oxford had three returning rowers with previous Boat Race experience: H. McLean (New College – number five), F.O. Wethered (Christ Church – number six) and D.H. McLean (New College – number seven). Cambridge went with five previous Boat Race rowers: C.J. Bristowe (Trinity Hall – stroke), S. Fairbairn (Jesus – number five), S.D. Muttlebury (Third Trinity – number-six), C. Barclay (Third Trinity – number seven) and G.H. Baker (Queens' – cox).

Race day was fine but with a stiff wind, which made the Thames choppy. Cambridge won the toss and chose the Surrey side of the Thames, leaving Oxford to push off from the Middlesex side of the river. Cambridge made off faster and were a good length ahead by Walden's Wharf. By the Crab Tree pub they had increased their lead to 1½ lengths. Oxford spurted several times and by Hammersmith Bridge the two boats were neck and neck. The two crews hit rough water, Cambridge coping better with the conditions, and by Chiswick they were 3 lengths clear. However, Oxford were determined not to lose for another year and by Barnes Bridge were level again. Just as it looked like Oxford were going to pull off an unlikely victory, Oxford's number seven Douglas McLean (New College) snapped his oar in half, effectively stopping Oxford making any further progress. Cambridge took full advantage of the situation and, racing ahead, passed the finish post with a 2½-length lead in a time of 20 minutes 52 seconds – the fastest time since 1876. Despite their victory they were still behind Oxford overall, 23–20. William Holland had lost his first Boat Race and didn't much like it.

45th Boat Race, 24 March 1888

The year 1888 started badly with the sad news that Oxford's Boat Club captain Hector McLean (New College), who had rowed number five and seven for Oxford between 1885 and 1887, had died of typhoid fever in January. Once again Cambridge went into the race as both champions and favourites. Oxford brought back G.C. Bourne (New College) who had rowed bow in 1882 and 1883 and coached the Oxford crew in 1885 (Oxford victory by 2½ lengths in a time of 21 minutes 36 seconds), F.P. Bully who had coached Oxford in 1886 (Cambridge victory by ⅔ of a length in a time of 22 minutes 30 seconds) and Tom Cottingham Edwards-Moss (Brasenose) who had rowed number seven between 1875 and 1878. Cambridge stuck with their successful coaches Charles William Moore (Christ's) and Herbert Edward Rhodes (Jesus). The old Cambridge rower Robert Lewis-Lloyd (Third Trinity) was selected to act as umpire.

Cambridge selected two former rowers for their 1888 boat: Percy Landale (Trinity Hall – number six) and Stanley Muttlebury (Third Trinity – number five). Oxford went with three previous rowers with Boat Race experience: W.F.C. Holland (Brasenose – bow), H.R. Parker (Brasenose – number six) and Guy Nickalls (Magdalen – number seven).

Oxford won the toss and selected the Middlesex station, with Cambridge taking the Surrey side. Lewis-Lloyd got the race started at 10.56 a.m. Cambridge pulled away quickly and took the lead. Outclassing the Oxford boat, by Hammersmith Cambridge were 6 lengths clear. They never looked back and eventually crossed the winning line 7 lengths clear in a time of 20 minutes 48 seconds. Although Cambridge were closing the gap, Oxford still held an overall lead of 23–21 victories. For the second time, Holland had to live with his disappointment.

46th Boat Race, 30th March 1889

Once again Cambridge went into the race as both champions and favourites. They used no fewer than five coaches during their training for the race: Fraser Emilie

Churchill (Third Trinity) who had rowed number five for Cambridge between 1883 and 1885, Charles William Moore (Christ's) who rowed number seven and three for Cambridge between 1881 and 1884, Frederick I. Pitman (Third Trinity) who rowed stroke between 1884 and 1886, Herbert Edward Rhodes (Jesus) who stroked and rowed seven for the Cambridge boat between 1873 and 1876, and the famous botanist Henry Tudor Trevor-Jones (although it is not exactly clear why).

Oxford, determined to stop the rot, were trained by Tom Cottingham Edwards-Moss (Brasenose), who rowed four times for Oxford between 1875 and 1878 as number seven and stroke, and William Grenfell (Balliol), who rowed number four for Oxford between 1877 and 1878. The former Oxford rower Frank Willan was selected to umpire the race for the first time.

There were no changes to the Cambridge Eight who had won the race in 1888 – the only time this had happened in the history of the race. The Oxford crew on the other hand contained three former rowers with previous Boat Race experience: H.R. Parker (Brasenose – number six), W.F.C. Holland (Brasenose – Stroke) and G. Nickalls (Magdalen – number seven).

Cambridge won the toss and selected the Surrey side of the river, leaving Oxford the Middlesex side. Willan got the race of at 1.15 p.m., and Cambridge went into an early lead. By the Crab Tree pub, Cambridge were clear. In an effort to keep up with the Cambridge Eight, Oxford spurted but it made little impact and by Hammersmith Bridge Cambridge were a 1½ lengths ahead. They maintained their lead, crossing the finishing line 3 lengths ahead of the Dark Blues in a time of 20 minutes 14 seconds. It was the fastest winning time since 1882 (Oxford). The overall score was now 23–22 to Oxford.

47th Boat Race, 26 March 1890

For the third year in a row Cambridge went into the race as champions and favourites. There is no record of who coached Cambridge for the 1890 race but it is safe to assume that they were made up of the previous year's successful team: Churchill, Moore, Pitman and Rhodes. Oxford were coached by F.P. Bully, F. Fenner, who had won the Silver Goblets at Henley with J.C.F. May, rowing for the London Rowing Club in 1865, William Grenfell (Balliol), who rowed number four for Oxford between 1877 and 1878, Frederick Smith, 2nd Viscount Hambleden MP (owner of WH Smith), W.F.C. Holland in his fourth race, along with the cox John Pemberton Heywood-Lonsdale who had steered the Dark Blues in 1889.

Cambridge brought back three former rowers: Stanley Muttlebury (Third Trinity – number five and six), J.C. Gardner (Emmanuel – stroke) and T.W. Northmore (Queens' – cox). Oxford were more conservative, bringing back six rowers with previous Boat Race experience: W.F.C. Holland (Brasenose – bow), H.E.L. Puxley (Corpus – bow), R.P.P. Rowe (Magdalen – number seven), G. Nickalls (Magdalen – number four), J.P.H. Heywood-Lonsdale (New College – cox) and Lord Ampthill (New College – number five). Frank Willan umpired once again.

Although the weather was fine, a strong westerly wind created rough water between Hammersmith and Barnes bridges. Cambridge won the toss and selected the Surrey station, leaving the Middlesex side to Oxford. Willan got the race off at 4.44 p.m. on the dot. Cambridge made the better start and soon had a ¼-length lead. They were still ahead by the Crab Tree pub and looked to be on for another victory. Cambridge were ½ a length ahead by Hammersmith Bridge and by The Dove pub were almost clear. Oxford fought back, however, and by Chiswick Steps had almost drawn level. Oxford pushed on and were clear of Cambridge by Barnes Bridge. Cambridge were not giving up and pushed back hard but just couldn't quite reach the Oxford boat, which crossed the winning line with a 1-length lead in a time of 22 minutes 3 seconds. Oxford now had an overall lead of 24–22. Holland had his Boat Race victory at last.

★★★

This wasn't the end of Holland's association with rowing, Oxford or the Boat Race, as he went on to coach the Oxford Eight and train the Leander team that won the World Championships in Stockholm in 1912. He married Kate Gilbey Gold and they had two children, William James and Elizabeth.

During the First World War Holland took a commission into the 4th Battalion, Durham Light Infantry, serving with them for two and a half years and rising to the rank of captain. He later served as a draft conducting officer attached to No. 1 Section, Tyne Garrison, stationed at Seaham Harbour. Due to the conditions Holland contracted frostbite in his left foot and had to be returned home for treatment at Hammerton House between 8 July and 10 August 1917. He was found dead in his room at Seaham Harbour on 8 September 1917, at the age of 52. It left his many friends and regiment surprised and shocked. A later inquest went some way to explain his early demise:

Inquest of Body:

In view of his sudden death an inquest was held last night by Coroner Burnicle on the body, which had been brought to Sunderland for a Post Mortem at the War Hospital Chester Road.

Colonel William Hylton Briggs O/C the DLI at Seaham Harbour stated that neither he nor Captain Holland himself was satisfied with the progress towards fitness he was making. Deceased suffered great pain and did not sleep at all well

Memorial to William Francis Claude Holland.

and he had in consequence been much depressed. On Wednesday night however, when he saw him, he seemed more cheerful. At about 8am yesterday morning he was called to the Captains rooms and found him lying in bed dead. As the result of enquiries he found that the deceased had been heard to be out of bed at about 6 o' clock that morning. Luke Gerald Dillon, Major RAMC, said he saw Captain Holland on September 10th when he said he was feeling ill and suffering great pain in the left foot. He examined his foot and found the toe much swollen and bad with septic poisoning and the foot and ankle so swollen. He treated him and the deceased said it was the first peaceful time he had had for some months. On September 10th he removed two pieces of bone from the toe and his condition improved. He attended him until September 25th and with his advice wore a special boot and was able to walk with care. On October 30th he said his foot was quite tolerable and that was the last time he saw him alive. He examined him after death and found all the organs were healthy with the exception of the heart. Death was due to valvular disorder of that organ accelerated by his long septic poisoning of the toe. A verdict in accordance with the medical evidence was returned.

A memorial service was later held for him at Bishop's Stortford. The Reverend H. T. Malaher, Chaplain to the Forces, and the Reverend E. W. Bolland, vicar of Dawdon, conducted the service. Among those present were Brigadier General F. English DMG DSO, Lieutenant Colonel W.H. Briggs, with about thirty officers and men of the Holland's regiment, Mrs Streatfeild and Miss Briggs of Hammerton Hill Hospital, Major L.G. Dillon and Malcolm Dillon together with a large number of NCOs and men of the regiment and civilian friends. Lance Corporal Abbey played Chopin's *Funeral March* on the organ and Lieutenant D.H. Farquharson sang 'Rest in the Lord'. At the close, Bugler Elliot played the 'Last Post'.

Holland is buried in Birchanger (St Mary) Churchyard. He is also commemorated at Eton College, the Marlow Rowing Club and Brasenose College, Oxford.

38

LIEUTENANT COLONEL RONALD HARCOURT SANDERSON

Boat position: Number Six
Race: 56th Boat Race, 25 March 1899
          57th Boat Race, 31 March 1900
College: Trinity College, Cambridge
Served: 148th Brigade, Royal Field Artillery
Death: 17 April 1918, aged 41

*I don't think I ever knew any man who was so entirely above and beyond
the mean things of life.*

Lieutenant Colonel Ronald Harcourt
Sanderson.

Ronald Harcourt Sanderson was born on 11 December 1876 at the Vicarage, High Hurstwood, Uckfield, Sussex. He was the only son of the Reverend Edward Sanderson of Uckfield Rectory, Sussex, and Mary Jane Sanderson. He was educated at Harrow School before going up to Trinity College, Cambridge. He rowed for three years in the Head of the River boat and won the University Fours and the Lowe Double Sculls twice, as well as the Colquhoun Sculls. He was selected to row number six for the Cambridge Eight in both 1899 and 1900.

56th Boat Race, 25 March 1899

Oxford began the 1899 race as champions, having won the 1898 race with some ease. Oxford were coached by the former Oxford bow G.C. Bourne (New College), who had rowed for Oxford in both 1882 and 1883, Douglas McLean (New College), who had rowed number five for Oxford between 1883 and 1887, and, finally, another established Oxford rower, R.P.P. Rowe, who had rowed number two and seven for Oxford on four occasions between 1889 and 1892.

Cambridge were trained by the former Oxford Blue William Fletcher (Christ Church), who had stroked for Oxford four times between 1890 and 1893, and R.C. Lehmann (First Trinity), a former captain of the First Trinity Boat Club. For the tenth year in succession, Frank Willan (Exeter) was selected to umpire. Willan had rowed number four, seven and six for Oxford and had been in the winning boat four years in succession between 1866 and 1869.

Cambridge had three rowers with previous Boat Race experience: Claude Goldie (Third Trinity) who had rowed number seven in 1898, William Dudley Ward (Third Trinity) who had rowed number seven in 1897 and Raymond Broadly Etherington-Smith (First Trinity) who had rowed number six in 1898. The Oxford crew contained four men with previous Boat Race experience: Harcourt Gilbey Gold (Magdalen) who had stroked the Oxford boat between 1896 and 1899, R.O. Pitman (New College – bow, 1898), F.W. Warre (Balliol – number four, 1898) and A.T. Herbert (Balliol – number seven, 1898).

Cambridge won the toss and decided on the Surrey side, Oxford being handed the Middlesex side of the Thames. It was a fine, if cold, day with a poor tide. Willan started the race promptly at 12.58 p.m. The crews matched each other stroke for stroke until they reached the Mile Post, by which time the Oxford boat had established a ¼-length lead. However, Cambridge fought back and began to reduce the Oxford lead. With a favourable bend in the river, Harcourt Gold, the Oxford stroke, increased the rate in an attempt to put clear water between the two boats. However, John Gibbon, the Cambridge stroke, was having none of it and matched them, increasing the rate. As a result the Cambridge boat begin to forge ahead and had a good lead by The Dove pub. Cambridge continued to lead, finally winning the race by 3¼ lengths in a time of 21 minutes 4 seconds. It was Cambridge's first win in ten years, although Oxford still maintained their overall lead 32–23.

57th Boat Race, 31 March 1900

Sanderson was selected to row number six once again in the 1900 Boat Race – no blame for Oxford's loss in 1899 being attached to him. Cambridge had the unusual distinction of going into the race as champions. Oxford were coached by Harcourt

Gilbey Gold (Magdalen) who had stroked in the losing Oxford boat only the year before and Douglas McLean (New College) who had continued as coach from the previous year. Oxford also suffered more than their fair share of misfortune. One of the new boys, M.C. McThornhill, was instructed by his doctor not to row, the Oxford president Felix Warre (Balliol) caught scarlet fever and H.J. Hale (Balliol) suffered an injury.

Cambridge brought in two new coaches: James Brooks Close (First Trinity) who had been bow and number three in the Cambridge boat on three occasions between 1872 and 1874, and Stanley Muttlebury (Third Trinity) who rowed number six and five for Cambridge between 1886 and 1890. The umpire was once again Frank Willan (Exeter).

Oxford went with three members of the 1899 losing crew: C.E. Johnston (New College – number three), C.W. Tomkinson (Balliol – number four) and G.S. Maclagan (Magdalen – cox). Oxford's stroke, H.H. Dutton (Magdalen), was an Australian and the only non-British rower. Cambridge unsurprisingly went with six members of their victorious crew: William Dudley Ward (Third Trinity – number seven), Raymond Broadly Etherington-Smith (First Trinity – number five), J.E. Payne (Peterhouse – number four), R.H. Sanderson (First Trinity – number six), J.H. Gibbon (Third Trinity – stroke) and G.A. Lloyd (Third Trinity – cox). Eight of the nine Cambridge crew were students at Trinity College; J.E. Payne was at Peterhouse.

This time Oxford won the toss and chose the Surrey side, as Cambridge had the year before, and it was Cambridge's turn to take the Middlesex side of the Thames. For the second year in succession the weather was fine and Willan got the race off on time at 2 p.m. Cambridge pulled hard from the start and took an early lead; by the Craven Steps they were 3 lengths ahead. They continued to pull away from Oxford, finally winning the race by 20 lengths in a time of 18 minutes 45 seconds. It was the fastest winning time in the history of the race (matching the time established by Oxford in 1893). Overall Oxford still led 32–24, but the gap was narrowing.

★★★

In 1908 Sanderson rowed number six for the Leander Eight during the Olympic Games in London. The event took place during the Henley Royal Regatta, with the Leander crew defeating teams from Hungary, Canada and Belgium to take the gold medal. Sanderson decided to make his career in the army and took a commission into the Royal Field Artillery.

He served as a second lieutenant during the Second Boer War in 1899–1900, being promoted to lieutenant on 8 March 1902. In August 1916 he married Norah Dorothy, eldest daughter of Warwick and Frances Butler of Linden Lodge,

Dorchester. They had one son. He continued to serve with the artillery during the First World War, going to France with the 3rd Royal Horse Artillery Brigade. He fought with the British Expeditionary Force during the retreat from Mons and was involved in the heavy fighting through until Christmas 1914. He was mentioned in dispatches in October 1914 and made a Chevalier of the Legion of Honour by the French for his actions between 21 and 30 October 1914. In the fighting at Petit Morin, where all the officers of the battery were killed or wounded, he succeeded in bringing the battery safely out of action.

The 1899 Cambridge crew, with Sanderson top left.

Boat Race crew of 1899, with Sanderson standing
first left.

In January 1915 he was recalled home to train a fresh battery before returning to France with them the following May. In May 1916 he was appointed to command D (RHA) Battery and served with it until June 1917, when he was once again returned home to organise a command depot of some 6,000 men. He returned to the Front in March 1918 as a lieutenant colonel and was given command of a brigade. He was killed in action by a shell while trying to discover the headquarters of a neighbouring group.

Brigadier General White later wrote:

We have had some stirring times since the offensive began, and Sandy did splendidly and was a great help and comfort to me. He was always cool, and one could invariably place reliance on his sound judgment. I should most certainly have recommended him for a DSO, and I think it is safe to say he would have got it.

Another wrote:

I don't think I ever new any man who was so entirely above and beyond the mean things of life. They simply did not figure on his horizon.

He is buried at Lijssenthoek Military Cemetery, grave ref. XXVII. G. 3. He is also commemorated in the chapels of Trinity College, Cambridge, and Harrow School, and there is a memorial plaque to him in Ripon Cathedral.

39

CAPTAIN JAMES SHUCKBURGH CARTER

Boat position: Number five
Race: 60th Boat Race, 1 April 1903
College: King's College, Cambridge
Served: 1st Battalion, Grenadier Guards
Death: 27 September 1918, aged 37

I should think that its quite true to say that Jim never had an enemy, for he was one of those genial large-hearted giants, with whom it is impossible to feel anger …

Captain James Shuckburgh
Carter, Grenadier Guards.

James Shuckburgh Carter was born in 1881 in Buckinghamshire, England. He was the son of John Proctor Carter and Isabel Mary Carter. He was educated at Eton College where he was president of Pop, keeper of the wall and captain of the shooting eight. After leaving Eton he went up to King's College, Cambridge, where he rowed for his college and then in 1903 was selected to row number five in the Cambridge boat in the annual Boat Race.

60th Boat Race, 1st April 1903

Cambridge went into the 1903 race as champions, having won the 1902 competition by 5 lengths in a time of 19 minutes 9 seconds. It was the third time Cambridge had won the race in four years. They also went into the race as favourites. However, no one was expecting what was to happen as a result of an inexperienced umpire.

Oxford selected the very experienced G.C. Bourne (New College) to coach the crew once again, together with the four-time Blue C.K. Philips (New College, 1895) to 1898. Cambridge put their faith in Charles John Bristowe (Trinity Hall), who had rowed bow for Cambridge in 1886–87, and Claude Goldie (Third Trinity), who had rowed number seven twice for Cambridge in 1898 and 1899. Later, the former Cambridge rower William Dudley Ward (Third Trinity), who had rowed number seven in 1897, took over the training. The race umpire for the first time was Frederick I. Pitman (Third Trinity).

Oxford's preparation was hampered by a series of accidents and illness including influenza, which created problems with crew selection. Despite this Oxford went into the race with four rowers who had previous Boat Race experience: A. de L. Long, (New College – number three), G.C. Drinkwater (Wadham – number seven), H.W. Adams (University – number five) and the American D. Milburn (Lincoln – number six), the only foreign rower in the race. Cambridge selected six rowers from the 1902 winning crew: W.H. Chapman (Third Trinity – bow), H.B. Grylls (First Trinity – number six), C.W.H. Taylor (Third Trinity – number four), R.H. Nelson (Third Trinity – stroke), P.H. Thomas (Third Trinity – number three) and J. Edwards-Moss (Third Trinity – number seven).

On the day of the race there was a strong tide running up the river. However, the 1903 race is probably best known for its poor start, which affected the entire race. Oxford won the toss and chose to row from the Surrey side, leaving the Middlesex side of the river to Cambridge.

Umpire Pitman, starting his first race, tried to get the boats under way at 3.35 p.m. Tom Tim handed him the antique gun, which he had for as long as anyone could remember. However, as Pitman pulled the trigger the pistol struck on a half cock and refused to go off for several seconds. As Pitman had shouted his instructions, 'are you ready', the Cambridge crew had squared their blades and against the strong tide. The man in the stakeboat was unable to hold them back. The Oxford crew on the other hand was held more firmly and Cambridge took an early ⅓ of a length lead. Pitman, still trying to sort out his faulty firearm, failed to notice. The dismayed Oxford crew did what they could to try to make up the distance but never really got it together. Cambridge crossed the finish line with a 6-length lead in a time of 19 minutes 33 seconds. Oxford's overall lead was now reduced to 33–26. Carter had been in the winning crew in his one and only Boat Race.

The 1903 Cambridge crew, with Carter
standing far left.

★★★

On leaving Cambridge Carter became an assistant master at Radley School, where
he taught between 1904 and 1909. From Radley he went on to teach at Warren
Hill. On 16 April 1914 he married Diana Violet Gladys Cavendish of Houghton
Green, Playden, Sussex. Leaving Warren Hill, he went into partnership with a
Mr Hales and together they ran a private school in Cromer. On Mr Hales' death
in 1917, Carter decided it was time to 'do his bit'. He had always been a keen
member of the Territorials and in 1917 took a commission into the 2nd Battalion,
Grenadier Guards. Second Lieutenant James Shuckburgh Carter arrived in France
on 8 January 1918, joining 1st Company. At some point he was transferred to
the 1st Battalion. In July 1918 he was appointed as a bombing officer and in
September 1918 was promoted to captain. Captain Carter was killed in action on
27 September 1918 during the Guards attack near Canal du Nord (for which the
regiment received honours). An account of his death later reported that, on nearing
Flesquières, the enemy's machine-gun fire from the direction of Graincourt became
very heavy, and Captain Carter was hit in the head. It was during this battle that
Lieutenant Colonel John Standish Surtees Prendergast Vereker and 6th Viscount
Gort received the Victoria Cross. The action eventually led to the capture of over
200 prisoners, two batteries of field guns and numerous machine guns. A fellow
master at Radley later wrote of Captain Carter:

> I should think that its quite true to say that Jim never had an enemy, for he was
> one of those genial large-hearted giants, with whom it is impossible to feel
> anger, and who was popular with everyone. Naturally when he was here he
> associated himself with the river and coached the crew of 1909, but his interests
> were wide and varied. He had stayed some moths in Athens and took a keen
> interest in archaeology, white he was more than an enthusiastic entomologist.

Many a night have I been out 'sugaring' with him, and he was always ready to lend a helping hand to anyone who was keen on the subject. He was a first-class skater and competed two or three times for the 'Open Bowl' at Davos, while at Leuzerheide he was deservedly the most popular man in the place. It was only this time last year that he came down to Radley to sing in a concert and perform in the 'Radley Quartette' which for five years enjoyed some popularity while he was here. It is hard to realize that poor old Jim is gone too, like Sammy Hales and Lance Vidal. Truly Radley has had some cruel losses, but the loss of these three leaves a sorrow that will never fade away. In his last letter, only three weeks ago he wrote, 'I would not miss this for anything. The men are simply splendid, and it is a real privilege to be with them. Keep the home fires burning and some day I shall be sitting by your fireside with a pipe, boring you stiff with what we did in the Great War.' And now he has joined all those other hero's, but he still lives enshrined in the hearts of many devoted and sorrowing friends.

He is buried in Sanders Keep Military Cemetery, Graincourt-lès-Havrincourt, grave ref. II. A. 1. His brother, Major Richard Thellusson Carter MC, an assistant master at Eton College, died of wounds received in action at Harbonnières on 18 August 1918.

40

CAPTAIN EDWARD PARKER WALLMAN WEDD MC

Boat position: Number five
Race: 62nd Boat Race, 1 April 1905
College: Caius College, Cambridge
Served: Essex Yeomanry attached Royal Army Medical Corps attached
53rd Brigade, Royal Garrison Artillery
Death: 13 July 1918, aged 34

He was a splendid medical officer and all the batteries swore by him.

Edward Parker
Wallman Wedd.

Edward Parker Wallman Wedd was born on 1 September 1883 in Great Wakering, Essex. He was the son of Edward Arthur and Katherine Wedd of Whitehall, Great Wakering. He was educated at Stubbington, Fareham, Hampshire, before being sent to Cheltenham College where he stroked the Cheltenham Eight in both 1901 and 1902, winning the 1901 race against the old boys and beating St Paul's School in 1902. From Cheltenham College he went up to Caius College, Cambridge. He was in the winning boat during the University Trials in 1903 and, rowing for his college, won the Thames Cup at Henley Royal Regatta but lost in the final of the Wyfold Cup to the Birmingham Rowing Club. In 1905 he was selected to row number five in the annual Cambridge *v*. Oxford Boat Race.

62nd Boat Race, 1 April 1905

Having won the race in 1904 by 4½ lengths, Cambridge went into the 1905 race as reigning champions and Wedd must have had high hopes of being in the winning boat. However, due to various misfortunes and illness they were not the favourites. The Cambridge coaches were John Edwards-Moss (Third Trinity) who had rowed number seven in 1902 and 1903, Francis Escombe (Trinity Hall) and David Alexander Wauchope (Trinity Hall) who stroked for Cambridge in 1895. The Oxford coaches were William Fletcher (Christ Church) who had stroked and rowed number six and seven for Oxford between 1890 and 1893, C.K. Philips (New College) who had rowed number three for Oxford during their four victories between 1895 and 1898. Frederick I. Pitman (Third Trinity) who had stroked the Cambridge between 1884 and 1886 was the umpire for the third year.

The Cambridge crew had four returning rowers, including P.H. Thomas (Third Trinity) who replaced Stanley Bruce (who had himself replaced W.P. Wormald due to illness) at the last minute due to ill health. This was his fourth appearance in the race, having been in the winning crew during the previous three years 1902–04, but this time he joined straight from an African expedition – not the best preparation for such an important race. The other three were H. Sanger (Lady Margaret Boat Club – bow), R.V. Powell (Third Trinity – number seven) and B.C. Johnson (Third Trinity – number three). The Oxford crew contained five rowers with previous experience, including A.K. Graham (Balliol – number seven), E.P. Evans (University – number six), A.R. Balfour (University – number four), A.J.S.H. Hales (Corpus Christi – number three) and R.W. Somers-Smith (Merton – bow).

Cambridge University won the toss and chose the Middlesex station, leaving Oxford with the Surrey side. Pitman began the race at 11.30 a.m. Oxford took the lead quickly and by the Mile Post they were in a commanding position. They continued to dominate the race and eventually won by 3 lengths in a time of 20 minutes 35 seconds. It was Oxford's first victory in four years. It was a disappointing result for young Wedd's only Boat Race.

★★★

He graduated as a BA in 1906 and continued his education at St Bartholomew's Hospital qualifying with a Membership of Royal College of Surgeons and Licentiate of the Royal College of Physicians diploma and becoming House Surgeon to the West London Hospital. Wedd also took a commission into the Essex Yeomanry and it was with them that he went to the Front in November 1914, in the first months of the First World War. In January 1916 he was mentioned in dispatches, and served on the staff for fifteen months before transferring to the

Royal Army Medical Corps in 1917. He became attached to the 53rd Brigade, Royal Garrison Artillery, as their medical officer and it was while serving with them that he was decorated with the Military Cross. His citation read:

> For unswerving devotion and courage throughout the period of active operations South-West of Ypres between 23rd and 29th March 1918 and on many previous occasions in travelling shell-swept roads and crossing beyond which his duty called him to tend the many casualties the batteries suffered. On 25 April it was reported that a battery at St. Hubert's Loch was suffering severely. He immediately went down to it without a thought of himself he searched from shelter to shelter amid the rain of shell until he found and relieved the wounded. By his personal fearlessness and devotion in visiting batteries under fire he set a magnificent example never failing to cheer all ranks as he went around.

While at the Front he wrote the following letter to his sister Muriel Tidman:

> My dear M   6.5.18
> So sorry to hear that Oscar is seedy, but hope by this time the West country has set him up. We are now in a farm which the inhabitants evacuated the day after we arrived. It is a sad sight – that of refugees. We put up a Battalion of our Allies the other night, who much appreciated a couple of bottles of whisky. They are a wonderful nation of fighters; sanitation is not their strong point, nor is horsemastership.
>
> Any calves that were found roaming about these deserted farms were not long before they were in their field kitchens. Incidentally we have done well with veal, & we bought a pig at 100 francs which did us very well indeed, enabled us to send handsome joints to the Batteries.
>
> The trees are just bursting into leaf & affording a little cover. Had lunch today with one of the Batteries I had when we were with Gen. Crampton. A very good lunch in charming company.
>
> Charles has got his new coat & is looking A1. He still is very gun shy, & even a flash brings him round in a hurry.
>
> We had an extraordinary heavy fall of rain last night.
>
> With all best wishes & much love
>   Yours ever
>   Parker

He was killed in action on 13 July 1918 by a stray shell at Ypres while motorcycling to tend some wounded at a casualty clearing station. He is buried in the Canada Farm Cemetery, grave ref. IV.B.12.

His loss was keenly felt. His former brigadier wrote to his family:

I knew him when he was a Staff Captain to the XI. Corps and he joined by Brigade last year as our doctor. We were simply delighted to get him. He was a splendid medical officer and all the batteries swore by him ... I left the Brigade last April so was not there when he got the Military Cross, which he gained by very gallant work. I don't think a straighter fellow ever went over the border than your son.

He is also commemorated at Cheltenham College, Caius College Cambridge and Great Wakering (Essex) war memorials.

41

LIEUTENANT EDOUARD MAJOLIER

Boat position: Number Four
Race: 67th Boat Race, 23 March 1910
College: Christ Church College, Oxford
Served: 5th Battalion, Yorkshire Regiment
Death: 26 November 1918, aged 30

Died at home but his place of burial still a mystery.

Edouard Majolier was born on 12 May 1888 in London. He was the eldest son of Edouard Majolier (Huguenot descendant), a cornbroker and factor, who had two sons and four daughters, and Suzanne Majolier (née Edouard). The family resided at No. 20 Bramham Gardens, Earl's Court. Edouard was educated at Eton College before going up to Christ Church College, Oxford, in 1907. He rowed for his College Eight, winning the Grand Challenge Cup, sadly in the same year his father died. He was selected to row number four for the Oxford Eight during the 1910 annual Boat Race.

Lieutenant Edouard Majolier.

67th Boat Race, 23 March 1910

Oxford went into the race as champions and favourites, having won the 1909 race by 3½ lengths in a time of 19 minutes 50 seconds. It was Oxford's first victory in four years. The Oxford coaches were G.C. Bourne (New College) who had represented Oxford between 1882 and 1883, Harcourt Gilbey Gold (Magdalen) who represented Oxford on four occasions between 1896 and 1899, and was also president of Oxford for the 1900 race, and W.F.C. Holland (Brasenose) who also rowed for Oxford on four occasions between 1887 and 1890. Cambridge were coached by William Dudley Ward (Third Trinity) who rowed for Cambridge in 1897, 1899 and 1900, Raymond Etherington-Smith (First Trinity) who had represented Cambridge in 1898 and 1900, and David Alexander Wauchope (Trinity Hall) who had rowed in the 1895 race.

This year the Boat Race was scheduled during Holy Week, which caused much disquiet and threatened the race going ahead at all. It wasn't until after the race celebrations were all cancelled that the Bishop of London finally gave his consent for the race to go ahead. Had he not, it is doubtful, even if the race had gone ahead, that key members of the crews would have taken part in it. The race day was beautiful with a warm sun and a mild breeze. Cambridge won the toss and chose to take the Middlesex station, with Oxford on the Surrey side. Fredrick I. Pitman was umpire for the seventh year in a row. Pitman (Third Trinity) had rowed for Cambridge in 1884 (Cambridge), 1885 (Oxford) and 1886 (Cambridge). Pitman, to the cheers of the assembled crowd, started the race promptly at 12.30 p.m. Cambridge made a quick start and began to leave Oxford behind until one of the

The Oxford Eight in 1910.

Cambridge crew caught a crab and the Oxford crew pulled quickly passed them. By Craven Steps, and despite being the slower boat, the Oxford crew were ¼ of a length ahead. However, Cambridge put on a spurt and by the Mile Post were in the lead. The Cambridge crew began to lose ground to Oxford as they rounded an unfavourable bend in the Thames, and Oxford began to push hard, gaining a length in 10 strokes. By The Dove pub, Oxford had a 1-length lead, which they finally extended to a 3½-length lead by the end of the race. Their time was 20 minutes 14 seconds, the slowest since 1907. Oxford's overall lead was now 36 to Cambridge's 30. Edouard Majolier had been in the winning crew in his one and only Boat Race.

★★★

On leaving Oxford he followed in the family business, becoming a cornbroker's clerk and residing at No. 20 Bramham Gardens, London. During the spring of 1916 he took the plunge and married Geraldine Briggs at Atcham, and they set up home at No. 131 Victoria Street, London. The couple had two daughters: Chloe, born in 1917, and Peggy, born in the summer of 1918.

During the war Majolier served as a lieutenant with the 5th Battalion, Yorkshire Regiment. He saw action during the Battle of St-Juilen and was wounded and awarded a wound badge in November 1917. Exhausted he was returned home to recuperate and died at his home on 26 November 1918 from pneumonia contracted while serving on the Western Front.

His death was registered at St George's, Hanover Square, London. He was laid to rest with full military honours on 29 November 1918 at Putney Vale Cemetary, Wandsworth. Probate was granted to a chartered accountant. He left £16,100 1d. He is commemorated at Eton College and on the Christ Church College Memorial.

42

Boat position: Stroke, Number Seven & Number Six
Race: 47th Boat Race, 26 March 1890
 48th Boat Race, 21 March 1891
 49th Boat Race, 9 April 1892
 50th Boat Race, 22 March 1893
College: Christ Church College, Oxford
Served: 2/6th King's Liverpool Regiment
Death: 14 February 1919, aged 49

Never in her long and varied history has Christ Church had a more loyal member or one more devoted to her best interests.

William Alfred Littledale Fletcher was born on 25 August 1869 at Holly Bank, Green Lane, Wavertree (near Liverpool). He was the eldest son of eight children (surviving to adulthood) of Alfred Fletcher, a former cottonbroker and director of the London and North Western Railway, the Liverpool and London Globe Insurance Company and the Shropshire Union Canal Company, and Edith Fletcher (née Littledale). The Fletcher family's

Lieutenant Colonel William Alfred Littledale 'Flea' Fletcher DSO.

wealth derived from Jacob Fletcher, a Whitehaven, Cumberland, ship owner and privateer, who moved to Liverpool in the 1750s.

William was educated at Cheam School, in Hampshire. After Cheam he went to Eton College. Although not greatly academic he was a fine athlete. He rowed for the Eton Eight in 1888 and in the Ladies' Plate at Henley Royal Regatta. He was also a member of the Eton College Volunteer Corps. On leaving Eton in 1899 he went up to Christ Church College, Oxford. Once again he failed to achieve much academically managing to squeeze out a 'pass' even though he never quite finished his course. However, continuing with his rowing he won the Ladies' Plate and the Thames Challenge Cup at Henley. His size, 6ft 3in, and weight, 13 stone, earned him the nickname 'Flea'. Because of both his talent and success he was chosen to row for Oxford on four occasions, rowing stroke, number seven and number six.

47th Boat Race, 26 March 1890

For the third year in a row Cambridge went into the race as champions and favourites. It is unclear who coached Cambridge for the 1990 race but it would be safe to assume they were made up of the previous year's successful team: Churchill, Moore, Pitman and Rhodes. Oxford were coached by F.P. Bully, F. Fenner, who had won the Silver Goblets at Henley with J.C.F. May rowing for the London Rowing Club in 1865, William Grenfell (Balliol), who rowed number four for Oxford between 1877 and 1878, and Frederick Smith, 2nd Viscount Hambleden MP (owner of WH Smith). The former Oxford rower Frank Willan (Exeter) umpired the race for the second year running.

Cambridge brought back three former rowers: Stanley Muttlebury (Third Trinity – number five and six), J.C. Gardner (Emmanuel – stroke) and T.W. Northmore (Queens' – cox). Oxford were more conservative and brought back six rowers with previous Boat Race experience: W.F.C. Holland (Brasenose – bow), H.E.L. Puxley (Corpus – bow), R.P.P. Rowe (Magdalen – number seven), G. Nickalls (Magdalen – number four), J.P.H. Heywood-Lonsdale (New College – cox) and Lord Ampthill (New College – number five).

Although the weather was fine, a strong westerly wind created rough water between Hammersmith and Barnes bridges. Cambridge won the toss and selected the Surrey station, leaving the Middlesex side to Oxford. Willan got the race off at 4.44 p.m. on the dot. Cambridge made the better start and soon had a ¼-length lead. They were still ahead by the Crab Tree pub and looked to be on for another victory. They were still ½ a length ahead by Hammersmith Bridge and by The Dove pub were almost clear. Oxford fought back, however, and by Chiswick Steps had almost drawn level. Oxford pushed on and were clear of Cambridge by Barnes Bridge. Cambridge were not giving up and pushed back hard but just couldn't quite reach the Oxford boat, which crossed the winning line with a lead of 1 length in a time of 22 minutes 3 seconds. Oxford now had an overall lead of 24 to 22.

48th Boat Race, 21 March 1891

Oxford University went into the 1891 race as champions and favourites. In preparation for the race Cambridge brought in Arthur Middleton Hutchinson (Jesus) who had rowed for Cambridge number six and two in 1881 and 1882. Oxford made a surprise choice by selecting Rudolph Chambers 'R.C.' Lehmann. Lehmann was a former president of the Cambridge Union Society and captain of the First Trinity Boat Club. He had taken part in the trials several times but never quite made the Eight. Frank Willan (Exeter), the old Oxford rower, was selected to umpire the race once again.

Cambridge selected four rowers from the previous year's race to compete again in 1891: Gerard Elin (Third Trinity – stroke), Edmund Towers Fison (Corpus – number four), Gilbert Francklyn (Third Trinity – number three) and John Friend Rowlatt (Trinity Hall – number six). The champions, Oxford, brought back five experienced rowers: Guy Nickalls (Magdalen – number four), R.P.P. Rowe (Magdalen – number two), Lord Ampthill (New College – number six), W.A.L. Fletcher (Christ Church – number seven) and J.P.H. Heywood-Lonsdale (New College – cox). Two Australians also rowed: F. Wilkinson (Brasenose – number five) and Edward Wason Lord (Trinity Hall – number two).

With the wind blowing from the north, Oxford won the toss and selected the Middlesex side of the Thames, leaving the Surrey side of the water to Cambridge. Willan got the race started at 11.09 a.m. Oxford took an early lead and were ¼ of a length ahead by the Craven Steps. By the Mile Post Oxford had extended their lead to ½ a length. However, Cambridge pushed hard and by Hammersmith Bridge had taken the lead. By The Dove pub Oxford were once again in the lead but only by a short nose. The lead changed several times, both crews fighting hard for the win. Finally Oxford managed to sustain a lead and were ¾ of a length ahead by Barnes Bridge. Cambridge managed to close the gap but it was too late and Oxford crossed the finishing line ½ a length ahead in a time of 21 minutes 48 seconds. The overall record was now 25–22 in Oxford's favour.

49th Boat Race, 9 April 1892

Once again Oxford went into the race as champions. They were coached by R.C. Lehmann and brought in: F.P. Bully, Douglas McLean (New College) who rowed number five and seven for Oxford between 1883 and 1887, and Guy

Nickalls (Magdalen) who rowed number two, seven, six and four for Oxford between 1887 and 1891. Oddly R.C. Lehmann had also coached the Cambridge Eight during the early part of their training. Once again Frank Willan (Exeter) was selected as umpire.

Cambridge brought back six rowers from the previous year's race: E.W. Lord (Trinity Hall – bow), G. Francklyn (Third Trinity – number three), E.T. Fison (Corpus – number four), W. Landale (Trinity Hall – number five), C.T. Fogg-Elliot (Trinity Hall – number seven), G. Elin (Third Trinity – stroke) and J.V. Braddon (Trinity Hall – cox). Oxford brought back four rowers with previous Boat Race experience: V. Nickalls (Magdalen – number five), R.P.P. Rowe (Magdalen – number seven), W.A.L. Fletcher (Christ Church – number six) and J.P.H. Heywood-Lonsdale (New College – cox). The crews had one non-British rower in Edward Wason Lord (Trinity Hall – bow) who came from Australia.

Conditions for the race were perfect with a light easterly breeze and a good tide. Oxford won the toss and decided on the Middlesex side of the river, leaving Cambridge the Surrey side. Oxford got a quick start and led from the beginning of the race; by the Craven Steps were ½ a length ahead. By Harrods Furniture Depository they had extended their lead to a length. Cambridge fought back by spurting and by Hammersmith Bridge had reduced Oxford's lead to ½ a length. However, by Barnes Bridge Oxford had pulled away and led by 4 lengths (this was largely due to a fault with one of the seats in the Cambridge boat). Oxford won the race by 2¼ lengths in a time of 19 minutes 10 seconds. It was Oxford and Fletcher's third consecutive victory. It was also the fastest winning time in the history of the race. The overall score was now 26–22 in Oxford's favour.

The 1891 Oxford crew, with Fletcher standing second from left.

50th Boat Race, 22 March 1893

Oxford went into the 1893 race as both champions and favourites, having won the 1892 race by 2¼ lengths in a time of 19 minutes 10 seconds. It was Oxford's third consecutive victory. For this year's race Oxford changed coaches, selecting G.C. Bourne (New College) who rowed bow for Oxford in both 1882 and 1883, Tom Cottingham Edwards-Moss (Balliol) who had rowed stroke and number seven between 1875 and 1878, and Douglas McLean (New College) who rowed number five for Oxford between 1883 and 1887. Cambridge went with experience, sticking with R.C. Lehmann (First Trinity) who, although having rowed in the trials and been the captain of the First Trinity Boat Club, had never rowed in the Boat Race. He was also happy to coach either side, Oxford or Cambridge, normally in the latter half of their training.

Cambridge selected two rowers with previous Boat Race experience for their Eight: Graham Campbell Kerr (First Trinity – number six) and Thurstan Fogg-Elliot (Trinity Hall – number three). Oxford kept faith with five of their previous rowers: W.A.L. Fletcher (Christ Church – number six), H.B. Cotton (Magdalen – bow), J.A. Ford (Brasenose – number two), V. Nickalls (Magdalen – number five) and C.M. Pitman (Magdalen – stroke).

Due to repairs at Barnes Bridge the race almost didn't take place; for one of the few times in its history it wasn't held on a Saturday but on a Wednesday. With a strong spring tide and an easterly breeze Cambridge won the toss and decided on the Surrey side of the river, leaving the Middlesex side to the Oxford Eight. Frank Willan (Exeter), who had been selected as umpire for the fifth year, got the race started promptly at 4.35 p.m. Although Cambridge made the better start and went into an early lead, Oxford quickly caught up and went ahead. By the Mile Post, Oxford were 1 length ahead. By Hammersmith Bridge, though, Oxford's lead had been cut to ½ a length and by The Dove pub the crews were level. However, Cambridge began to tire and Oxford took advantage, pushing ahead; by Barnes Bridge Oxford were 1½ lengths clear. With rough water slowing the Oxford crew, Cambridge attempted to take advantage but despite a big effort were unable to stop Oxford, taking the race by 1¼ lengths in a time of 18 minutes 45 seconds (it was the fastest time in the history of the race). Oxford now had an overall lead of 27 races to 22. Fletcher became only the third man in Boat Race history to win it on four occasions.

★★★

Fletcher went on to win the Silver Goblets at Henley with his old friend Vivian Nickalls in 1892 and 1893, and rowed in the winning Leander Club crews at Henley. He was also on the Varsity Water Polo team and on the committee of

William Alfred Littledale 'Flea' Fletcher.

the Vincent's Club (a sports club mainly for Oxford Blues founded in 1863 by the Brasenose rower Walter Woodgate who was also its first president). As well as coaching the Christ Church boat and introducing what became known as the 'Christ Church style', Fletcher went on to coach the Oxford Eight for seven years between 1894 and 1906. Interestingly in 1898 he was invited to coach the Cambridge crew, an honour that only three Oxford coaches in the history of the race have ever been granted. He went on to coach the Cambridge Eight to victory in 1899: the university's first win in ten years. The 'Christ Church style' is perhaps best summed up by Sir William Gladstone:

> The Style was introduced by W.A.L. Fletcher, a great coach of University crews in his own right. Evolving the ideas of Warre and de Havilland, he appreciated that with the longest existing (16") sliding seat, the 'quick catch' so vital to the English style might best be achieved by a broader blade and a shorter oar, with a relatively longer inboard length, than by an excessively long body swing with a long oar and thin blade which had seemed the best combination for many years in spite of its tendency to 'pinch' the boat and reduce the strength which could be applied at the beginning.

During the Second Boer War Fletcher took a commission into the 32nd Company, Imperial Yeomanry, and was appointed lieutenant into the 2nd Battalion. A natural soldier, during his time in South Africa he was mentioned in dispatches twice: 7 May 1901 for valuable services rendered in connection with operations and 10 September 1901 for special and meritorious service in South Africa. He was also made a Companion of the Distinguished Service Order (27 September 1901) – a rare award for such a junior officer. The award was made for the defence of an isolated Boer farmhouse near Colesburg in the Cape Colony, which helped to keep open a vital British supply line. Ambushed by upwards of 300 Boer farmers, Fletcher refused to surrender his position over two days of heavy fighting and held fast until the Boers finally gave up and withdrew. It was while serving in South Africa that he became a big game hunter, following his sport around the world. He also became a noted explorer, travelling with his uncle on a year-long expedition to Tibet. He only just failed to reach the forbidden city of Lhasa, returning via unmapped areas of Tibet to Ladakh and then across Kashmire. On his return he became a member of the Royal Geographical Society and presented a paper, 'A Journey toward Lhassa'.

In 1914 Fletcher inherited large sum of money (around £5 million in today's currency) after the death of his third cousin. He also spent more time at the family's 150-acre estate in Allerton, which had been purchased in 1815.

On 23 September 1914, at the outbreak of the First World War, Fletcher took a commission into the 2/6th Battalion, King's Liverpool Regiment (Territorial Force) being promoted to captain. He became the battalion's adjutant on 10 November 1914. On 6 August 1915 he was promoted to temporary lieutenant colonel and became commanding officer of the 2/6th Battalion. He was sent to France with the battalion on 14 February 1917 and was involved in some of the heaviest fighting of the war. On 18 July 1917 he was badly gassed (mustard gas) during the second gas attack of the war at Armentières. The battalion suffered 457 casualties during this attack. Despite returning to duty on 11 September 1917 his health had been broken and in spite of his best efforts he was forced to relinquish his command on 28 July 1918, being close to a breakdown. In the words of the battalion historian, he was 'never been able to recover his old vitality'. During the war he was mentioned in dispatches twice and was created a Chevalier of the French Legion of Honour (2 May 1918). He was also appointed brevet major for distinguished service in the field.

After the war Fletcher became acting chairman of the Henley Regatta, becoming responsible for organising what was to become known as the 'Peace Regatta'. However, a few days later, with his lungs badly damaged, he died from broncho-pneumonia during the deadly flu pandemic that killed more people than the war did. He was just a few months short of his fiftieth birthday. He was later buried in the family plot in the graveyard of St Nicholas' Church, Halewood, grave ref. West.2.16.

After his death one of his students wrote of him in *The Oxford Magazine*: 'Never in her long and varied history has Christ Church had a more loyal member or one more devoted to her best interests.'

A bronze tablet, featuring a profile of his head, wearing his Oxford University Boat Race cap, was erected in his memory in the Oxford University Boat House. Written beneath are the words, 'This Tablet is Placed Here by Rowing Men of Both Universities'. A fitting tribute indeed.

Appendix 1

HISTORY OF THE BOAT RACE

The Oxford and Cambridge University Boat Race was first held in 1829 and has been an annual event since 1856. The idea for the race came from a St John's (Cambridge) student, Charles Merivale, and his friend Charles Wordsworth who was at Christ Church College, Oxford. Christ Church College rowed in dark blue, which was their Boat Club colours and became Oxford's official colours. Cambridge seem to have a long list of claims as to why they race in light blue, the favourite being that in 1830 Cambridge put a light blue ribbon on the bow of their boat as an emblem, and since then the two universities have stuck to dark and light blue as their official colours. Oxford won the 1829 race easily. The women's race was first rowed in Oxford in 1927 but until 2015 was held in a different location.

The only periods the race hasn't taken place were during the First and Second World Wars. Since 2016 Cambridge had won the race on eighty-two occasions and Oxford on seventy-nine occasions (with one contested draw in 1877). The race is normally held in late March or early April. Around 250,000 people line the banks of the Thames every year to watch the race live. A further 15 million watch it on TV worldwide.

Appendix 2

THE RACE COURSE

The Boat Race is held on the Thames and covers a distance of 4.2 miles (6.8km), from Putney to Mortlake.

THE START – PUTNEY BRIDGE

The boats start from two stake boats moored so that the competitors' bows are in line with the first university stone.

The Black Buoy
Painted yellow to stop collisions.

Fulham Football Club

Craven Cottage (The Fulham Flats)
This part of the river is shallow with slack water.

The Mile Post
About 1 mile from the Boat Race start. The post is a memorial to Steven Fairbairn (Jesus) who rowed number six and seven between 1882 and 1883, and number five in 1886 and 1887. He was important in changing the style of racing, introducing such things as the sliding seats.

The Crabtree
'Crabtree Reach' after The Crabtree pub.

Harrods Furniture Depository
Once a warehouse for the famous shop now apartments.

Hammersmith Bridge

St Paul's School

Chiswick Eyot
A tree-covered river island in the middle of the Thames.

Fuller's Brewery
Just visible to the crews behind the Eyot.

Chiswick Pier

The Crossing
Marks the end of the long Surrey bend.

The Bandstand

Barnes Railway Bridge
Crews must pass through the centre arch. Of crews that have gone through the arch first, 95 per cent have gone on to win the race.

The Mortlake Brewery or the Stag Brewery

THE FINISH – CHISWICK BRIDGE

Previous Courses

The course for the main part of the race's history has been from Putney to Mortlake. However there have been three other courses.
1829 – Hambledon Lock to Henley Bridge
1839, 1842 – Westminster to Putney
1846, 1856, 1862, 1863 – Mortlake to Putney

Appendix 3

ROWING TERMS

Bandstand A public bandstand east of Barnes Bridge used as a landmark.

Barnes Bridge The fourth timing point – both crews must pass through the centre arch of Barnes Railway Bridge.

Beverley Brook A tiny stream approximately 2 minutes into the Boat Race, often used as a landmark by commentators.

Black Buoy A massive half-yellow, half-black floating drum marking the end of Putney Embankment.

Blade A rower's term for an oar.

Blue Doors A house with bright blue windows on the Middlesex Bank, which marks roughly the mid-point of the race.

Boat Can mean crew, or the vessel they row in (aka 'shell').

Bow Either the prow of the boat, or the person sitting in the seat nearest the prow.

Bow-ball The tennis ball-sized piece of rubber fixed over the sharp bow of the boat to prevent injuries in the case of a collision.

Bow-side The starboard side of the crew.

Catch The 'start' of the stroke when the oar enters the water – catches have to be in time or the crew will not go fast.

Chiswick Eyot A large island in the Thames marking approximately 9–11 minutes into the race.

Chiswick Steps The third timing point, between Chiswick Eyot and Chiswick Pier.

Clashing When the oars become interlocked in a race, leading to anything from crabs to stoppages and accusations of fouls.

Crab Catching a crab is when a rower's oar becomes stuck in the water, often throwing them off their seat and/or stopping the boat suddenly.

Crew A boat full of rowers. Not a team – ever.

Crossing A point west of Chiswick Pier where the river turns back to the north again, switching the station advantage back to Middlesex.

Drive The part of the stroke when the legs are shoving the oar through the water.

Finish (of the stroke) The point where the oars are pulled out of the water, which must be synchronised cleanly to avoid crabs.

Fulham Wall The Bishop's Park wall, along which the start of the race takes place.

Hammersmith Bridge The second timing point in the race.

Harrods Depository Now Harrods Village, a large building just before Hammersmith Bridge.

Loom The long shaft of the oar/blade, which should not be under water.

Milepost The first timing point in the race, 1 mile from the start.

Mortlake The beach where the crews will land after the finish, and where the winning coxes are ceremoniously thrown into the water.

Pressure How hard a rower pulls their blade through the water: full pressure means maximum effort.

Push A few (typically 10–15) strokes in which the crew adds extra effort, to try to get ahead of their rivals.

Rate Number of strokes per minute, typically 40–44 off the start and then settling to approximately 33–36 during the race, depending on wind conditions.

Recovery The period in the stroke when the blades are out of the water and the crew are effectively resting.

Rhythm The ratio of time a spoon spends in the water relative to the rest time spent sliding back for the next stroke. The more efficient the rhythm, the longer a rower can carry on working at full power.

Second Lamp Post The point on Hammersmith Bridge under which the coxes will try to pass for maximum stream advantage.

Spoon The coloured end of the oar/blade, which goes into the water.

Spurt To sprint; to row very quickly.

Stakeboat The moored boat that holds a crew in position before the race begins like a starting block.

Station The side of the river the crew is rowing on. The two stations are Middlesex (north) and Surrey (south).

Stern The back end of the boat, where the cox sits.

Stride A point 15–25 strokes after the start when the crews change gear to a longer, more powerful stroke rhythm, which gives them a sustainable cruising speed.

Stroke As well as the action of the rowing stroke itself, 'stroke' can also mean the rower who leads the crew, setting the rhythm and racing rate.

Stroke-side The port side of the crew.

Surrey Bend From the Milepost to the Crossing, a stretch of often very bumpy water in which the Surrey crew has the advantage.

Taking water Moving ahead of the other crew so that they are in line astern and being washed down.

University Post A large post marking the finish at Chiswick.

University Stone A small obelisk marking the starting point of the race at Putney.

Washing down When the oars of one crew are creating 'puddles' into which the other crew has to row, if it is too far behind – this slows the second crew down considerably.

Appendix 4

LIST OF NAMES

Oxford

Thomas Geoffrey Brocklebank: Eton & Trinity College (1904), captain, Royal Field Artillery, 5 August 1916.

John Julius Jersey De Knoop: Eton & New College (1896, 1897), captain, Yeomanry, attached Indian Camel Corps, 7 August 1916. Kantara War Memorial.

Geoffrey Otto Charles Edwards: Eton & New College (1897, 1898), second lieutenant, Duke of Wellington's Regiment, 7 July 1916.

William Augustine Ellison: MVO, Eton & University College (1878), colonel, Royal Berkshire Regiment, 1 November 1917.

Reginald William Fletcher: Eton & Balliol College (1914), Royal Field Artillery, 18th Battery 26th Brigade, 31 October 1914.

W.A.L. Fletcher: DSO, Eton & Christ Church (1890, 1891, 1892, 1893), lieutenant colonel, King's Liverpool Regiment, 14 February 1919.

A.J.S.H. Hales: Rugby & Corpus Christi College (1904, 1905), captain, Wiltshire Regiment, 5 July 1916.

Robert Prothero Hankinson: Winchester & New College (1913), lieutenant, Indian Army, 23 February 1917.

A.T. Herbert (later Lord Lucas): Bedford Grammar School & Balliol College (1898, 1899), flight commander, Royal Flying Corps, 4 November 1916.

M.B. Higgins: Melbourne University & Balliol College (1910), captain, Australian Light Horse, 7 January 1917.

W.F.C. Holland: Eton & Brasenose College (1887, 1888, 1889, 1890), captain, Durham Light Infantry, 8 November 1917.

G.E. Hope: Eton & Christ Church (1907), lieutenant colonel, Grenadier Guards, 10 October 1917.

F.S. Kelly: DSC, Eton & Balliol College (1903), lieutenant commander, RNVR, 13 November 1916.

A.G. Kirby: Eton & Magdalen College (1906, 1907, 1908, 1909), staff captain, Royal Artillery, 29 March 1917.

D. Mackinnon: Rugby & Magdalen College (1909, 1910, 1911), lieutenant, Scots Guards, 9 October 1917.

G.S. Maclagen: Rugby & Magdalen College (1899, 1900, 1901, 1902), second lieutenant, Royal Warwickshire Regiment, 25 April 1915.

E. Majolier: Eton & Christ Church (1910), lieutenant, Yorkshire Regiment, 26 November 1918.

C.P. Rowley: Winchester & Magdalen College (1889, 1890, 1891, 1892), major, Royal Garrison Artillery, 29 October 1916.

R.W. Somers-Smith: MC, Eton & Merton College (1904, 1905), captain, King's Royal Rifle Corps, 30 June 1915.

E.H.L. Southwell: Charterhouse & Pembroke College (1907, 1908), lieutenant, Rifle Brigade, 15 September 1916.

The Hon. R.P. Stanhope: Eton & Magdalen College (1908), captain, Grenadier Guards, 15 September 1916.

Cambridge

C.F. Burnand: Downside & Trinity College (1911), second lieutenant, Grenadier Guards, 13 March 1915.

J.S. Carter: Eton & King's College (1903), captain, Grenadier Guards, 27 September 1918.

O.A. Carver: Charterhouse & Trinity College (1908), captain, Royal Engineers, 17 June 1915.

W.H. Chapman: Eton & Trinity College (1899, 1902, 1903), captain, Yorkshire Regiment, 7 August 1915.

A.B. Close-Brooks: Winchester & Trinity College (1907), captain, Manchester Regiment, 10 January 1917.

S.P. Cockerell: Eton & Trinity College (1900), second lieutenant, Royal Flying Corps, 20 March 1915.

C.P. Cooke: Geelong & Trinity Hall (1910), second lieutenant, Shropshire Light Infantry, 22 August 1917.

D.I. Day: Repton & St John's College (1914), second lieutenant, Royal Field Artillery, 7 September 1915.

G.E. Fairbairn: Eton & Jesus College (1908, 1911), second lieutenant, Durham Light Infantry, 20 June 1915.

K.G. Garnett: MC, Croix de Guerre, St Paul's & Trinity College (1914), lieutenant, Royal Field Artillery, 21 August 1917.

H.M. Goldsmith: Sherborne & Jesus College (1906, 1907), lieutenant, Devonshire Regiment, 9 May 1915.

R.O. Kerrison: Eton & Trinity College (1893, 1894), lieutenant colonel, Cavalry Reserve, attached Australian Artillery, 18 September 1917.

C.R. le Blanc-Smith: Eton & Trinity College (1910, 1911, 1912), lieutenant, Rifle Brigade, 27 November 1915.

L.E. Ridley: Eastbourne & Jesus (1913, 1914), lieutenant, Royal Berkshire Regiment, 18 August 1916.

J.A. Ritson: Rugby & Trinity College (1914), captain, 5th Lancashire Regiment, 23 July 1916.

R.H. Sanderson: Harrow & Trinity College (1899, 1900), lieutenant colonel, Royal Artillery, 17 April 1918.

H.J.S. Shields: Loretto & Jesus College (1910), lieutenant, Royal Army Medical Corps, 25 October 1914.

E.P.W. Wedd: MC, Cheltenham & Caius College (1905), major, Yeomanry and Royal Army Medical Corps, 13 July 1918.

E.G. Williams: Eton & Trinity College (1908, 1909, 1910), lieutenant, Grenadier Guards, 12 August 1915.

B.R. Winthrop-Smith: Eton & Trinity College (1905), Scots Guards, 15 November 1914.

Appendix 5

BOAT RACE RESULTS
1829 to 1920

1. 10 June 1829.   Oxford

There was no race between 1830 and 1835

2. 17 June 1836.   Cambridge

There was no race between 1837 and 1838

3. 3 April 1839.   Cambridge
4. 15 April 1840.   Cambridge
5. 14 April 1841.   Cambridge
6. 11 June 1842.   Oxford

There was no race between 1843 and 1844

7. 15 March 1845.   Cambridge
8. 3 April 1846.   Cambridge

There was no race between 1847 and 1848

9. 29 March 1849.   Cambridge
10. 15 December 1849.   Oxford

There was no race between 1850 and 1851

11. 3 April 1852.   Oxford

There was no race in 1853

12.   8 April 1854.   Oxford

There was no race in 1855

13.   15 March 1856.   Cambridge
14.   4 April 1857.   Oxford
15.   27 March 1858.   Cambridge
16.   15 April 1859.   Oxford
17.   31 March 1860.   Cambridge
18.   23 March 1861.   Oxford
19.   12 April 1862.   Oxford
20.   28 March 1863.   Oxford
21.   19 March 1864.   Oxford
22.   8 April 1865.   Oxford
23.   24 March 1866.   Oxford
24.   13 April 1867.   Oxford
25.   4 April 1868.   Oxford
26.   17 March 1869.   Oxford
27.   6 April 1870.   Cambridge
28.   1 April 1871.   Cambridge
29.   23 March 1872.   Cambridge
30.   29 March 1873.   Cambridge
31.   28 March 1874.   Cambridge
32.   20 March 1875.   Oxford
33.   8 April 1876.   Cambridge
34.   24 March 1877.   DEAD HEAT
35.   13 April 1878.   Oxford
36.   5 April 1879.   Cambridge
37.   22 March 1880.   Oxford
38.   8 April 1881.   Oxford
39.   1 April 1882.   Oxford
40.   15 March 1883.   Oxford
41.   7 April 1884.   Cambridge
42.   28 March 1885.   Oxford
43.   3 April 1886.   Cambridge
44.   26 March 1887.   Cambridge
45.   24 March 1888.   Cambridge
46.   30 March 1889.   Cambridge
47.   26 March 1890.   Oxford

48.	21 March 1891.	Oxford
49.	9 April 1892.	Oxford
50.	22 March 1893.	Oxford
51.	17 March 1894.	Oxford
52.	30 March 1895.	Oxford
53.	28 March 1896.	Oxford
54.	3 April 1897.	Oxford
55.	26 March 1898.	Oxford
56.	25 March 1899.	Cambridge
57.	31 March 1900.	Cambridge
58.	30 March 1901.	Oxford
59.	22 March 1902.	Cambridge
60.	1 April 1903.	Cambridge
61.	26 March 1904.	Cambridge
62.	1 April 1905.	Oxford
63.	7 April 1906.	Cambridge
64.	16 March 1907.	Cambridge
65.	4 April 1908.	Cambridge
66.	3 April 1909.	Oxford
67.	23 March 1910.	Oxford
68.	1 April 1911.	Oxford
69.	30 March 1912.	NO RACE
70.	1 April 1912.	Oxford
71.	13 March 1913.	Oxford
72.	28 March 1914.	Cambridge

Between 1915 and 1919 there was no race due to the war

| 73. | 27 March 1920. | Cambridge |

Appendix 6

ROWERS BY BOAT RACE YEAR

1878

Lieutenant Colonel William Augustine **Ellison**. Royal Berkshire Regiment. Died 1 November 1917. University College, Oxford. Bow.

1887

Captain William Francis Claude **Holland**. Durham Light Infantry. Died 8 November 1917. Brasenose College, Oxford. Bow/stroke.

1888

Captain William Francis Claude **Holland**. Durham Light Infantry. Died 8 November 1917. Brasenose College, Oxford. Bow/stroke.

1889

Captain William Francis Claude **Holland**. Durham Light Infantry. Died 8 November 1917. Brasenose College, Oxford. Bow/stroke.

1890

Captain William Francis Claude **Holland**. Durham Light Infantry. Died 8 November 1917. Brasenose College, Oxford. Bow/stroke.

Lieutenant Colonel William Alfred Littledale **Fletcher** DSO. King's Liverpool Regiment. Died 19 February 1919. Christ Church College, Oxford. Stroke.

1891

Lieutenant Colonel William Alfred Littledale **Fletcher** DSO. King's Liverpool Regiment. Died 19 February 1919. Christ Church College, Oxford. Stroke.

1892

Lieutenant Colonel William Alfred Littledale **Fletcher** DSO. King's Liverpool Regiment. Died 19 February 1919. Christ Church College, Oxford. Stroke.

1893

Lieutenant Colonel Roger Orme **Kerrison**. Australian Field Artillery. Died 18 September 1917. Trinity College, Cambridge. Number seven.

Lieutenant Colonel William Alfred Littledale **Fletcher** DSO. King's Liverpool Regiment. Died 19 February 1919. Christ Church College, Oxford. Stroke.

1894

Lieutenant Colonel Roger Orme **Kerrison**. Australian Field Artillery. Died 18 September 1917. Trinity College, Cambridge. Number seven.

1896

Major John Julius Jersey **De Knoop**. Imperial Camel Corps. Died 7 August 1916. New College, Oxford. Bow.

1897

Lieutenant Geoffrey Otho Charles **Edwards**. West Riding Regiment. Died 7 July 1916. New College, Oxford. Number two.

Major John Julius Jersey **De Knoop**. Imperial Camel Corps. Died 7 August 1916. New College, Oxford. Bow.

1898

Lieutenant Geoffrey Otho Charles **Edwards**. West Riding Regiment. Died 7 July 1916. New College, Oxford. Number two.

Captain/Flight Commander Auberon Thomas **Herbert**. Royal Flying Corps. Died 4 November 1916. Balliol College, Oxford. Number seven.

1899

Lieutenant Gilchrist Stanley **Maclagan**. Royal Warwickshire Regiment. Died 25 April 1915. Magdalen College, Oxford. Cox.

Captain Wilfrid Hubert **Chapman**. Yorkshire Regiment. Died 7 August 1915. Trinity College, Cambridge. Bow.

Captain/Flight Commander Auberon Thomas **Herbert**. Royal Flying Corps. Died 4 November 1916. Balliol College, Oxford. Number seven.

Lieutenant Colonel Ronald Harcourt **Sanderson**. Royal Field Artillery. Died 17 April 1918. Trinity College, Cambridge. Number six.

1900

Lieutenant Samuel Pepys **Cockerell**. Royal Flying Corps. Died 20 March 1915. Trinity College, Cambridge. Bow.

Major Charles Pelham **Rowley**. Royal Garrison Artillery. Died 29 October 1916. Magdalen College, Oxford. Stroke.

Lieutenant Gilchrist Stanley **Maclagan**. Royal Warwickshire Regiment. Died 25 April 1915. Magdalen College, Oxford. Cox.

Lieutenant Colonel Ronald Harcourt **Sanderson**. Royal Field Artillery. Died 17 April 1918. Trinity College, Cambridge. Number six.

Lieutenant Colonel William Alfred Littledale **Fletcher** DSO. King's Liverpool Regiment. Died 19 February 1919. Christ Church College, Oxford. Stroke.

1901

Lieutenant Gilchrist Stanley **Maclagan**. Royal Warwickshire Regiment. Died 25 April 1915. Magdalen College, Oxford. Cox.

Second Lieutenant Graham Floranz Macdowall **Maitland**. Irish Guards. Died 1 November 1914. Trinity College, Cambridge. Stroke.

1902

Lieutenant Gilchrist Stanley **Maclagan**. Royal Warwickshire Regiment. Died 25 April 1915. Magdalen College, Oxford. Cox.

Captain Wilfrid Hubert **Chapman**. Yorkshire Regiment. Died 7 August 1915. Trinity College, Cambridge. Bow.

1903

Captain Wilfrid Hubert **Chapman**. Yorkshire Regiment. Died 7 August 1915. Trinity College, Cambridge. Bow.

Lieutenant Commander Frederick Septimus 'Cleg' **Kelly** DSC. Royal Naval Volunteer Reserve. Died 13 November 1916. Balliol College, Oxford. Number four.

Captain James Shuckburgh **Carter**. Grenadier Guards. Died 27 September 1918. King's College, Cambridge. Number five.

1904

Second Lieutenant Richard Willingdon **Somers-Smith**. King's Royal Rifle Corps. Died 30 June 1915. Merton College, Oxford. Number two, cox.

Captain Arthur John Shirley Hoare **Hales** MC. Wiltshire Regiment. Died 5/6 July 1916. Corpus Christi College, Oxford. Number three.

Captain Thomas Geoffrey **Brocklebank**. Royal Field Artillery. Died 5 August 1916. Trinity College, Cambridge. Bow.

1905

Captain Bernard Ridley **Winthrop-Smith**. Scots Guards. Died 15 November 1914. Trinity College, Cambridge. Number six.

Captain Arthur John Shirley Hoare **Hales** MC. Wiltshire Regiment. Died 5/6 July 1916. Corpus Christi College, Oxford. Number three.

Captain Edward Parker Wallman **Wedd** MC. Royal Army Medical Corps. Died 13 July 1918. Caius College, Cambridge. Number five.

1906

Lieutenant Henry Mills **Goldsmith**. Devonshire Regiment. Died 9 May 1915. Jesus College, Cambridge. Number three.

Captain Alister Graham **Kirby**. London Regiment. Died 29 March 1917. Magdalen College, Oxford. Number five, six, seven.

1907

Captain Alister Graham **Kirby**. London Regiment. Died 29 March 1917. Magdalen College, Oxford. Number five, six, seven.

Lieutenant Henry Mills **Goldsmith**. Devonshire Regiment. Died 9 May 1915. Jesus College, Cambridge. Number three.

Captain Evelyn Herbert Lightfoot **Southwell**. Rifle Brigade. Died 15 September 1916. Magdalen College, Oxford. Number seven.

Captain Arthur Brooks **Close-Brooks** MC. Manchester Regiment. Died 10 January 1917. Trinity College, Cambridge. Bow.

Lieutenant Colonel George Everard **Hope** MC. Lancashire Fusiliers. Died 10 October 1917. Christ Church College, Oxford. Number three.

1908

Captain Oswald Armitage Guy **Carver**. Royal Engineers. Died 7 June 1915. Trinity College, Cambridge. Number three.

Second Lieutenant George Eric **Fairbairn**. Durham Light Infantry. Died 20 June 1915. Jesus College, Cambridge. Number two.

Lieutenant Colonel William Alfred Littledale **Fletcher** DSO. King's Liverpool Regiment. Died 19 February 1919. Christ Church College, Oxford. Stroke.

Lieutenant Edward Gordon **Williams**. Grenadier Guards. Died 12 August 1915. Trinity College, Cambridge. Number six.

Captain Evelyn Herbert Lightfoot **Southwell**. Rifle Brigade. Died 15 September 1916. Magdalen College, Oxford. Number seven.

Captain the Rt Hon. Richard Philip **Stanhope**. Grenadier Guards. Died 16 September 1916. Magdalen College, Oxford. Bow.

Captain Alister Graham **Kirby**. London Regiment. Died 29 March 1917. Magdalen College, Oxford. Number five, six, seven.

1909

Lieutenant Edward Gordon **Williams**. Grenadier Guards. Died 12 August 1915. Trinity College Cambridge. Number six.

Captain Alister Graham **Kirby**. London Regiment. Died 29 March 1917. Magdalen College, Oxford. Number five, six, seven.

Lieutenant Duncan **Mackinnon**. Scots Guards. Died 9 October 1917. Magdalen College, Oxford. Number five.

1910

Lieutenant Hugh John Sladen **Shields**. Royal Army Medical Corps. Died 25 October 1914. Jesus Collegem Cambridge. Stroke.

Lieutenant. Edward Gordon **Williams**. Grenadier Guards. Died 12 August 1915. Trinity College, Cambridge. Number six.

Lieutenant Charles Ralph **le Blanc-Smith**. Rifle Brigade. Died 27 November 1915. Trinity College, Cambridge. Number seven.

Captain Mervyn Bournes **Higgins**. Australian Light Horse. Died 23 December 1916. Balliol College, Oxford. Bow.

Second Lieutenant Cecil Pybus **Cooke**. Shropshire Light Infantry. Died 22 August 1917. Trinity Hall, Cambridge. Number four.

Lieutenant Duncan **Mackinnon**. Scots Guards. Died 9 October 1917. Magdalen College, Oxford. Number five.

Lieutenant Edouard **Majolier**. Yorkshire Regiment. Died 26 November 1918. Christ Church College, Oxford. Number four.

1911

Second Lieutenant Cyril Francis **Burnand**. Grenadier Guards. Died 11 March 1915. Trinity College Cambridge. Number four.

Second Lieutenant George Eric **Fairbairn**. Durham Light Infantry. Died 20 June 1915. Jesus College, Cambridge. Number two.

Lieutenant Charles Ralph **le Blanc-Smith**. Rifle Brigade. Died 27 November 1915. Trinity College, Cambridge. Number seven.

Lieutenant Duncan **Mackinnon**. Scots Guards. Died 9 October 1917. Magdalen College, Oxford. Number five.

1912

Lieutenant Charles Ralph **le Blanc-Smith**. Rifle Brigade. Died 27 November 1915. Trinity College, Cambridge. Number seven.

1913

Lieutenant Lancelot Edwin **Ridley**. Royal Berkshire Regiment. Died 19 August 1916. Jesus College, Cambridge. Cox.

Second Lieutenant Robert Prothero **Hankinson**. Punjabi Rifles. Died 23 February 1917. New College, Oxford. Number three.

1914

Second Lieutenant Reginald William **Fletcher**. Royal Field Artillery. Died 31 October 1914. Balliol College, Oxford. Bow.

Second Lieutenant Dennis Ivor **Day**. Royal Field Artillery. Died 7 September 1915. St John's College, Cambridge. Bow.

Captain John Andrew **Ritson**. South Lancashire Regiment. Died 23 July 1916. Trinity College, Cambridge. Number four.

Lieutenant Lancelot Edwin **Ridley**. Royal Berkshire Regiment. Died 19 August 1916. Jesus College, Cambridge. Cox.

Lieutenant Kenneth Gordon **Kenneth Garnett** MC. Royal Field Artillery. Died 21 August 1917. Trinity College, Cambridge. Number five.

Appendix 7

ROWERS BY COLLEGE

Cambridge

TRINITY COLLEGE

1. Lieutenant Colonel Roger Orme **Kerrison**. Australian Field Artillery. Died 18 September 1917. Number seven. 1893, 1894.
2. Captain Wilfrid Hubert **Chapman**. Yorkshire Regiment. Died 7 August 1915. Bow. 1899, 1902, 1903.
3. Lieutenant Colonel Ronald Harcourt **Sanderson**. Royal Field Artillery. Died 17 April 1918. Number six. 1899, 1900.
4. Lieutenant Samuel Pepys **Cockerell**. Royal Flying Corps. Died 20 March 1915. Bow. 1900.
5. Second Lieutenant Graham Floranz Macdowall **Maitland**. Irish Guards. Died 1 November 1914. Stroke. 1901.
6. Captain Bernard Ridley **Winthrop-Smith**. Scots Guards. Died 15 November 1914. Number six. 1905.
7. Captain Arthur Brooks **Close-Brooks** MC. Manchester Regiment. Died 10 January 1917. Bow. 1907.
8. Captain Oswald Armitage Guy **Carver**. Royal Engineers. Died 7 June 1915. Number three. 1908.
9. Lieutenant Edward Gordon **Williams**. Grenadier Guards. Died 12 August 1915. Number six. 1908, 1909, 1910.
10. Lieutenant Charles Ralph **le Blanc-Smith**. Rifle Brigade. Died 27 November 1915. Number seven. 1910, 1911, 1912.
11. Second Lieutenant Cyril Francis **Burnand**. Grenadier Guards. Died 11 March 1915. Number four. 1911.
12. Captain John Andrew **Ritson**. South Lancashire Regiment. Died 23 July 1916. Number four. 1914.

13. Lieutenant Kenneth Gordon **Kenneth Garnett** MC. Royal Field Artillery. Died 21 August 1917. Number five. 1914.

TRINITY HALL

14. Second Lieutenant Cecil Pybus **Cooke**. Shropshire Light Infantry. Died 22 August 1917. Number four. 1910.

JESUS

15. Lieutenant Henry Mills **Goldsmith**. Devonshire Regiment. Died 9 May 1915. Number three. 1906, 1907.
16. Second Lieutenant George Eric **Fairbairn**. Durham Light Infantry. Died 20 July 1915. Number two. 1908, 1909, 19101911.
17. Lieutenant Hugh John Sladen **Shields**. Royal Army Medical Corps. Died 25 October 1914. Stroke. 1910.
18. Lieutenant Lancelot Edwin **Ridley**. Royal Berkshire Regiment. Died 19 August 1916. Cox. 1913, 1914.

ST JOHN'S

19. Second Lieutenant Dennis Ivor **Day**. Royal Field Artillery. Died 7 September 1915. Bow. 1914.

CAIUS

20. Captain Edward Parker Wallman **Wedd** MC. Royal Army Medical Corps. Died 13 July 1918. Number five. 1905.

KING'S

21. Captain James Shuckburgh **Carter**. Grenadier Guards. Died 27 September 1918. Number five. 1903.

OXFORD

UNIVERSITY

1. Lieutenant Colonel William Augustine **Ellison**. Royal Berkshire Regiment. Died 1 November 1917. Bow. 1878.

BRASENOSE

2. Captain. William Francis Claude **Holland**. Durham Light Infantry. Died 8 November 1917. Bow/stroke. 1887, 1888, 1889, 1890.

CHRIST CHURCH

3. Lieutenant Colonel William Alfred Littledale **Fletcher** DSO. King's Liverpool Regiment. Died 19 February 1919. Stroke. 1890, 1891, 1892, 1893.

4. Lieutenant Colonel George Everard **Hope** MC. Lancashire Fusiliers. Died 10 October 1917. Number three. 1907.

5. Lieutenant Edouard **Majolier**. Yorkshire Regiment. Died 26 November 1918. Number four. 1910.

NEW

6. Major John Julius Jersey **De Knoop**. Imperial Camel Corps. Died 7 August 1916. Bow. 1896, 1897.

7. Lieutenant Geoffrey Otho Charles **Edwards**. West Riding Regiment. Died 7 July 1916. Number two. 1897, 1898.

8. Second Lieutenant Robert Prothero **Hankinson**. Punjabi Rifles. Died 23 February 1917. New College, Oxford. Number three. 1913.

BALLIOL

9. Captain/Flight Commander Auberon Thomas **Herbert** (later Lord Lucas), Royal FLying Corps. Died 4 November 1916. Number seven. 1898, 1899.

10. Lieutenant Commander Frederick Septimus 'Cleg' **Kelly** DSC. Royal Navy Volunteer Reserve. Died 13 November 1916. Number four. 1903.

11. Captain Mervyn Bournes **Higgins**. Australian Light Horse. Died 23 December 1916. Bow. 1910.

12. Second Lieutenant Reginald William **Fletcher**. Royal Field Artillery. Died 31 October 1914. Bow. 1914.

MAGDALEN

13. Lieutenant Gilchrist Stanley **Maclagan**. Royal Warwickshire Regiment. Died 25 April 1915. Cox. 1899, 1900, 1901, 1902.

14. Major Charles Pelham **Rowley**. Royal Garrison Artillery. Died 29 October 1916. Magdalen College, Oxford. Stroke. 1900.

15. Captain Alister Graham **Kirby**. London Regiment. Died 29 March 1917. Number five, six, seven. 1906, 1907, 1908, 1909.

16. Captain Evelyn Herbert Lightfoot **Southwell**. Rifle Brigade. Died 15 September 1916. Number seven. 1907, 1908.

17. Lieutenant Duncan **Mackinnon**. Scots Guards. Died 9 October 1917. Number five. 1909, 1910, 1911.

18. Captain the Rt Hon. Richard Philip **Stanhope**. Grenadier Guards. Died 16 September 1916. Bow. 1908.

MERTON

19. Second Lieutenant Richard Willingdon **Somers-Smith**. King's Royal
    Rifle Corps. Died 30 June 1915. Number two, cox. 1904, 1905.

CORPUS CHRISTI

20. Captain Arthur John Shirley Hoare **Hales** MC. Wiltshire Regiment. Died
    5/6 July 1916. Number three. 1904, 1905.

TRINITY

21. Captain Thomas Geoffrey **Brocklebank**. Royal Field Artillery. Died
    5 August 1916. Bow. 1904.

Bibliography

Burnell, Richard Desborough *One Hundred and Fifty Years of the Oxford and Cambridge Boat Race: An Official History* (London: Precision Press for Guinness, 1979)

Clutterbuck, Colonel L.A., Dooner, Colonel W.T., Denison, Commander the Hon. C.A. *The Bond of Sacrifice: A Biographical Record of all British Officers Who Fell in the Great War* (The Anglo-African Publishing Contractors, 1915)

Craig, E.S. ed. *Oxford University Roll of Service (1914–1918)* (Oxford: Clarendon Press, 1920)

De Ruvigny, the Marquis *The Roll of Honour* (Uckfield: N&M Press, 1922, 2003)

Dodd, Christopher *The Oxford and Cambridge Boat Race* (London: Paul and Co. Ltd, 1983)

Drinkwater, GC. and Sanders T.R.B. *The University Boat Race, Official Centenary History* (London: Cassell and Company Ltd, 1929)

Great War Forum, www.1914-1918.invisionzone.com/forums/index.php

Harrow School Memorial Books

Hugh Shield's War Diary (Army Medical Services: Keogh Museum Barracks, 1914)

Kelly, Frederick Septimus *Race Against Time: The Diaries of F.S. Kelly* (National Library of Canberra: Australia, 2004)

Malmichael, William F. *The Oxford and Cambridge Boat Race 1829–1869* (Europaischer and Hochschulverlag, 2014)

Medals Forum, www.britishmedalforum.com/

Ross, Gordon *The Boat Race: The Story of the First Hundred Races Between Oxford and Cambridge* (London: The Sportsman's Book Club, 1956)

Ruby School Memorial Books

Ryan, Eugene P. *Haig's Medical Officers: The Papers of Colonel Eugene 'Micky' Ryan CMG DSO RAMC* (Barnsley: Pen and Sword, 2013)

The Dragon Book (pupils from the Dragon School killed in the First World War)

Vaughan, E.L. & Littlejohn E. *List of Etonians who fought in the Great War 1914–1919* (Eton: Eton College, 1921)

Winchester School Memorial Book

Index

You may also be interested in …

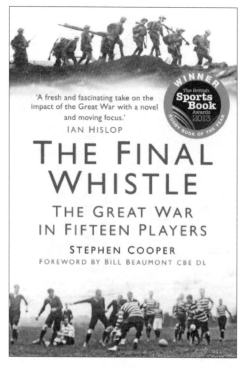

'A fresh and fascinating take on the
impact of the Great War with a novel
and moving focus.'
IAN HISLOP

THE FINAL
WHISTLE

THE GREAT WAR
IN FIFTEEN PLAYERS

STEPHEN COOPER
FOREWORD BY BILL BEAUMONT CBE DL

9780 7524 9900 0

'A fitting tribute not simply to 15 individu-
als cut down in their prime, but a paean to
all those who died in the First World War.'
– Mark Souster, *The Times*